Alfred J. Goodrich

Complete Musical Analysis

A system designed to cultivate the art of analyzing and criticising and assist in the

performance and understanding of the works of the great composers of the

different epochs

Alfred J. Goodrich

Complete Musical Analysis
A system designed to cultivate the art of analyzing and criticising and assist in the performance and understanding of the works of the great composers of the different epochs

ISBN/EAN: 9783337402594

Printed in Europe, USA, Canada, Australia, Japan

Cover: Foto ©Thomas Meinert / pixelio.de

More available books at **www.hansebooks.com**

COMPLETE MUSICAL ANALYSIS

❖

A SYSTEM DESIGNED TO
CULTIVATE THE ART OF ANALYZING AND CRITICISING
AND TO ASSIST IN THE PERFORMANCE
AND UNDERSTANDING OF
THE WORKS OF THE GREAT COMPOSERS OF
DIFFERENT EPOCHS.

❖

BY A. J. GOODRICH,

AUTHOR OF
"GOODRICH'S PIANO MANUAL," "THE LANGUAGE OF MUSIC,"
"THE ART OF SONG,"
"THE MYSTERIES OF MUSIC" (MS.), ETC.

❖

PUBLISHED BY
THE JOHN CHURCH CO.,
CINCINNATI.   NEW YORK.   CHICAGO.

PREFACE.

AMONG the vast army of music students busily engaged in acquiring technical skill in manipulating instruments and voices, there are comparatively few who cultivate the critical faculties in listening properly to music, or have sufficient analytical knowledge to enable them to name and classify a composition after a single hearing. Some interesting books have been written in which certain music is recommended to be performed for pupils; but listening to music is an art, and can be acquired only through a systematic series of exercises and instructions, unless one is content to wait for the gradual absorption of this information through a professional career of many years.

Acknowledgment is also made of the fact that even in small cities one may have the privilege of listening to the greatest artists, including such birds of passage as von Bülow, Rubinstein, d'Albert, Klindworth, Rosenthal, Essipoff and Aus der Ohe.

But, in truth, considerable of this heavy cannonading is (so to say) fired over the heads of the average student. Every embryo pianist is improved by hearing a recital by any of these artists; but in the majority of cases they should descend somewhat from their lofty pedestal to the common earth upon which the student stands, if others than advanced students are to be hit by their artistic missiles. But it is often impossible for these distinguished virtuosi (who, in addition to their inherent gifts, have enjoyed every possible advantage) to comprehend the chaotic state of musical culture outside the radius of our large cities.

The text-books, the laws of the country which permit the titles of " Professor " and " Doctor " to be bestowed upon persons who are ignorant of the very nomenclature of music, and that spirit of American impatience which seeks to acquire everything by a patent process, these are responsible for the present uncultivated state of musical taste.

3

Aside from the preliminary exercises in listening to and naming different tones and rhythms, it is highly important that the student shall be able to say, after hearing a certain opus, that it was a Sarabande, Loure, Musette, Tambourin, Saltarello, Barcarolle, Spinning-song, Fantasie, or Sonata. A skilled listener should, moreover, name the epoch to which the composition belongs, and specify whether it be Italian, French, German, Hungarian, Norwegian, Spanish, Scotch, Chinese or Persian. And it is of equal importance to the proper interpretation of music that these and very many other peculiarities should be understood analytically. For instance, sequence, echo, repetition, and canonic imitation, all have a certain resemblance on the printed page, yet each one is to be played in a different manner, and these distinctions can be ascertained only by analysis. Indeed, the analyzation of the hundred or more details and devices of high-class music is more than important—it is absolutely essential.

The author makes no apology for introducing a considerable number of new terms to designate either newly discovered or neglected details of composition, nor for rejecting certain accepted analytical names and conclusions. He would merely call attention to the fact that "semitone" is the accepted definition of a minor second or chromatic interval; that "bar" is the word used to denote a certain measure; and that "time" is applied not alone to metre and movement, but to rhythm. Yet these and many other terms and deductions of common acceptance have, if analyzed, no relevant significance whatever. As to the very homely elementary chapters of this book, the writer's experience has led him to presuppose on the part of the average student little more than native good sense and a disposition to learn. The sole object has been to explain and set forth the various topics as plainly as possible—a task far more difficult than the analysis of a symphony.

The descriptions of various styles, devices, forms, etc., in this book may be found at variance with what is understood of those topics; but these explanations are derived from the works of the great tone poets, and not copied from musical dictionaries and text-books.

TO THE TEACHER.

ATTENTION is first called to the two-fold character of this book
The auricular exercises go hand in hand with the numerous
bits and scraps of information which are necessary to the proper
enjoyment or performance of music, and to the analysis of compositions away from the instrument. The mere act of hearing music
will not cultivate the *art of listening*. Even pupils who are
technically well advanced will, as a rule, require *systematic* practice
in listening to single tones (first diatonic, then chromatic), different
kinds of rhythm, chord combinations, etc. When a preliminary
exercise is played, the class must know whether they are to appre-
hend the distance of the intervals, or the value of the notes. Otherwise the ear receives but little benefit, because the mind does not
co-operate. The lessons must penetrate beyond the auricle, and to
the vestibule.

Another requisite to intelligent listening is that the hearer shall
not *see* the actual performance. This is why the blind have such
acute auditory nerves; they perform but the single act of listening,
whereas we attempt the double task of seeing and hearing at the
same time. The matter of watching a performance of music is
merely the result of morbid curiosity, for certainly the music is
invisible, and those who see the most hear the least of a musical
performance. Therefore the class is always to be so situated that
they cannot see the key-board, and if the performer can also be
hidden from view it will be still better. At a regular recital we
admit the propriety of an occasional visual observation in order to
discover the position of the performer's hands in producing certain
effects. But this does not invalidate the rule that music is to be
heard, not seen.

The first lessons, which are necessarily dry and uninviting,
should be made as pleasant as possible, for whatever one learns
drudgingly is poorly learned. Therefore, as soon as the mechani-
exercises in melody and rhythm are comprehended they should

5

superseded by or interspersed with short, simple pieces. The auricular exercises are to be continued throughout the book by devoting a few moments of each lesson to some example in tones and rhythm.

Whenever a certain style or form is described the description should be followed by a performance of that particular type, in order to stamp the unsealed impression of the worded explanation upon the mind. In these cases the questions are to be omitted until the chapter has been concluded.

Notwithstanding every member of the class will require a copy of the work, the author recommends the use of a common note-book in order to make a condensed statement or epitome of certain prominent features. Thus, the Sarabande may be described in the note-books (from your dictation) as briefly as this: *metre*, 1; *mode, generally minor, accent on second beat; movement, slow*. These are the main features; and where so many styles are described this much is sufficient, for the Sarabande can be easily recognized from this description. Afterwards, as a review of the lesson, the class would be more interested in knowing some historical or esthetic details. Aside from these advantages, the art of writing such synopsis serves to reinforce the memory and produce an impression, where the mere reading might leave no impress. The metre, mode, rhythm, movement, etc., are to be ascertained by the class after hearing a section or period of any style or form under consideration.

In such chapters as XV, XXVII, XXXV, and all of Parts X and XI, the substance of the text should at first be extracted by reading certain paragraphs and questioning the class as to the meaning or application. As soon as a conclusion is reached it should be written, briefly as possible, in the note-books. Some of the chapters may require practical examples at certain points not indicated in the text. In a chapter like XXVII almost every sentence should be analyzed. After an opus has been played and analyzed auricularly, the students are to be allowed to see the printed copy.

Some persons have a gift of recognizing at once the absolute pitch of any tone. If your class contains such an exception, give them questions like rhythm, periods, form, etc., not alone for the benefit of that particular person, but to prevent any embarrassment to those not possessing this gift. If, on the other hand, you discover a backward or obtuse member of the class, be patient and assist them; not by answering their questions, but by giving the question in such manner that they will be induced to instigate comparisons, and thus acquire that all-important possession—*the ability to think.* Do this as the clever lawyer questions the witness from whom he desires favorable testimony. This is the art of class teaching. And the fact should be constantly remembered that many cases of apparent stupidity are the result of our false system of education, rather than inherent obtuseness.

Attention is now called to what the author considers the most important part of this system: that is, the analyzation (according to the analytical key) of every possible point of distinction and constituent element which influences the performance, the construction, or the effect. This is to be done principally *away from the instrument,* and at first by the class collectively. If, in analyzing a certain opus, a sequence, transition, or counter-subject is overlooked, call attention to the oversight and have the neglected detail pointed out before proceeding. When the symbols and the details to which they refer are understood, each student should be required to analyze, by means of the symbols, a few Sonatinas from Reinecke and Löschhorn, followed by one or more Sonatas by Em. Bach, Haydn, Mozart, Dussek, and Steibelt. Some of the single forms are also to be marked according to the analytical key. (The application of the symbols may be gathered from the analysis of the Clementi Sonata, Chapters XXXVII and XXXVIII.) Insist upon the indication of every constituent element and peculiarity that is observable. A bell motive, a hunting-horn signal, or an anticipation may be detected and marked, away from the piano, but the esthetic or suggestive nature of a certain opus will frequently require an actual performance to determine. Hence, these latter peculiarities are not mentioned in the key.

The author's experience in using this system during the past eleven years has demonstrated to his own mind that many important features of classical music are observable in this mode of analysis which would not be detected by merely reading the music at sight as in actual performance. Music has become too complex and many-sided to be comprehended in this *prima vista* manner. Indeed, those who never study a work away from their instrument know but little of what the music contains.

With regard to reading from the book, that is left entirely to the judgment of the instructor. In nearly all cases the information for the class is easily distinguished from the mere *modus operandi* laid down for the guidance of the teacher. The language is not sufficiently poetic to justify one in always adopting it, especially as certain topics may in certain cases require a different mode of treatment from that of the text.

The compositions mentioned as illustrations at the end of each chapter were, in most cases, indicated at the time of writing and necessarily selected from the author's library. But frequently some other piece of similar style would answer the same purpose. For instance, in Chapter XVII, a Bourrée by Couperin, Rameau, Scarlatti, Nardini, Matthison, or Benda, would serve as good a purpose as the one recommended. But in reference to the Bolero and Saltarello care must be taken to select examples containing the disproportionate rhythm, at least until the class has heard several standard examples.

A few words of caution are also here included in reference to the roccoco pieces which have recently found such favor with composers and listeners. A great many enterprising scribblers have assumed the names of old dances for their inane effusions, hoping that what would not pass current as a Main Street March or a Sawdust Waltz might find favor in the guise of a Gavotte or Minuet. Beware of these counterfeits, for should the class form opinions of roccoco music from such precedents they would some time be obliged to erase those impressions. So it will be better to select illustrations from the master-works quoted, and thus build upon solid foundations.

When the various styles are well understood it would be well to play a few roccoco suites, such as those mentioned in the Compendium. Where a certain opus is specially analyzed it will, of course, be necessary to procure a copy of that particular composition. In other cases selections may be made from the Compendium, which will be found complete so far as this system is concerned. The teacher's own collection of music may also be utilized.

In view of the fact that many successful teachers are not skillful executants, care has been taken to include in the Compendium, as well as throughout the book, selections of medium difficulty, which may be used as illustrations of the various chapters.

THE AUTHOR.

MARCH 4, 1889.

CONTENTS.

PAGE

PREFACE . . . . \

TO THE TEACHER 5

PART I.

CHAPTER 1. **Auricular Exercises:** Major and Minor Scales . .   13

CHAPTER 2. **Chromatic Scale. Chromatic Intervals** . . .   17

CHAPTER 3. **Metre (Measure)** 19

CHAPTER 4. **Rhythm, Rhythmic Device** 20

CHAPTER 5. **Movement, Character of.** (Errors in Musical Nomenclature) 23

PART II.

CHAPTER 6. **Major and Minor Concords** 28

CHAPTER 7. **Natural Transitions.** Tonality 30

CHAPTER 8. **Dominant, Diminished and Secondary Seventh Chords.** Peculiariites of 37

CHAPTER 9. **Harmonic Cadences:** Half, Authentic, Complete,
Avoided, and Plagal 41

PART III.

CHAPTER 10. **Phrase, Semi-phrase, Motive.** Melodic and
Rhythmic Construction 46

CHAPTER 11. **Phrases beginning upon fractional parts
of a measure** 53

CHAPTER 12. **Section.** Different Kinds 56

CHAPTER 13. **Periodic Construction.** Type 59

CHAPTER 14. **Ballad Model.** (Two Periods) 67

PART IV.

CHAPTER 15. **Primary Forms.** (Three Periods) . .   72

CHAPTER 16. **The Dance Form.** Common Species 80

CHAPTER 17.   "   "   " Roccoco Species 85

CHAPTER 18.   "   "   " Modern Classical Species . . 90

9

PART V.

                                                        PAGE
CHAPTER 19. Prelude, Introduction, Intermezzo   98
CHAPTER 20. Uneven Phrases and Sections. United
             Periods   101
CHAPTER 21. Coda (Postlude). Curtailed Period, Extend-
             ed Period   105
CHAPTER 22. Dispersed Harmonies. Abrupt Transitions   111

PART VI.

CHAPTER 23. Characteristic Styles: Lyric, Thematic, Har-
             monic, Antiphonal, Canonic, Fugal and Bravura . .   114
CHAPTER 24. Intermediate Details: Eingang, Second Theme,
             Episode, Termination, Recollection, Stretto, Sequence,
             Passage and Cadenza   122
CHAPTER 25. Intermediate Details—continued: Echo, Rep-
             etition, Anticipation, Parenthesis, Pedal-Note   129
CHAPTER 26. Miscellaneous Single Forms: Spinning Song,
             Hunting Song, Boat Song, Cradle Song, Bell Piece
             (Carillon), Night-Song, Serenade, Romance, Bagatelle,
             Invention, Toccata, Etude, Song Without Words, Pif-
             ferari, Scherzo, Humoresque, Idyl   133
CHAPTER 27. Romantic Single Forms: Feu Follet, Will-o'-the-
             Wisp, Fairy Revel   140

PART VII.

CHAPTER 28. Canonic Imitations: Free, Strict, Contrary, and
             Partial   144
CHAPTER 29. Old Cyclical Forms: Suite, Old Sonata, Partita .   148
CHAPTER 30. Mixed Forms: Potpourri, Medley, Common Over-
             ture, Theme and Variations. Imperfect Forms . . .   150
CHAPTER 31. The Rondo Form   156

PART VIII.

CHAPTER 32. Auricular Exercises: Pitch, Force, and Quality of
             Tone ; Number of Voice-Parts, Location of Principal
             Theme, Style of Performance, Phrasing. Analysis of
             Toccata by Paradisi   160
CHAPTER 33. The Small Sonata Form. In major   169
CHAPTER 34.   "   "   "   "   In minor   178
CHAPTER 35. Analysis of Thematic and Irregular Peri-
             odic Construction. Thesis continued. Liszt's
             "Waldesrauschen." Apotheosis   182

PART IX.

Chapter 36. **Abbreviated Symbols, and Key to this Analysis.** Explanation of the same 185

Chapter 37. **Analyzation of the Sonata Movement.** Application of the Key 197

Chapter 38. **Analyzation of Entire Sonata.** Further application of the Key 204

PART X.

Chapter 39. **Origin and Development of the Sonata Form** . . . . 212 ✔

Chapter 40. **Development of the Sonata continued** . . 223

Chapter 41. **Enlargement and Perfection of the Sonata concluded** 232

Chapter 42. **Symphonic Form. Overture, Concerto, String Quartette** . . . . 238 ✔

PART XI.

Chapter 43. **Program Music:** Dramatic, Characteristic, Descriptive and Realistic 248

Chapter 44. **The Anti-Classical Epoch. Modern Romantic, Romantic-Classical and Realistic Styles** 255

Chapter 45. **American Orchestral and Choral Works** 285

COMPENDIUM.

COMPLETE MUSICAL ANALYSIS.

PART I.

Chapter I.

AURICULAR EXERCISES.

NATURAL INTERVALS.

WE will presuppose a class of from six to twelve pupils, all of whom have some practical knowledge of music. The class should be so arranged that they cannot observe the key-board of the instrument. The teacher at the piano sounds the different intervals of the major scale of *C*, from 1 to 8; explaining that 1 is the tonic, or key-tone; that the scale is based upon this fundamental tone, and that the other intervals naturally revolve around and end upon this tone. To make this plain to all, play the scale ascending and descending, stopping upon different tones, as the seventh, sixth, fifth, or second: then ask if the effect is complete and final. Then play 3, 2, 1, asking the same question. After this, sound 5, 6, 7, 8, and demonstrate that the scale naturally ends upon the key-tone, either ascending or descending. When this is comprehended, begin upon the key-tone, 1, sound the next degree of the scale and ask what was played last. If answered incorrectly, repeat the question until some one answers 2. Then sound *c, f, g, a, b*, and *c*, and require the number of each interval to be named after it is sounded. Repeat the lower *c* frequently, in order that the class may

Ex. 1.

judge of the distance of each tone from the tonic. These intervals
may then be sounded as written:

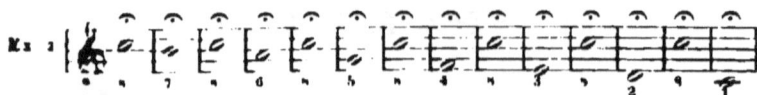

Pause after sounding each tone until the correct answer is given.
When this has been well practiced, select such intervals as these:

After naming the number of each tone as above, the class may call
it by intervals, thus c to f, a fourth; f down to d, a third; d to g, a
fourth etc. The exercise consists of a sequence of fourths, and is
easily recognized after the first two measures. If the class fail to
name a certain interval, they may be allowed to sing the intermediate tones, thus. If they fail to recognize g as the fifth, sound the
key note and require the class to sing the scale diatonically until
they come to the tone in question, as here:

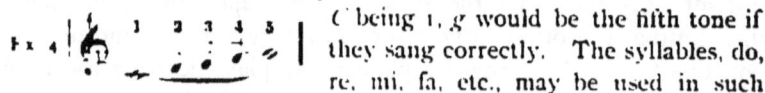

C being 1, g would be the fifth tone if
they sang correctly. The syllables, do,
re, mi, fa, etc., may be used in such
case. The author has often found this of benefit to certain pupils.
Other arrangements of the natural intervals will suggest themselves
to the teacher, and when the class is backward in naming the tones
in these exercises it would be well to play in succession several
thirds, as c e; d, f; e, g; etc., not simultaneously but alternately.
Then give examples in fourths, fifths, sixths, sevenths, and octaves.

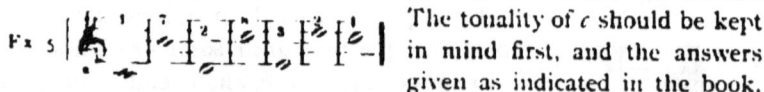

The tonality of c should be kept
in mind first, and the answers
given as indicated in the book.
Afterwards the numerical intervals may be called for as thus in the
first example seventh (c to b), sixth (b to d), seventh (d to c), etc.
American students, especially those who have heard but little good
music require much practice upon these auricular exercises, until
they can name an interval as soon as it is heard.

The teacher should play each form of the minor scale, ascending and descending, until any of the forms can be recognized from hearing. Here are the scales in regular order:

THE OLD MINOR SCALE.

Ex. 6.

This is the minor scale of Palestrina, known as the Eolian mode.* Before the chromatic scale was introduced, the above was much used, being the nearest approach to our modern minor scale; in fact, the descending form of the melodic minor scale is identical with this. It would be well to have the class name the whole and half-steps in the above scale. The half-steps or minor seconds are indicated by slurs.

THE MELODIC MINOR.

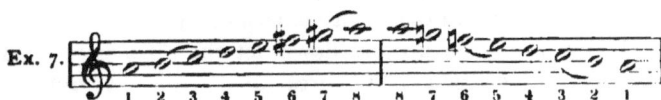

Ex. 7.

Modern tonality requires that the seventh of every key shall be a minor second below the tonic, in order to be a leading tone to the tonic. This necessitates sharpening the seventh, which is also the major third of the dominant chord, *c, g*-sharp, *b*. But inasmuch as the augmented second (*f* to *g*-sharp) is not a melodic sound, composers have, for melodic purposes, sharpened the sixth as well as the seventh, making the last half of the scale like that of *A* major. The result may be seen in the last exercise. Let the class become familiar with this form, ascending and descending; also have them analyze the scale auricularly, by calling the whole and half-steps, and the order in which they come. The last and most important form of minor scale is this:

THE HARMONIC MINOR.

Ex. 8.

---

* See Ecclesiastical Modes in the Histories of Naumann, Grove, or Langhans.

This is the most characteristic, and is called harmonic because *every tone occurs in the harmonics of the tonic, subdominant,* and *dominant* which are employed in a perfect cadence :

Ex. 9.

(The class should discover in these chords every tone in the harmonic scale.) It is also remarkable that the principal diminished seventh chord, with its natural tonic resolution, will likewise include every tone of the harmonic scale:

The first chord includes the second, fourth, sixth and seventh of the scale, while the concord includes 1, 3, 5; these together making the entire harmonic minor scale.

Ex. 10.

Another advantage of this form of scale is that it contains one more minor second (half-step) than any other scale, and this fact has not escaped the attention of the great modern composers.

After playing the scale up and down, let the class discover the three half-steps. Then repeat the three forms (Ex. 6, 7, and 8) in different order until the class are able to name each one as soon as it is sounded.

At this point the class should be made to understand the difference between "key" and "mode." Key refers merely to the *foundation* of any recognized series of diatonic tones; as when we say that a piece beginning and ending upon *A* is in the key of *A*, or that there are twelve major keys and twelve minor keys. Key is the index to the scale. Mode refers to a characteristic series of sounds, the fundamental of which is the key-tone. Our normal major scale constitutes the major mode; and when this is transposed above or below we say the key has changed, but the mode remains the same.

Before the time of Monteverde there were seven modes, each one being characteristic. These still exist, though not now recognized as tonal scales. At present we have but two modes—major and minor.

Intervals somewhat similar to those in Ex. 2, 3, and 5 may now be played in minor. As soon as the class becomes more proficient, the intervals may be played less slowly.

ILLUSTRATIONS.

1. Sarabande in D minor, from Bach's First French Suite. (Mostly harmonic form.)

2. Gipsy Rondo in G, Haydn. (Both strains in G minor contain examples of the harmonic and melodic minor scales.)

3. Kuhlau, Op. 55, No. 1. (The Allegro contains scales in major and melodic minor.)

4. Second Lieder ohne Worte, Mendelssohn (A minor). (The harmonic minor scale descending appears in melody, measures 5 and 6.)

Play these pieces (or parts specified) until the class can recognize the different scales, especially the major, harmonic and melodic minor, and chromatic.

Chapter II.

-- --

CHROMATIC INTERVALS.

HAVING had considerable practice in naming the natural, unaltered intervals we may now introduce chromatic or altered intervals. Explain to the class that you propose to sound some of the chromatic tones, not contained in the diatonic scale. Play the chromatic scales slowly, ascending and descending. Sound c, then e-flat, and call for name of last note. If answered d-sharp it is correct, for d-sharp is the enharmonic equivalent of e-flat, being the same upon the key-board.

Then sound f-sharp and require the note which represents that sound to be named rather than the theoretical designation, for theorists are not agreed as to whether this is an imperfect fifth, a minor fifth, or a diminished fifth. (The author in his Harmony Treatise calls it by the first name.)

Ex. 11.

The following intervals may now be sounded, and in each case the answer is to be accepted if either of the enharmonic equivalents is mentioned, as these exercises are practical, not theoretical:

Ex. 12.

The first tone only is to be named to the class; after which they must judge the distance from the key-tone to each succeeding sound; though in the sixth measure it is easier to recognize a from its being a half-step below the b-flat, and so in the eighth measure, if one member of the class names the f-sharp correctly, it will be easy enough for the next member to recognize the g, because it is a minor second above. In case of failure to name certain tones, the teacher may play the chromatic scale from c up to the tone in question, and the class may ascertain the correct answer in this way

NOTE.—The practice of other intervals is left to the discretion of the teacher. Some classes require much practice in naming tones; others are more proficient and need but few lessons in these preliminary matters If the class is not proficient it will be well to intersperse short melodic exercises with the following lessons in metre and rhythm. This, however, should not be done before the second or third lesson in metre.

The teacher may now perform certain short pieces and ask the class to tell the mode, major or minor.

ILLUSTRATIONS.

1. Kuhlau, Op. 55, No. 1. (The *Vivace* contains chromatic scales ascending. These occur in the second period and again just before the coda. Play the entire movement.)

2. Rubinstein, Op. 3, No. 1. (La Melodia in F.) The first intermezzo consists of a chromatic melody in the bass descending from c to c. The second intermezzo contains the same design reversed, ascending in the bass one octave. Play entire piece and ask the class to tell where the chromatics take place, and in which voice-part.

Also third period of the Heller Tarantella, Op. 85, No. 2.

The teacher should bear in mind that the object is not merely to cultivate in the pupil the sense of hearing as applied to tones and rhythms, but also a taste for music that has meaning as well as charm, a soul as well as a body.

Chapter III.

METRE.

FROM one bar to another comprises a *Measure*, and the peculiarity of the measure as indicated by the metrical signature (numerator and denominator) constitutes the *Metre*. If the metrical signature is ¾ the piece is in three-quarter metre, because three quarters, or the value thereof, fill a measure. The metre is always indicated by the numerator and denominator.* Here are examples of duple, triple, and quadruple metre, with the proper accents for each:

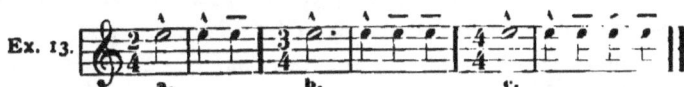

Ex. 13.

This mark of accentuation ∧ is the most forcible; this > is not so strong, and this ‒ is very slight. The first of every measure in all kinds of metre receives the strongest accent. Each succeeding note which corresponds to the denominator also receives an accent. In common metre the third quarter note falls upon an equal division of the measure and receives an accent somewhat more pronounced than the second and fourth quarters.

Therefore, as the first quarter is accented the loudest, it becomes necessary to use two other degrees of accent—making in all three. These have been recommended by Von Bülow and should be more generally used and understood. (See Ex. 13, *c*, second measure.)

No note of less value than a quarter in these examples is to be accented, except it fall upon one of the accented parts, or metrical divisions of a measure.

Thus, we might recognize the difference between four eighths in ⅜ metre and four quarters in ¼ metre, both being performed at the same rate of speed. The former would have but two accents, while the latter would have four:

---

* The word metre is usually applied to what is here called rhythm.

In order to make this perceptible to the class the teacher might play the two examples like this:

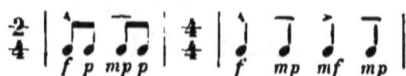

The quarters are to be played as fast as the eighths. Reverse the examples and repeat them until the class can recognize the difference between $\frac{2}{4}$ and $\frac{4}{4}$ metre.

The class should also make copies of the printed examples, showing the manner of accenting the various kinds of metre. A few short pieces should now be performed for the class to hear. Choose for the present only $\frac{2}{4}$, $\frac{3}{4}$, and $\frac{4}{4}$ metre and allow the question, metre, to be a general one. The class may also endeavor to beat with the notes indicated by the metrical signature. In this case their beats must correspond to the accented parts of the measure.

The first pieces should be simple, followed by more difficult selections. The waltzes and marches of Schubert are good for this purpose. One or two periods will generally suffice. Selections from the works of Löschhorn, Tours, Löw, Kirchner, or Heller will prove interesting and instructive.

Chapter IV.

RHYTHM.

RHYTHM signifies symmetry, proportion, and division. The latter definition is more applicable to our first lessons in rhythm, as we wish to indicate by that word the peculiar division or arrangement of the notes in a measure in comparison to the metrical division. For instance, a March is in $\frac{4}{4}$ metre, with this peculiarity of the rhythm: A Bolero is in $\frac{3}{4}$ metre, with this rhythm in the accompaniment: The rhythm is, therefore, any characteristic arrangement of the notes in a measure, corresponding in value to the metrical signature.[*]

The class may now be questioned in reference to the following section:

Ex. 14.

The metre should be ascertained first and the example repeated until all realize that it is ¾. Then call for the rhythm of the accompaniment. (The answer should be *three quarters*.) The rhythm of the theme (first two measures) comes next. The answer is, *a dotted eighth, sixteenth*, and *two quarters*. In the third measure they have but to recognize the four notes to a beat in order to answer *twelve sixteenths* (three times four). This instance is not simple to an elementary class; therefore it should be played moderately, with strong accents as indicated.

In the following example the class should name the rhythm (valuation) of every measure. Explain to them that the exercise is in ¼ metre throughout, and that the beats are to continue at the same rate of speed—moderate movement. Indicate the four metrical beats audibly while the examples are being played. This may be done by tapping on a book or chair with a pencil. If they recognize two notes to a beat they say "eighths," if they hear three to a beat they say "triplets," and if four to a beat the answer is "sixteenths," and so on:

Ex. 15.

Repeat each measure, that the class may answer without stopping the movement. Each member of a class of six might have a question, as indicated by the figures above the notes. Then play the exercise backwards, so that the order will be different and each

pupil will have a different question.　Finally vary the order as here:
1, 3, 2, 4, 6, 1, 5, 3, etc.

Exercises like this should now be practiced, asking the class, first, the metre, and then the rhythm: $\frac{3}{4}$ The answer should be "¾ metre, one quarter and four eighths." Play this exercise next. $\frac{3}{4}$ and finally some examples like these:

$\frac{2}{4}$

If necessary the class may count eight sixteenths in the last measure, thus: 1 and, 2 and, 3 and, 4 and, which would give the solution. The author's experience is that pupils at the present time are deficient in practical arithmetical knowledge, which is sacrificed by our schools and seminaries for less useful branches of study. The exercises in rhythm (which are merely musical fractions) should, therefore, be often repeated and long continued. Such exercises, properly conducted, sharpen the mental faculties, and the class should pursue the matter until they can recognize any characteristic rhythm instantly.

The Etudes of Lemoine, Op. 37, Nos. 40, 41, and 42, may be played in connection with this chapter; also "Soliloquies for Piano," by S. G. Pratt, Nos. 2 or 3; "At the Forge," by Jungmann, and "The Mill," by Jensen, Op. 17, No. 3.

Chapter V.

MOVEMENT.

AN important feature of a musical composition, and one that assists us in determining its character, is Movement, *i. e.*, the rate of speed at which it moves. In this the student must not be influenced by the rapidity of the unaccented notes, but by the movement of the accented (metrical) beats. A quick movement may contain notes of long duration, and a slow movement may contain rapid notes. Endeavor to ascertain, first, the metre, by counting regularly a given number of metrical accents in each measure. The movement may then be determined by the manner in which these regular accents follow each other—whether fast, moderate, or slow. (The word "time" has unfortunately been applied indiscriminately to metre, rhythm, and movement.) The following example would be recognized as a slow movement:

because the regular beats are indicated by the notes, and these beats follow each other slowly.

The next example is easily classified as a fast movement:

The six eighths here are played in the same space of time that is consumed by one quarter of the previous measure, thus: $\frac{4}{4}\left(\text{\musicalnote} = 80\right)$ $\frac{6}{8}\left(\text{\musicalnote.} = 80\right)$ In other words, the last quotation is three times as fast as the first.

We will now present an example of rapid notes in a slow movement:

Ex. 18.

In the first measure we recognize an Andante movement on account of the slow metrical beats $\left(\begin{array}{cc} | & | \\ \bullet & \bullet \end{array}\right)$ In the second measure the movement remains the same, though the right hand executes eight notes to a beat. Only the first note of each group of thirty-seconds is accented, and this shows that the regular beats (1 and 2) move slowly

One more similar example will be presented:

Ex. 19.

At (a) the four accented quarters represent the beats indicated by the metrical signature $\frac{4}{4}$. At (b) the beats and the movement remain unaltered, because the groups of thirty-seconds are recognized as accessory, or passing tones, in form of a Cadenza. Eight thirty-seconds being equal to a quarter, only the first of each group is accented, as the group merely represents a quarter note, or one beat.

Movement is also influenced by rhythm, and in this respect there is a seeming contradiction with regard to movement as indicated by the metronome. For example, a Sarabande in $\frac{3}{4}$ metre may be marked $\left(\downarrow = 88 \right)$ to indicate a slow dance, and a Bolero in the same kind of metre is metronomized identically to indicate a quick dance $\left(\downarrow = 88 \right)$ But a Sarabande seldom contains more than *one note to a beat*, and this gives to the dance a slow and deliberate character. On the other hand the Bolero contains sixteenths and thirty-second notes; the rhythm of the acccompaniment is much more animating, and altogether there is an impulse of sprightliness that suggests quick motion. Compare the following examples:

(♩ = 88) SARABANDE, KUHNAU.

Ex. 20.

This suggests slow and rather ponderous dance movements. Now play the next example according to the same metronomical beats:

(♩ = 88.)   BOLERO. MOSZKOWSKI.

Ex. 21.

The accompaniment alone is indicative of a sprightly dance; but the dotted sixteenth and consequent thirty-second notes of the theme add still more of vivacity to the movement. The fact is to be considered, however, that these quick notes are *melodic* ones, and not in the nature of variations or mere rapid parenthetical groups such as frequently occur in an Andante or Adagio. The Adagio in Beethoven's F minor Sonata, No. 1, will illustrate this. The matter ought to be well understood, otherwise there will ever be a misunderstanding as to the movements of certain compositions.

The quick notes in the Bolero are melodic, and consequently all receive sufficient accent to make them prominent. But in Ex. 18 and 19 the rapid notes are mere intermediate and accessory tones which receive no accent except upon the first of each group, where the metrical accents naturally occur. Ex. 16 should be played for the class while they beat two to each measure, slowly. The movement is indicated by Italian terms such as *Allegro*, quick; *Moderato*, neither slow nor fast; *Andante*, slow, etc.; or by metronomical figures following a note of any denomination. (♩ = 60) signifies that the sliding weight on the pendulum of the metronome is to be set at sixty, which is one quarter to a second. This is rather slow. Six-eighth metre should be indicated in reference to the movement by an eighth or dotted quarter. Sometimes it is marked like this: ($\stackrel{|}{\bullet} \dot{=} 72$) which is erroneous; as we must have either two $\stackrel{|}{\bullet}_{\bullet}$ or six $\stackrel{|}{\bullet}$ in a measure (or one $_{\bullet}\stackrel{|}{\bullet}$).

It would be well for the class to learn to distinguish the three common movements first, as already indicated. These are *Allegro*. *Moderato*, and *Andante*. In the following selections the teacher should observe a difference of about twenty degrees between the *Allegro* and the *Moderato*, and also between the *Moderato* and the *Andante*, in order to make the matter plain to the class.

ILLUSTRATIONS.

Sarabande (*Andante*), Gavotte (*Moderato*), Gigue (*Allegro*). (These may be selected from any of the Suites.) One or two periods from La Chasse, by Heller, Op. 29. Op. 15, No. 11, from Schumann. (Alternate slow and fast movements.) Adagio, Op. 2, No. 1, Beethoven. (Such measures as the second after the Coda begins are to be executed with but three accents in a measure—one to the first of each group. The exceptions to this rule occur not in the parenthetical passages, but in the melodic notes.) The following questions should be given out separately: 1. Metre (¾, ⅜, ⅔, or ⅝). 2. Rhythm of the Melody. 3. Rhythm of the accompaniment. 4. Movement. 5. Mode.

If the class is large give the same question to several members, and such difficult questions as rhythm to the greater number. Continue the illustrations and distribute the questions differently, until they are answered promptly and correctly.

Before concluding Part I the author would call attention to several common errors, principally in the nomenclature of music.

1. *Note* is often confounded with *tone* and *vice versa;* but it would be better to say, *we read the notes*, and *listen to the tones.* One is a character, the other a sound.

2. The expression "¾ time" or "⅔ time" is very common; but as time is a part of eternity it is manifestly improper to speak of the metrical signature as a part of eternity. Nor is it proper to say we increase or retard the "time." Time cannot be increased or retarded—it is everlasting and unvarying. Better to say we increase or retard the movement.

3. Referring to a certain measure musical writers have a habit of saying "bar" so and so, when they mean *measure* so and so. The mensural divisions of music are indicated by perpendicular lines called bars, which constitute equal measures. The word *bar*, when used in this sense, has no real meaning, though it is understood to refer to a certain measure.

Here, for example, is a measure included between the two bars:

Ex. 22.

The substitution of *bar* for *measure* is, therefore, both incorrect and indefinite.

4. The word "accidental" is also employed incorrectly in referring to a foreign tone not contained in the scale in which a composition is written. In such cases it would be preferable to speak of the foreign tone in a general way as a chromatic alteration, or be specific and say *b*-flat, *g*-sharp, *e*-natural; for it is not reasonable to presume that the composer used the tone accidentally.

5. We often hear that a certain note is *"sharped"* or *"flatted,"* yet both words are grammatically incorrect. When the pitch is raised or lowered by means of a chromatic alteration it may be said to have been *sharpened* or *flattened*.

PART II.

Chapter VI.

MAJOR AND MINOR CONCORDS

A CONCORD contains a major or minor third and a perfect fifth from any fundamental tone considered as root. The first, third, and fifth natural degrees of any major scale will constitute a major concord; the same degrees of any minor scale will comprise a minor concord. All concords, whether major or minor, have a perfect fifth. If the third be small, as *a* and *c*, it is minor. (Minor means *less*.) If the third be large, as *a* to *c*-sharp, it is major (which means *more*, or larger).

Sound several major and minor concords in their first position (fifth uppermost) and ask which are major and which minor. (If the class has studied that all-important subject, Harmony, they can pass rapidly over this and the two following chapters; the auricular exercises are, however, of importance to all students.) Repeat such exercises as Ex. 23, until every one can recognize major from minor:

Ex. 23.

The chords should be played both arpeggio and simultaneously, as in the example. Explain that when the fifth is at the top and the root at the bottom the chord is in its first or original position, having originated in this way.

When the root of a chord is at the top it is in its second position, the letters being re-arranged. When the third appears at the top the concord is re-arranged in its third position. The last three paragraphs should be committed to memory, as the directions apply equally to major and minor chords. (This must not be confused with inversion, in which the bass has some other tone than the root.)

The re-arrangement of a concord can be easily accomplished by re-arranging the letters of the chord in regular order, thus: *C e g*, 1. *e g C*, 2. *g C e*, 3. (The figures show the position and the capital letters give the location of the root.) Every one in the class should arrange a concord in its three close positions as indicated. If correct, play the different positions as here:

Ex. 24.

After this, play several major and minor concords in their first position:

Ex. 25.

Let the class become accustomed to the sound of these chords in their first position. Then play an example in second position:

Ex. 26.

Finally play example of chords in their third position:

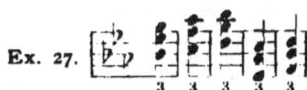

Ex. 27.

Play these up and down that they may leave an impression upon the class by their peculiar effect.

A few exercises like the following should be played, the class to tell mode and position:

Ex. 28.

(Give the name of the first chord only.) Repeat the examples with the root of each chord in the bass.

If any chord is named incorrectly, either with regard to its character or position, it may be played slowly in arpeggio form, always sounding the notes from bottom to top, and sustaining the tones that they may vibrate. Continue such example as 28 until the answers are generally correct.

The next step is this: Play in whole notes, *Moderato*, certain natural chord progressions in four parts, and require class to name root note and mode of each. Ex. 29 will answer our purpose, though even this is more difficult than any previous lesson:

Ex. 29.

(Sound each chord distinctly and with equal force.) The answers should be "C major, second position" (or root highest), "A minor, third position" (or third highest), "F major, first position," etc.

Similar exercises may be improvised by the teacher until their object has been accomplished.

As illustrations of this chapter, play the first two periods of the Sarabande in D minor, by Händel (among the twelve easy pieces by Händel). Also the first two periods of the Chorale in Schumann's Opus 68, No. 4.

There are a few discords in both selections, but most of the chords can be named, and without stopping the performance.

Chapter VII.

NATURAL TRANSITION.

TONALITY.

TRANSITION is the act of passing from one key (not from one chord) to another. This is accomplished by introducing some tone which belongs to the new key and does not belong to the old one. The simplest transitions are those to the related keys, as follows: Tonic, 1; Subdominant, 4; Dominant, 5; and the relative ьainor to each of these:

Ex. 30.

In a minor mode this order is reversed:

Ex. 31.

The simplest way of effecting these transitions is by means of the Dominant (or dominating) chord. This is founded upon the fifth degree of the scale and contains a major third and perfect fifth. This dominant chord contains the leading-tone to the key we may wish to establish, and in five cases out of six this leading-tone will be a chromatically altered tone.

ILLUSTRATIONS.

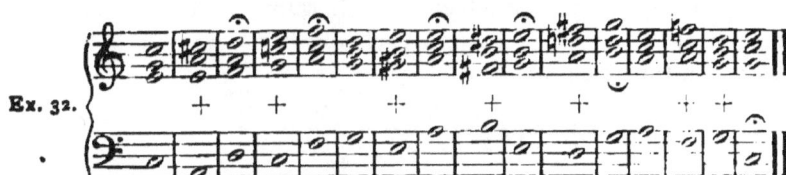

Ex. 32.

At the end of each transition there is a pause. After naming the first chord and its position, the questions are: What is the following chord, its position and root? Then play the D minor chord and ask if any transition has been made. (The class should recognize the c-sharp as a tone foreign to C major.) The chords marked are the ones which change the tonality from what it was before that chord was played. In the fourteenth measure the chord of F assists in restoring the key of C, because in the twelfth measure the tonality was decided as that of G, and the f-natural destroys that key.

The example may be played through without the pauses in order to detect the transitions.* Finally play the example through in a different position as here:

Ex. 33.

*The author's object is to effect these transitions with concords only, as discords have not yet been introduced.

The substance of this chapter may be brought out by the performance of a few pieces, such as the No. 1 (Courante) of the twelve easy pieces by Händel (Augener & Co., No. 8153). The class should simply listen for the modulations. A transition occurs in the fifth, sixth, and seventh measures of the first period. In the second period the transitions are: Measures 3, going to Dominant; 5, to the relative minor; 9, to C major; 10, back to the key-tone (by means of *b*-flat , 12 and 13. These transitions to dominant and back to tonic are repeated. At 14 there is a temporary transition to subdominant and back to tonic. No. 16 of the "Wonderland Series" by W. Cooper. Transitions to G major and D minor are to be observed. The strain in *F* is not to be considered as transition. No. 13, from Schumann's "Scenes of Childhood," may be played, omitting Cadenza.

Following are brief explanations of a few technical terms, which should be understood on account of their frequent use:

VOICE-PART.

The term is borrowed from musical theory, where it is used to distinguish four-part harmony, as well as counterpoint, from a mere chord accompaniment, or adventitious harmony. The different *parts* are thus referred to as though each one was sung by a different *voice*. In this example:

there are two voice-parts, the contralto (a) being imitated by the soprano (b). But in the next example there is only one voice-part:

If the performer sustains the contralto tone firmly, so that it will be heard singing while the upper voice-part executes the canonic imitation, the listener can recognize the two voice-parts; but if the holding tone (*c*) be forsaken, the effect will be as in the next example, only one voice-part being recognized.

The technical names of the different kinds of human voices, as Soprano, Contralto, Tenor, Baritone and Bass, are also used in similar manner:

Ex. 36.

as when we say the principal theme is here in the baritone part, or that the tenor and bass have pedal notes. This is done in piano and orga:. music, as well as in vocal quartettes and quintettes, because it is both convenient and suggestive.

THE SCALE DEGREES.

The technical names applied to the different degrees of the scale should also be understood. The first note of a scale is called Tonic, *i. e.*, key-tone. The second, Supertonic, the next degree above the tonic. The third, Mediant, midway between tonic and dominant. The fourth, Subdominant, beneath the dominant. The fifth, Dominant, that is, the dominating or controlling tone in harmony. The sixth, Submediant, being the same distance below the tonic that the mediant is above the tonic. The seventh, Leading-tone, being a minor second below the tonic (its natural resolution when forming part of the Dominant harmony is up to the key-tone).

A related concord is formed upon each of the first six degrees of every major scale, and these concords are generally called by that name which indicates their root note. If we say the transition is to the Mediant from *a*-flat, C minor would be indicated. The triad founded upon the seventh of a major scale is not a concord, and so the word leading-tone is seldom used to denote a chord' or a key, but merely the half-step below any tonic. The names apply to both modes, as may be seen below:

Ex. 37.

If the seventh in the lower staff (G minor) should appear as *f*-natural, it would cease to be the leading-tone.

Iu its general application this refers to our entire eighty-eight chromatic tones; to the twelve major scales; the several forms of the minor scale; to our system of related and unrelated keys; and the science of Harmony. But the application in this book is to our impression of the key at any particular point, and the relationship between the new and old fundamental. A few examples will set this forth in plainer light:

Ex. 38.

The tonality in the first measure is plainly that of C major. At (b) the tonality is recognized as that of D minor, even before the resolution on the third beat. The chord at (d) destroys the impression of D minor because *b*-natural does not occur in that key. The discord at (e) establishes the tonality as that of G. The concord at (f) does not affect the tonality; but when the *f*-sharp is canceled at (g) the key of the dominant disappears and the ear anticipates the return of the original tonality as at (i). So soon as the C major chord is sounded the ear comprehends the entire series of natural tones in the scale of *C*. In the second measure the entire minor scale of *D* is comprehended; and in the third measure we can readily appreciate the tones which belong to G major. The difference between these related scales is very slight, as may be seen from this:

Ex. 39.

All the tones in the *G* scale occur in *C*, except *f*-sharp. Consquently the only difference in the actual tones is between *f*-natural of *C* and *f*-sharp of the *G* scale. Aside from these slight distinctions between the related keys, there is a still more important difference which ought to be considered under tonality. That is the transfer of the base of operations to a higher or lower plane. The following quotation from the principal subject to Beethoven's First Symphony will illustrate our meaning:

Ex. 40.

(b) is a repetition of (a) transferred from the key of C major to D minor—a major second higher. The foundation of the series of tones at (b) is located a whole step above that of (a); though the second scale contains the same sounds that belonged to the first scale, excepting the *c*-sharp. These transfers or changes of base have an important bearing upon Form in music, aside from the variety of tone-color which they impart. The mere difference in signature being but one sharp or one flat between the related keys, the ear can comprehend them and their relationship to the original key without special effort; but it is not the difference of one tone between two related keys in a musical work which produces the effect. It is rather the change in the foundation of tones, or the transfer of the base of operations to a different location—a higher or a lower plane —from which we are enabled to see objects which were invisible from the first standpoint. The chromatic alteration is merely the *means* of arriving at the new key or location; the *view* from the new location is the *end* to be arrived at.

Every chromatic alteration does not necessitate a change of key. For example, these melodic tones (+) may be harmonized so as not to create any new key, as thus:

Ex. 41.

The diminished seventh chord is used as a mere passing harmony, and the key of *C* still remains. In the next example we modulate at (a) to the key of E minor. At (b) we pass to the key of *G* major, creating in each case a different tonality, and transferring the fundamental to a different plane.

Ex. 42.

ILLUSTRATIONS.

Händel, twelve easy pieces, Minuet I and II.
Bach, Gavotte and Musette in D.
Bach. Gavotte and Musette in G.
A. Durand, Pomponnette, Op. 80.
A. Durand, Valse, Op. 83.

Distinction should be made between these selections. In the Minuets from Händel there is a prevailing key-tone, with but few temporary transitions. In the selections from Bach the mode is altered from major to minor, and minor to major, but the key-tone remains the same. Therefore, the bass or fundamental is not altered so much as the order of the scale intervals and the tone-color. The first period of the Pomponnette is in A major; then the scene is shifted to the plane of E major. This is a change of base.

In the Valse the scene changes frequently, as from *E*-flat to *B*-flat, then back to the original fundamental, then there is a period in *A*-flat, and again the bass is changed to F minor, a third lower, etc.

Chapter VIII.

PRINCIPAL AND SECONDARY SEVENTH CHORDS.

THE DOMINANT SEVENTH CHORD.

THIS is also known as the "essential seventh chord," and is
founded upon the fifth degree of any scale—major or harmonic
minor. It consists of a major third, perfect fifth (the major fifth of
Marx and Weitzmann), and a minor seventh from the root. This is
the most agreeable of all so-called discords, and though built upon
thirds, yet from 1 to 7 (g to f) is a dis-
cordant interval, the ratio of vibrations
being as 16 to 9—or $\frac{16}{9}$. The interval of
a seventh also requires resolution to a
more consonant interval and is accordingly called a *discord*. This is more noticeable when the interval is heard alone (or
inverted to a major second):
The dominant seventh chord is in its first
position when the seventh is above:
In the second position the root is at the top; in the
third position the third of the chord is above, and
in the fourth position the seventh is below and the fifth above:
Play these in regular order up and
down; then change order and ask number of each position. Other dominant
sevenths should be played, and the class
ought to become familiar with the peculiar intervals which constitute the chord. In modulating from
tonic to subdominant the minor seventh
performs the transition, as it represents
the difference between the two keys, thus:
In modulating by fourths we might proceed in the same manner by means of the

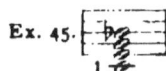

Ex. 43.

Ex. 44.

Ex. 45.

Ex. 46.

Ex. 47.

seventh to the old key, which becomes the subdominant of the new key, as here:

Ex. 48.

At (a) (b) and (c) the class should recognize the element of transition, which occurs on the second half of each measure.

Only a superficial knowledge of this subject can be gathered here, but even this will be of much assistance in our future work.

THE DIMINISHED SEVENTH CHORD.

This is produced by raising the root of an essential seventh chord one chromatic step, the third, fifth, and seventh remaining stationary: Ex. 49.

The second chord contains componently, three minor thirds; or, fundamentally, a minor third, imperfect fifth, and diminished seventh. The different positions of this chord are obtained in the same manner as with the dominant seventh:

Ex. 50.

The positions are numbered from 1 to 4. The class should re-arrange this diminished seventh chord in its three other close positions, by placing the lowest note an   Ex. 51.
octave higher each time:

The diminished seventh being an enharmonic, not a tonal discord, the different positions are not susceptible of recognition by the ear, except where the tonality is distinctly established. There are but three essentially different diminished seventh chords, and yet as a chord of this kind is found upon the leading-tone of every minor scale, it follows that each of the three diminished seventh chords can be so written enharmonically as to equally represent four minor keys. This chord, for example, can represent E minor, G minor, B-flat minor or D-flat minor—depending upon the notation :

Ex. 52.

The first chord in each measure here is the same, as far as sounds are concerned, *b* double flat being the enharmonic equivalent of *a*. So at 2 the *d*-sharp of 1 becomes *e*-flat. The two discords with which we have become familiar should be played alternately, and interspersed with concords, until the class can recognize and qualify the difference between them. Give to each pupil a question. The answers are :

Ex. 53.

1. "Diminished seventh chord;" 2. "Dominant seventh chord;" 3. "Major concord;" 4. "Dominant seventh;" 5. "Major concord;" 6. " Diminished seventh;" 7. "Minor concord." The positions might also be given of all except 1 and 6.

SECONDARY SEVENTH CHORDS.

In connection with the dominant and diminished seventh chords the student may cultivate at least a passing acquaintance with the secondary discords. These are founded upon the first, second, third, fourth, sixth, and seventh natural degrees of every major scale, and in their original positions appear like this :

Ex. 54.

These are called secondary discords, because they lack the elements of transition and cannot be used as principal transition discords. (The No. 3 has been employed as a principal discord, as it contains the essential elements of transition, *i. e.*, the subdominant and leading-tone. But it is weak and very often appears as a secondary discord.) The principal discords are: the Dominant seventh, founded upon the fifth of the scale; the Diminished seventh, chords of an extreme sharpened sixth, and the Dominant ninth chords—major and minor.

The Secondary discords serve as connecting links in the harmonic chain, and by their dissonant character prepare the ear for the more important principal discords which follow. Those marked 5 are extremely harsh, being a product of suspension. Those numbered 4 are less harsh; No. 3 is still less so, and the Nos. 1 and 2 are perfectly euphonious:

The secondary discords usually occur in some such situation as this:

The discords numbered 4 follow each other naturally, and finally lead to the terminal discord, 1, of which the previous seventh chord contains two connecting tones (*f* and *d*). This is a better effect than to employ so many concords, which may be compared to dinner of pie and cake. Where the harsher discords are used they will be found to resolve themselves into the more agreeable species, something like this example from the author's Harmony Treatise:

Observe that only one voice moves at a time, and that the dissonances are gradually reduced. Certain short pieces should now be played, the pupils naming the discords as they occur, *i. e.*, whether Dominant, Diminished, or Secondary Seventh Chords. After this distribute these questions: 1. Name the Key-tone; 2. Name the Mode or Modes; 3. Metre; 4. Rhythm; 5. Number of Dominant Seventh Chords; 6. Number of Diminished Seventh Chords; 7. Number of Secondary Seventh Chords; 8. Was the last chord major or minor? 9. Its position. (If other questions are required include number of Periods, Form, Species, etc.)

Play the last part of Mozart's Fantasia in D minor (No. 13, "Album Classique," Litolff), beginning just before the mode changes to tonic major. The diminished seventh chord in arpeggio should be recognized, also the essential seventh in the next measure. The chord in the middle of the Cadenza had better be played: that the class may recognize the dominant seventh with its fifth above. Instances of this kind need a few words of explanation from the teacher:

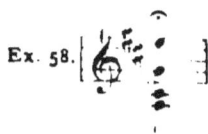

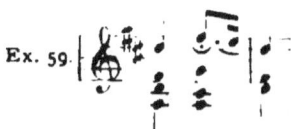

Ex. 58.

Ex. 59.

The *f*-sharp marked > is an appoggiatura. and the following harmonic note (*e*), together with the chord in the bass, gives us the complete dominant seventh chord to *D*; *a*, *c*-sharp, *e*, and *g*.

SELECTIONS FOR THIS CHAPTER.

Schumann, Op. 15, No. 13. The last period will suffice. (This contains discords 1, 2, 3, and 4.)

Kirchner, Op. 7, No. 1. Contains principal discords (1 and 2), and Secondary discords in measures 7 and 10. (In the second, fourth, and sixth measures the *d* above is to be considered as a suspension; therefore the class could not at present analyze such examples, except by omitting the upper tone.)

Introduction to the Pavan by H. F. Sharpe. (Discords 1, 2, and 4.)

Chapter IX.

HARMONIC CADENCES.

HALF CADENCE; AUTHENTIC CADENCE; PLAGAL CADENCE; COMPLETE CADENCE; AVOIDED CADENCE.

THE definition of Cadence in music is, close or ending. This is applicable to most of the above, but in respect to the avoided cadence it must be understood to refer to the harmonic progression, as no close is accomplished in such case. The various harmonic cadences will be presented and explained for the purpose of showing their general application and effect at different points in a musical composition.

1. *The Half Cadence* consists of the tonic followed by the dominant or dominant seventh harmony, while the fifth of the tonic is usually placed below as a real bass, being the root of the dominant chord. The effect of the half cadence is incomplete wherever it may occur.

Ex. 60.

The last measure is a half cadence and leads us to expect something else. Hence it is most appropriate in the middle of a period as just illustrated. (In the classical sonatas it was customary to introduce a half cadence before the second subject.) This cadence may also occur at the natural close of a period, in which case it results in an extended period, as shown in the previous chapter. The application is similar in the minor mode, as here:

Ex. 61.

In transitional passages the student must know what is the tonic (for the time being) in order to recognize the last chord as dominant.

2. *Authentic Cadence.* This is a regular terminal cadence and consists of the principal resolution of any transition chord to that key to which it naturally belongs. Following are examples of authentic cadence:

Ex. 62.

* This discord is a combination of the dominant and diminished seventh chords (1 and 2) and is called the dominant ninth.

The effect of these is decided and more or less terminal. (No. 3 is the least decided). They bring the music to an harmonic close, and their best effect is at the end of a period or isolated phrase.

3. *Plagal Cadence.* This is also known as the Amen cadence, and embraces the harmonies of the subdominant and tonic; in other words, the chords of the fourth and first degrees. This is true of both modes. The plagal cadence is frequently used in the Episcopal and Catholic services to the word "Amen," which occurs at the end of chants and anthems. It was likewise known as the Ecclesiastical cadence in the time of Palestrina, when it was employed in certain "modes" which contained no dominant for the authentic close. It is really an after, or sub-cadence, and comes after a full cadence; in which case it is the foundation of a short coda, as the mensural proportion is generally complete before the plagal cadence is introduced. It is more mild and less decided than any of the others, having in reality very little transitional strength:

Ex. 63.

Each of these is a plagal cadence and is supposed to come after the close of a period or form; hence the tonic chord is introduced first in each case, though the cadence itself merely consists of two chords, thus:

Ex. 64.

4. *The Complete Cadence.* This embraces the three principal harmonies in any major or minor key, following in their natural order:

Ex. 65.

Ex. 66.

This is the most complete and final of all the har
The reason for this is, that in either mode *it compr*
the scale. The chords 1, 4, 5, are generally known
dominant and Dominant, followed of course by th
ample). The complete or perfect cadence has the
end of a terminal period, where completeness is
The perfect cadence may also be written in the fo

Ex. 67.

1, 2, and 3 might be made minor by including the
canceling *b*. It would be well to play these in the
positions and then transpose them. These are all te
    5. *Avoided Cadence.* This takes place when a tr
followed by any other chord than that to which the
resolves.* The regular cadence being thus avoide
the interest is kept up, instead of being satisfied, ur
cadence takes place. The ordinary effect of an av
to extend the period beyond its natural duration.
the composer may be to express disappointment or
to keep the interest from subsiding, but the prac
extend the limits of a period by postponing the t
or to avoid the effect of a perfect cadence. An inst
may be observed in the Op. 12, No. 4, by Schumann
the first period in G-flat major (where one measu
introduced) and constitutes an extended period o:
of eight measures.
    Another instance may be mentioned in which th
ent: The avoided cadence takes place on the first
teenth full measure in the Rondo from Beethover
period contains nine measures; but the extension
after cadence in the sixteenth measure, not from the
in the fourteenth measure. However, the effect of

* The third, fourth, fifth, and sixth resolutions of the dominal
stitute avoided cadences.

deuce in this and all other instances is to avoid the impression which an authentic cadence would create.

The various harmonic cadences just described play an important part in the construction, division, and effect of musical compositions. If well understood they will be of material assistance in our future analytical work. The teacher is therefore advised to perform the examples again, in different order.

[The author of this work has made a distinction in "The Mysteries of Music" (from which this chapter is abridged) between deceptive and avoided cadences. But this distinction need not enter here.]

ADDITIONAL ILLUSTRATIONS.

Renunciation, W. Tappert. (Avoided cadence in second measure of the Coda. The last cadence is authentic.)

Heller, Op. 49, No. 1. Last eight measures of the Arabesque.

No. 4, same opus. Last ten measures. Plagal cadences at the close of each.

The last measure of Bertini's Seventeenth Etude, Op. 32, contains a complete cadence.

Measures 1 and 2, 7 and 8 of the first movement of Beethoven's Op 81a, are examples of the esthetic effect of an avoided cadence. See "Lebe wohl" written over the notes in the reprint of the Stuttgart edition.

Also the Andante con moto to Schubert's B-flat Symphony contains many instances like this:

Ex. 68.

PART III.

Chapter X.

PHRASE, SEMI-PHRASE, AND MOTIVE.

THE analytical terms, Phrase, Section, and Period, are retained in this book to designate the constructional parts of a musical composition. A complete musical sentence or Period is divided, firstly, into two equal parts called Sections, and, secondly, into subdivisions, called Phrases, thus:

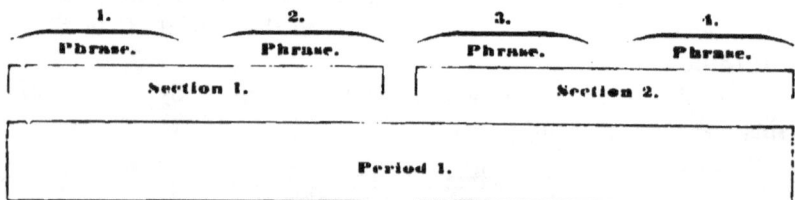

The period, therefore, contains two sections, four phrases and eight (or sixteen) measures. These terms are generally understood in this sense, and, what is more important, they are perfectly proper and suggestive.

SEMI-PHRASE.

We will make a still farther distinction, or subdivision, in this system. There are many instances in which the phrases are subdivided by the composer into two equal parts, and these are not to be ignored. We have, therefore, applied the term Semi-phrase to this smallest constituent part of a period. Following is a practical example of the phrase and semi-phrase:

Ex. 69.

What we have quoted includes the usual length of a phrase, *i. e.*, two measures. This phrase is subdivided by the composer into two equal parts, and these we call semi-phrases. These usually go in pairs; the first is a brief question, the second is the answer. The next example is similar:

Ex. 70.

This phrase, like the other included in the brackets, naturally divides itself into semi-phrases. The second part of the Rondo from which the last extract is taken contains the same feature as regards the division of the phrases.

PHRASE.

We will now consider the phrase in its entirety. A phrase may contain two, three, or four measures; though two measures is the rule, and this being the simplest, naturally comes first. This merely refers to the mensural proportion, or the length of the phrase. In addition to the proportion of the phrase it has two characteristic features, Melody and Rhythm. Melody we will illustrate by means of a negative statement:

Ex. 71.

This is not melody. Yet if the example at (a) were played upon a trumpet or kettle-drum it would constitute a phrase. The melodic feature of a phrase therefore consists of the tones comprised in the phrase, and the distance between each of these tones as they follow one another successively.

there is a simple melodic figure ascending from the tonic by regular diatonic degrees to the third of the scale and then skipping over one degree to the tonic where it began. This is a diatonic phrase and contains more of the melodic than the rhythmic element.

In the following phrase the *melodic element* is also most prominent:

Ex. 73.

The intervals are an ascending fifth and two descending thirds, constituting what we call a chord motive, being composed of the intervals of a common chord.

The next example is principally rhythmical:

GURLITT

Ex. 74.

In a general way we might say that the harmony to this is of first importance; but what the ear seizes upon is principally this characteristic rhythm: which is continued throughout the piece. In such cases the rhythm becomes a means of uniting the entire piece into a consistent whole, and accordingly, an element of construction.

DIABELLI.   BELLINI.

Ex. 75.   Allegro.   Andante.

This first example is a Gipsy rhythm, and becomes a most prominent feature of the music in which it occurs. The rhythm of this, for example, played upon a drum, (after the above phrase has been sounded) would not only suggest Hungarian music but serve to recall the principal motive as quoted in the example. The introductory phrase from "Norma" is more serious, but not so characteristic. However, as the rhythm is more prominent than the melody, the former enters more into the construction and connection of the period than does the latter.

Following is an example that is both melodious and rhythmical:

Ex. 76.

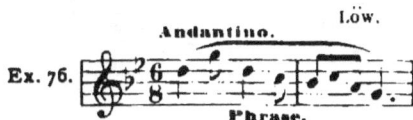

This contains some diatonic degrees; but it is principally a chord motive. The rhythm is also peculiar, and the ear will seize upon this almost as readily as upon the melodic features. Indeed, rhythm exercises a more important influence upon music than is commonly supposed. The principal works of Bach, Beethoven, Berlioz, and Schumann illustrate this fact.

We will now present a few examples of four-measure phrases. (Three-measure phrases, being exceptional, are explained in a separate chapter.) Phrases of four measures usually occur in ⅜ or ⅞ metre, and in a quick movement. Here is an illustration from a Galop:

Ex. 77.

The movement is vivace, and it is equivalent to the following in common measure:

Ex. 78.

This is a diatonic phrase, ascending from the dominant to the tonic and descending back to the dominant.

The next example is in ⅜ metre, and also contains four measures:

Ex. 79.

This is not materially different in mensural proportion from the other phrases. The four measures naturally belong together and are necessary to the completion of the sense of the phrase.

The next example contains a short and a long phrase for comparison:

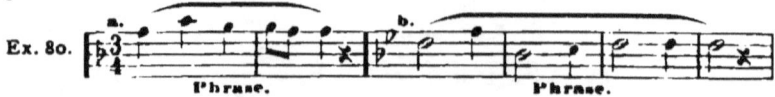

In both cases the movement is slow and the metre ¾; but at (a) the sense of the phrase is completed in two measures, whereas at (b) the sum and substance of the phrase includes four measures. The period beginning at (a) will contain eight measures; but in the next example the period will contain sixteen. (This will be more readily comprehended when we come to Period.)

MOTIVE.

The text upon which a musical work is written is called Motive. The motive is the seed from which the trunk, branches, leaves, etc., issue and develop. From this definition it is apparent that no exact mensural proportion can be prescribed for the motive. Here is a lengthy text: "The Future of Republicanism in France." Tyndall wrote his great acoustical work upon the text, "Sound." So in music. Some motives are so terse and significant that when we hear them the effect is like reading the heading of an editorial on Animal Magnetism. They suggest the general nature of the composition and give us a clew as to thoughts and emotions which are set forth. This is especially so where we analyze the motive first, or ponder upon a text before reading the article. In fact, the motive is the germ from which the composition grows and develops, and to which its various ramifications may be referred and compared. Haydn was in the habit of asking his friends for a motive, and if they gave him merely this:

it was sufficient for him to build a very clever composition upon. How he developed this semi-phrase we shall see.

In the majority of cases the first phrase of the principal period is the motive. In the last example the motive constitutes but half of a phrase; and sometimes the motive exceeds the limit of a phrase. These exceptional cases will be presented after the rule has been first established.

A variety of motives are contained in the following examples, which should be examined attentively, and then performed:

Ex. 82.

* The motive from Onslow requires three measures for its completion; but on the first of the third measure the second phrase enters as a response in the treble, so that the even mensural proportion is thus preserved.

Each of these motives constitutes the first phrase, with exception of Nos. 3, 5, and 9. The remainder of this phrase (3.) is:

Ex. 83.

The first semi-phrase, however, is a complete motive. The fermata placed by the composer over the fourth note is proof of this. In each of the nine motives we have a complete text. What follows after these is the continuation of the motive, or melodic development —in other words, the antithesis. As a rule the motive will consist of two long, or four short measures, and must be sufficiently significant or suggestive to form a text.

The motive of the Oratorio "Naaman" is simply this:

Ex. 84.

These portentous intervals run like a thread throughout the entire Oratorio. The quotation No. 3, from Beethoven's great Fifth Symphony, is another instance of a concise but significant short motive.

Ex. 85.

This motive, the text upon which Mr. Goldbeck wrote his *Petite Etude*, contains but one short measure, which is exceptional. The notes are taken from the song "Kelvin Grove."

In the following quotation from Haydn we have the continuation of the semi-phrase:

Ex. 86.

(The motives in Wagner's music dramas contain any amount of measures that may be required to typify a certain person or sentiment. This is a wider application than our present one and cannot be considered here.)

ILLUSTRATIONS FOR THIS CHAPTER.

* Diabelli, Op. 149, Books 1, 2, 3 and 4. Grateful Tasks, Gurlitt, Op. 102: Nos. 1, 3, 5, 6, 7, 8, 9, 10, 11, 13, 14 and 25. Enke, Op. 8: Nos. 2, 3 and 5. Pabst, Scherzino, Op. 15, first period only. Dussek, Rondo, "Les Adieux."

The class should name each phrase as it is played, giving the number of measures which the phrases contain. To do this the metre and movement must first be ascertained. The semi-phrases are also to be specified.

---

* These are known as "Melodious Exercises."

Chapter XI.

PHRASES BEGINNING UPON FRACTIONAL PARTS OF A MEASURE.

WHEN a phrase commences upon the fractional part of a measure it will generally appear that the second phrase also begins in like manner. Therefore, if the first phrase of a theme commences upon the fourth quarter in ¼ metre it must end upon the third beat, so that the second phrase may also commence upon the fourth beat. An illustration will make this more plain:

Ex. 87.

Observe that each phrase consists of exactly two full measures, just as if written thus:

Ex. 88.

This produces a different effect on account of the reversed accents, though the notes are identical—both melodically and rhythmically. (Play examples 87 and 88 as written.)

Thus it is with a Gavotte; each phrase and period begins upon the third quarter in common metre, and terminates upon the second quarter of a measure. Therefore the eight measures of a period are counted in this way: Seven full measures and two half measures (one at the beginning and one at the end), making in all, eight measures:

Ex. 89.

The first period commences upon the last half of a measure at (a),
and ends upon the first half of a measure at (b). The second period
also commences upon the third beat, at (c). The phrases are included in brackets.

Play the *Andante* to Kuhlau's Op. 20, No. 1, until the class can
say upon what part of a measure the different phrases begin. The
Rondo will serve as another illustration.

The fractional part of a measure is not counted at first, but
carried over and counted in with the last incomplete measure, which
requires the carried fraction to complete it:

The first two notes (a) added to the last half note in the eighth
measure will complete the rhythm of the period—eight measures.
But the numbers do not begin until the first full measure. (See 1,
2, 3, 4, etc.) The commencement of each of the four phrases is indicated by the letters (a), (b), (c) and (d). A second period similar
in construction begins at (e). (These phrases are subdivided by the
slurs into semi-phrases. In such cases the two subdivisions are
counted as one phrase.)

A few more examples will be presented in exemplification of
this subject:

The first piece begins upon the fourth eighth note; and so the phrases and periods end upon the third eighth. See (a) and (b). The next example begins upon the last three sixteenths; consequently the phrases and semi-phrases terminate upon the third quarter—or the thirteenth sixteenth note. In the second period it is still more necessary to observe these fractional beginnings, in order to properly punctuate and phrase the different divisions. See (e), (f) and (g). The last note at the end of each slur must be extremely staccato. The phrasing is indicated in the example. The quotation from Kuhnau commences upon the second eighth note, and so the phrases must end upon the first eighth in the measure following.

ILLUSTRATIONS.

First movement, Sonatina, Op. 66, No. 1, Lichner.

"After the Ballet," Pratt.

Nos. 9, 10 and 15, from "Grateful Tasks," by Gurlitt, Op. 102.
In the No. 15, omit the "trio."

Album Leaf, No. 1, Gade.

Sonatina, Reinecke, Op. 47, No. 1.

Each movement begins upon the fractional part of a measure. This the class is to discover; also the particular part of the measure upon which the phrases begin. In the Lichner Sonatina the periods are even and may be specified by the class; also in the Nos. 9 and 10 from Gurlitt the periods are even and ought to be distinguished. In the slow movement from Reinecke the periods are easily recognized until we come to the Coda. The first movement contains both curtailed and extended periods, and cannot be analyzed by the class at present.

The following questions should now be given: 1. Mode; 2. Rhythm of the theme; 3. Rhythm of the accompaniment; 4. Metre; 5. Indicate what part of a measure the periods commence upon; 6. The Movement; 7. Number of Phrases.

Chapter XII.

SECTIONS—VARIOUS MODES OF CONSTRUCTION.

AFTER the first phrase there follows another phrase, composed of the same number of measures, and usually constructed of the same melodic or rhythmic material, thus:

STEIBELT.

Ex. 92.

When the two phrases follow each other in this close relationship of antecedent and consequent, they form a section. A section consists, therefore, of two equal phrases, or four measures. Should the phrase contain four measures, the section will necessarily have eight. There are scarcely any exceptions to this rule; but with regard to the construction of the consequent phrase (second half of the section), there are various modes of procedure. The simplest arrangement is to continue the first phrase in sequence, as thus:

Ex. 93.

This is a continuation of the phrase quoted in Ex. 72. The slurs show the Phrases and the bracket embraces the Section. The second phrase is similar to the first, played a degree higher in the scale.

The continuation of the first phrase in Ex. 94 is after the same fashion:

Ex. 94.

Compare the second phrase with the first and analyze the intervals. The melodic features are almost the same, and the rhythm is identical.

In the next example the method employed is not so primitive:

Ex. 95.

The tones at (b) have an ascending rather than a descending tendency, and the rhythm is considerably altered. The second phrase here affords a better illustration of antithesis following the thesis. Somewhat similar is the following extract from a Romanesca of the sixteenth century:

Ex. 96.

Both melodic and rhythmic features of the two phrases are different, yet the continuation is natural and effective.

The ascending and descending features, as applied to the two phrases of the section, play an important part in the construction and the effect. Observe the following quotations:

Ex. 97.

Ex. 98.

The second phrase in each example is in contrast to the first—the ascending groups being answered by descending ones.

The next example is by repetition:

Ex. 99.

The first phrase is repeated almost literally to complete the section; but the second phrase being an echo of the first, becomes a substitute for the consequent phrase. Examples of this kind are numerous, especially in old music.

(Play a number of sections in reverse order, to show the natural tendency of the antecedent phrase. In the majority of cases the class will be able to recognize the inversion of the order in which the phrases ought to occur.)

Here is the continuation of a four-measure phrase:

By comparing (b) with (a) the affinity between the antecedent and consequent will be noticed; (a) is the thesis, (b) the antithesis. Play the second phrase first, and then as a continuation of this, play the first phrase. This will prove what we have said.

We will quote but one more eight-measure section:

The rhythm of the second phrase is similar to the first, but the melody ascends in the first, and descends in the second. The skips of the first phrase are omitted in the second, and this has a tendency to prevent monotony.

ILLUSTRATIONS.

"La Matinée," Rondo, by Dussek

(The first phrase is this:

'and the other phrases correspond, so far as mensural proportion is considered.)

The Sarabande in D minor, by Händel.

"Les Moutons" and the "Romance," from Padre Martini, and the Couperin Gavotte-Rondo, in F.

The Mazurka, by Pabst, Op. 15, No. 2.

Any of the duets mentioned in the last chapter.

These selections should be analyzed first from the printed notes, merely for the phrases and sections.

Then distribute the following questions before playing the illustrations: 1. Metre and Movement; 2. Rhythm of the Theme; 3. Modes; 4. Phrases and Semi-phrases; 5. Sections (how many and of what length).

The last two questions might be general during the first few selections.

———————————

Chapter XIII.

SINGLE PERIOD, OR TYPE.

DIFFERENT MODES OF PERIODIC CONSTRUCTION.

WE have become familiar with the construction of phrases and sections; and as two sections or four phrases constitute a Period, we have but to add another section to those of our previous lesson in order to arrive at a simple musical Type, or what is called a Tune. A satisfactory period or pattern cannot be composed of less than eight measures. Period is therefore to be understood in its literal sense as indicating a termination, fulfillment, or something completed.

The second section, though generally similar to the first, should be more final, and end upon the key-tone. Let us copy a previous section :

Ex. 103.

This is an ascending sequence, and is incomplete;

* The fermata ⌢ indicates the period.

The first phrase at (b) is a retrograde imitation of the first phrase at (a). And the last phrase is arranged to end on the key-tone, thus forming a cadence and a period. Accordingly, two sections, or four phrases, constitute a regular period. Consequently if the phrases have two measures the period will have eight; but if the phrases contain four measures the period will be found to contain sixteen.

Before proceeding it will be necessary to call attention to the Half Cadence, and the Authentic Cadence, which play such important roles in periodic construction. The Half Cadence consists of the tonic harmony followed by that of the dominant, and this has the best effect at the end of the first section:

The last two chords marked (K. H.) indicate the half cadence. (The thorough bass figures are included for the benefit of those who understand them.) As the piece cannot end on the dominant harmony (unless there be a transition to the dominant) it is evident this is incomplete, and that more must follow, as here:

The Authentic Cadence occurs in the last of the second section, and brings the strain to a satisfactory terminaton.

The Authentic Cadence is simply this:

These two cadences might be transposed into various keys by the class in order to familiarize them with the application and effect:

1 and 2 are half cadences; 3, 4, 5 and 6 are authentic and final. At 5 the melody ends upon the third of the key-tone; and at 6 the fifth of the key-tone is uppermost. Any of these may occur in the final cadence, though Nos. 3 and 4 are most common. These should be transposed on paper theoretically, and at the piano by sound.

The simplest periodic construction is by means of a repetition of the first section, with a more final ending in the last phrase.

Compare the first and third with the second and fourth phrases in this example, "Birdie's Burial":

Ex. 108.

Ex. 109.

These phrases are more than similar; they are rhythmically identical. First there is the thesis; then the antithesis, and so the period is completed in the most natural and primitive manner. Chopin's Prelude, Op. 28, No. 7, is constructed in this way. A quotation of the rhythm will show this:

This is the same in what follows.

The second mode of construction is to slightly vary the second phrase, thus:

Ex. 110.

The first and third phrases are identical, also the second and fourth. The second period, though different in rhythm, is on the same plan.

The first section of this period quoted in Ex. 100, ended upon a half cadence; this second section ends upon the key-tone with an authentic cadence. A similar instance is Le Tambourin, by Rameau.

The third arrangement is, to write the second phrase in contrast to the first.

The second phrase differs from the first both in melody and rhythm. The following example from Padre Martini is similar:

Nos. 2 and 5 from Enke's Op. 8 are in this style. This resembles the second scheme, but there is more variety and contrast between the antecedent and consequent phrases. In all these cases the first and third, and second and fourth phrases correspond.

The fourth arrangement is, to repeat the first phrase in sequence, with identical rhythm, and then vary the last section :

Ex. 114.

The first period of Rubinstein's Valse Caprice (after the Introduction) affords another instance of this arrangement. The Eglogue by Heller, Op. 40, No. 4, also contains something of this fourth arrangement, though the second phrase is an exact repetition of the first. After these the style is varied.

The fifth arrangement is the subdivision of the phrases into semi-phrases. This style is more fragmentary. Such an instance has been quoted in this chapter; but a more uniform example is the second period of Chopin's Mazurka, Op. 67, No. 2. This will be analyzed:

Ex. 115.

When the phrases are joined together into one section, and not separated by apparent punctuation marks, the effect upon the period is the same. Therefore in the analysis the united phrases can be counted as usual; *i. e.*, two measures to a phrase, though the actual performance might require no punctuation. Such instances may result from a sequence carried beyond the limits of a phrase, as in the last example, or from a continuous passage of three or four measures in which *two phrases are united into a section*. In the example from Chopin there are two regular phrases, first with this rhythm:

Following this are four more measures to complete the period, but all joined into a section by the sameness of the rhythm. The analysis of this would be:

But the periods are so short, and the melody so well defined, that these punctuations are not necessary in the performance.

In the following example from Haydn's Gipsy Rondo the connection of the third and fourth phrases is more perfect and continuous:

The motive is sequenced by the second phrase, the melody being similar, and the rhythm identical, thus:

The third and fourth phrases are joined into the last section by the continuous theme and this unvarying rhythm:

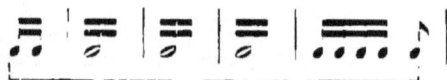

The slurs in the example indicate the phrases for analysis, while the bracket shows the manner of performance, and how the second section is joined together. This mode of connecting the phrases has an important esthetic effect, and that is to relieve the sameness of similar phrases by uniting two phrases into one section.

RECAPITULATION.

This matter of regular periodic construction by phrases and sections is so important that it will not be sufficient for the class to know that two long or four short measures usually constitute a phrase. As certain parts of classical music are not composed of phrases, it is necessary for us to know what constitutes regular periodic construction. The fact has been stated that the first phrase is the thesis, and the second phrase the antithesis, or natural consequent of the first. This may be illustrated by a familiar quotation: "To be," that is the thesis; then follows the antithesis, "or not to be." The next sentence refers to the first proposition: "Whether 'tis nobler in the mind to suffer," etc. The antithesis to this also follows: "Or to take arms against a sea of troubles, and, by opposing, end them?" The meditation is upon life or death—the state of existence or non-existence. *Life* is the thesis; the natural or unnatural *end of life* is the antithesis. Though the two propositions are directly opposite, the connection between them is intimate. In music, regular periods are constructed in this way. The first phrase is usually the thesis, and the second phrase the antithesis:

Ex. 117.

The second phrase here is the natural continuation of the motive. A motive sometimes includes both thesis and antithesis, as, for example, first phrase in the Minuet to Mozart's G minor Symphony. See (a) and (b). In the Finale these two contrasting features of the motive (c) and (d) require two phrases for their exposition. This is the more frequent occurrence; in fact, the example from the Minuet is exceptional.

Ex. 118.

Ex. 119.

The first is a three-measure or uneven phrase, but it contains the two contrasting features which usually belong to two different phrases. Compare (a) and (b). In the example in common metre the first phrase contains the chord feature, while the second phrase has the answer, or consequent. Thus (c) in the second example corresponds to (a) in the first.

Ex. 120.

In like manner (d) corresponds to (b).

We will also meet with instances in which there is no antithesis following the thesis, but these will be found outside the regular periods, either in the Introduction, or Coda, or in a transition, sequence, or anticipation. Sequence affords a good example of this:

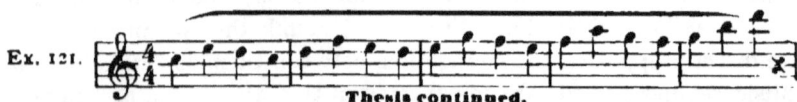

Ex. 121.

Thesis continued.

which merely represents but one phase of the same thought. Music composed in this manner would be very monotonous and unsatisfactory. A familiar instance is to be found in the Andante to Beethoven's Fifth Symphony, where a fragment of the second subject appears in C major. But this occurs in an intermediate passage, not in a regular period. This will be explained later.

The complete period, as we have found it, expresses a perfect sentence, or a short verse of poetry. This we call a musical type, or the smallest embodiment of a complete tune or subject.

KUHLAU.

Ex. 122.

The complete period is indicated in the performance either by a slight pause, a *rallentando*, or by separating the principal tone or tones from what follows.

ILLUSTRATIONS.

Prelude, Op. 28, No. 7, Chopin.

Prelude, Op. 28, No. 20, Chopin. (End on the eighth measure, as the second section is repeated.)

Nos. 11 and 21, in the 50 Children's Songs by Reinecke. (These may be played or sung as examples.)

"The Hunt is Up," old English song.

The first repeated period in the Rondo from Kuhlau's Op. 20, No. 1.

One period from any of the examples quoted.

(It would be well to have the class construct a regular period from a simple motive.)

1. Metre; 2. Rhythm; 3. Movement; 4. Mode; 5. Phrase (number of measures); 6. Section; 7. Period.

(Phrases beginning on a fractional part of a measure should be specified.)

Chapter XIV.

TYPE—ONE PERIOD. MODEL—TWO PERIODS.

WE have become acquainted with the principal features of natural periodic construction; and as the single period represents a complete strain, or melody, we have but little more to accomplish in this direction, for the Consequent Period is constructed out of the same melodic and rhythmic materials as was the Type, or Pattern Period.

Where the single period represents a complete musical theme we call it a Type. It has a natural beginning and ending; thesis and antithesis; constructional divisions and subdivisions—sections and phrases. Therefore it becomes a standard or pattern for other periods and parts; or may stand by itself as the expression of a poetic idea. The simple type of one period may contain eight or sixteen measures, provided there are four phrases, and this constitutes but one period, *however often it may be repeated.* The little Prelude by Chopin (already quoted) is a beautiful pattern of this primary musical type.

THE DUPLEX PERIODS OR BALLAD MODEL.

In simple Ballads, Ballad Dances, and short instrumental movements, the single period becomes the type for another similar period *corresponding to the first*, and constructed in the same manner. The most natural mode of constructing the consequent period is this: The first phrase of the second period commences on a different part of the scale, and usually the direction ("motion") of the melody is reversed or otherwise altered from what it was in the Pattern Period. The second phrase would naturally correspond to the first; and then the last section of the first period is repeated as a completion of the second. Here is an example:

Ex. 123.

The first period begins and ends in G major; the second period begins in E minor, then passes into D major (second phrase), and the last section (d) is an exact repetition of the last two phrases of the first period (b). In other words, the second sections are identical. Many of Schubert's Dances, besides innumerable songs, are in this style.

The next example is different in character, but similar in construction:

Ex. 124.

(The first period of this has been quoted in Ex. 104 and 105, which see.)

The first phrase here commences with the dominant, in place of the tonic harmony, but the rhythm is similar. Observe that the last section is exactly the same as the last section of the first period, Ex. 105. The second period of the Andantino quoted in Ex. 111 is completed in this manner. The well-known American song,

"Old Folks at Home," and the Doll's Cradle Song by Reinecke are good illustrations of this mode of construction.

The second plan of constructing the consequent period is to write it in a similar style to that of the pattern period, but without repeating any part of the latter literally. We will select the second period to the Gavotte-Rondo from Martini, as the pattern period has been quoted, Ex. 113:

Ex. 125.

The first two phrases here have a descending tendency, whereas the first section of the pattern period ascends. The only resemblance between the two periods consists in the rhythm, and the descending scale passages, thus:

Ex. 126.

(a) is from the first period (second section); (b) is from the second period (first section). In other words, there are two separate strains constructed of the same material, in a similar manner, and having the same periodic length. Yet they belong together by their very resemblance and conformity; the first period being the pattern, and the second the duplicate, or consequent. The two periods being similar in rhythmic and melodic structure, as well as in outline, they form a union, or what we shall call a Duplex or Ballad Model. Here is another example:

SCHUBERT WALTZ.

Ex. 127.

The rhythm of these two periods is identical except in the seventh measure. The second part of the Funeral March from Chopin: the

Turkish Rondo, by Steibelt, and the Rondo already cited, from Dussek, are in this style. The second arrangement presents more variety and is of more frequent occurrence.

The third arrangement consists in writing a new section for the second period, and then repeating the first period verbatim. The well-known Boccherini Minuet in A answers to this description:

Ex. 128.

This commences with the second period; but after the first four measures, which are new, the first period of eight measures is repeated.

The second part of the song quoted in Ex. 109 of the previous chapter begins like this:

Ex. 129.

which is the commencement of the second period. But immediately following the above the first period of eight measures is repeated.

The fourth plan, somewhat the reverse of the last, consists in writing the consequent period entire, so far as mensural proportion is considered, and then leaving the cadence incomplete so that the last section of the original period may be repeated.

The Musette to Bach's G minor Gavotte (in the third English Suite) is an instance.

The last twelve measures of the Gavotte II, from Bach's Sixth 'Cello Suite is a similar instance. (This occurs in the third period, commencing like this:

Ex. 130.

The last four measures are the same as the last section of the pattern period.) These instances result in an extended period of twelve measures, which will be more fully explained in Chapter XXI.

In each case we have a full second period without the repetition of the last section from the first period.

All these arrangements come under the general title of what we call the Ballad Model. It is the natural corresponding expression of popular rhymes, and both poetry and music of this kind have for their principal outward charm a certain mensural proportion and rhythmic cadence.

Before the practical exemplifications of this chapter are performed the different methods of constructing a Ballad Model should be briefly restated, and the class should be expected to distinguish each one from the others. Perform one example of each, and allow this question to be a general one.

ILLUSTRATIONS.

First Mode.—Schubert, Ecossaisen No. 4 (from the Schubert Dances); Gurlitt, No. 9 or 11, from the "Grateful Tasks"; Diabelli, Op. 149, No. 5 (omitting the Trio); Kuhlau, Op. 20, No. 1, Andante.

Second Mode.—Schubert Waltz No. 1 (from Dances); "Trio" to Chopin's Funeral March in B-flat minor; first two periods of the Rondo Turc, by Steibelt; the Rondo "Les Adieux," Dussek, and the Gavotte "Les Moutons," Martini.

Third Mode.—Boccherini Minuet in A (two periods); the song by Claribel, "We'd better bide a wee."

Fourth Mode.—Musette in G minor from Third English Suite, Bach, and Gavotte in D, already indicated (last twelve measures).

QUESTIONS.

1. Metre and Movement; 2. Rhythm of the theme; 3. Number of Phrases; 4. Length of Phrases; 5. Number of Sections; 6. Number of Periods (including Repetition).

In pieces like Nos. 2 and 4, from Diabelli's Op. 149, the second period looks on paper twice as long as the first period; but the first period follows the second in the repetition, and so there are but two periods, or one Ballad Model, in all such instances.

PART IV.

Chapter XV.

FORM—PRIMITIVE EXAMPLES.

RECAPITULATION.

THE simplest pattern in music is the single period of eight or sixteen measures, which we call a Type. The Chopin Prelude, No. 7, is an example. The next approach is the Duplex, or Ballad Model of two corresponding periods—the first being the Type or Pattern, and the second the Duplicate or Consequent Period. Ballads, Ballad Dances (as we shall term them), and such short pieces as the Andante to Kuhlau's Sonatina, Op. 20, No. 1, are Ballad Models.

We now approach the instrumental form of three periods. The simplest illustration of this is that popular vocal style which the author calls Narrative-Song-Ballad. In this we find two single periods as a Ballad Model, and then a third, and differently constructed period, which is the Refrain—or strictly and technically, the Trio. The reason for applying the word "Trio" to the third and fourth periods of a Dance has never been satisfactorily explained. The surmise that a third instrument was called upon to assist in the performance of the second half of a dance tune is too conjectural and supposititious to be accepted; for the so-called Trio is not a third period, but second half, or third and fourth period added to the first two; both halves being of the same proportion and having the same subdivisions. (Perhaps we have accidentally found the solution in this *third single period.*)

In old ballads the Ritornello, or instrumental Intermezzo, assumes the shape of a third period, thus showing the incompleteness of the ballad model and the desire for something more satisfactory and less monotonous than the twin periods of the ballad. This latter does not constitute a Form, in the general application of that important term.

FORM.

Few words have such a variety of definitions, applications, and synonyms as Form; and it has proved to be far more elastic than consistent in the case of music. Thus, two twin periods are called a "Ballad Form;" two ballad forms (i. e., "two principal periods and a trio" of two more) are called a "Dance Form;" a piece like Jensen's "Mill," with four periods, intermezzo, and coda, is called a "Single Form;" Haydn's "Gipsy Rondo" contains seven periods, an intermezzo, and coda, and is known as a "Rondo Form." A set of dance pieces, such as constitute a Suite, or Partita, is called a "Cyclical Form." In the first movement to a Sonata we have an extended period as first subject, and then a second subject in contrast to the first; and this (so we are told) constitutes a "change of form." In the development, according to this definition, the form may change again, and then we have the Reprise. Following this is what some German authors have called a "Binary" or a "Ternary Form;" then for the third movement a "Dance Form;" and finally a "Rondo Form," or another "Sonata Form." Now observe the catastrophe: All these movements and forms bound together under one cover, and following each other in regular order, are called the "Sonata Form." The contradictions and inconsistencies do not end here; but certainly these are sufficiently numerous and confusing to claim our immediate and patient attention. A curious person may very pertinently inquire, What is Form in Music? and what is the Sonata Form? Can a form contain any number of forms? Is a house having several partitions a Partition? All this is an obvious confusion of genus with species.

The most important definitions of Form are: " 1. The shape and structure of anything, as distinguished from the material of which it is composed; particular disposition of matter, giving it individuality or distinctive character; external appearance; the outline of a person. 2. Constitution; organization; mode of construction; system. 3. Established method; fixed way of proceeding; conventional scheme." The less important synonyms are: "Figure, Mold, Pattern, Type, Model."

We naturally associate form, or outline, with structure; and when *form* is applied to music we understand it to signify some kind of embodiment of constituent parts, systematically and artistically joined together into a complete and satisfactory whole. Therefore, since the twin periods of the Ballad Model simply constitute a melody, without preface or conclusion, we will apply to it a word of less general significance than Form, which is too comprehensive and too confusing. Moreover, there is no instance in which a reputable modern composer has attempted to create a complete instrumental form within the limits of sixteen measures, or out of two equal periods. The Duplex period of the Ballad becomes the Model in the Dance form; and so we will say that in the second half of a dance piece ("trio") the *Style*, not the *Form*, changes. Some of the ancient dances, such as the Pavan, Sarabande, Courante, contained but two repeated periods, or a simple model. These we will call Ballad-Dances, especially as some popular ballad was frequently sung in connection with the dance of two periods. Bach and Händel did not use the word "trio" for the second theme, or second part of their Minuets and Gavottes; they simply marked the divisions I and II. This was both sensible and proper; but in modern editions the word "trio" has been applied to the third and fourth periods, and without any good reason, except that Trio is easily said. The smallest single instrumental form which will be recognized in this Analysis is a composition like Rubinstein's La Melodia (in F); the Venetian Gondola-song, in F-sharp minor, by Mendelssohn; a Toccata; Prelude and Fugue, and the three period pieces already mentioned. The best informed writers upon music are mostly agreed that the "basis of form" includes at least a complete period, with a "contrasting theme in the middle" (not a mere consequent period) and a repetition of the first part. This is very good reasoning, and excludes the Ballad from the list of Instrumental forms. The student is advised in the first place that Form in music depends upon three requisites, namely: Outline, Rhythm, and Tonality. Let us analyze these:

1. Suppose we conclude to write a composition with a First Part of sixteen measures (two similar periods), and a Second Part of the same number of periods; and, finally, a repetition of the First Part. That is the Outline, or draught.

2. In the First Part the rhythm is about the same, making the duplicate period similar to the pattern period. This would soon become monotonous; so we change the value of the notes in the Second Part (third and fourth periods) in order to present variety of style. This is Rhythm.

3. We now come to the third requisite. Suppose our first two periods were in D major, with, perhaps, temporary transitions to the dominant or relative minor. We now change the tonal foundation in order to present a different view, and write the first period of the second part in F-sharp minor, and the second period in A major. The rhythm and melody of these two periods of the second part being similar, the difference between F-sharp minor and A major is slight, but sufficient to afford some contrast to the scale of D major. After finishing the second part and ending in A, we can naturally repeat the first part, A being the dominant to our original key-tone, D. This is an example of Tonality. We have here something corresponding to the processes of drawing, i. e., Outline, Sketch, and Delineation. According to this plan (which is of common occurrence) we have two periods in the principal key, D, one in F-sharp minor and one in A major. In this case Part I is played again after Part II (D. C.), which gives considerable prominence to the original key, D, and at the same time the change in Tonality in Part II introduces but two foreign tones to D major, i. e., g-sharp as leading-tone to A, and e-sharp as leading-tone to F-sharp minor.

ELEMENTARY FORMS OF THREE PERIODS.

There are three methods of constructing the Simple Form of three periods.

1. The most primitive is derived from the simple Ballad, in which the vocal model of two similar periods is sung to the first stanza, and then a Ritornello or Interlude is introduced to afford the singer a rest, and as a relief to the sameness of the two vocal periods. Interludes played between the verses of hymn tunes illustrate this. In these cases the Interlude is usually a slight development of the principal motive, and becomes a third period. Observe the following quotation from a popular song:

Ex. 131.

The Ballad Model ends in the sixteenth measure, being composed of two similar periods. The Interlude then commences, and this contains one regular period. It is constructed out of the first and seventh measures of the first period. In these instances the third strain is in the same key, and bears considerable resemblance to the model. This plan affords relief to the regular Ballad, and presents us an example of Elementary Form. It has been employed in numerous songs, and in variations for solo instruments (such as violin or flute) with piano accompaniment. After the soloist performs a variation of the two periods of the theme, the piano alone takes up a third period, similar to the Interlude. Several similar instances occur in the Op. 149, by Diabelli.

The second arrangement is this: First, a Ballad model of two periods, usually repeated; then a third strain in another key, and with *different rhythm*. The third period, or Trio, is also repeated, and then the first two periods are repeated in order to end in the original key:

This third period in C minor affords us a consistent example of Trio, *i. e., a third strain.* The mode is changed from C major to tonic minor (with a temporary transition to E-flat), and the rhythm, which was at first [rhythm notation] becomes in the Trio [rhythm notation] There is, however, sufficient analogy between the model and the Trio, and the mensural proportion of each period is the same. Observe that the phrases in every period contain four measures, and that each strain has sixteen measures. Similar examples will be found among the illustrations.

The third arrangement consists in adding a third period in the same key, after the repetition of the two principal periods; and ending with the Afterlude in place of the Da Capo. In some cases this third period has the appearance of a Coda; but in the examples we shall quote there is a regularly constructed third strain, and sometimes a short Coda as final ending:

Ex. 133.

The third period here is repeated with the second, to which it is joined in the accompaniment. The first period ends in the dominant major; the second ends in the subdominant minor, and the third in the tonic, D.

The Sarabandes in the second and third French Suites, and several of the Minuets, are constructed in the same manner. Some of the short pieces in the Op. 149 of Diabelli come under this heading; but as the third period has a different relationship, we will analyze one of these:

Ex. 134.

The first period of eight measures (a) is repeated; then we have a second period of the same length (b), beginning and ending in the dominant. This leads to a repetition of the first period (a), and at the end of this the two periods are repeated. So far we have but two periods, though the first has been heard four times, and the second (b) twice. After this we have a third period of eight measures (c) as an Afterlude. As a conclusion to the whole, there is a Coda of four measures commencing at (d). Nos. 3, 9 and 13 are in the same style.

Another plan, similar to the last, consists of a Ballad Model and a Coda. (The Coda is added after the natural termination of the movement, and is usually less regular in construction.) The Larghetto in Kuhlau's Sonatina, Op. 20, No. 3, is a good example. First there are two double periods repeated, the first sixteen and the second eighteen measures. The last eleven measures form a Coda. This is of sufficient length and import to constitute a third period, though its construction is less regular and tuneful than the other two periods. The Coda contains eleven measures. The Adagio to Op. 20, No. 2, is similar, though the Coda is more brief. In the slow movement to the Sonatina by Reinecke, Op. 47, No. 1, the third period in form of Coda consists of seventeen measures in canon style.

The class should learn to recognize the main features of a Regular Period which is to be counted but once, however many times it may be repeated. And in the repetition of a certain period the composer often varies it somewhat; or it may appear in a different key. Hence it becomes necessary, even in simple music, to recognize and remember each strain as it is heard; and in enumerating the various periods care must be exercised not to confuse a *repeated period* with a *second* or *third period*. Attention is called to the paragraph in explanation of the No. 8 from Diabelli. This must be read in connection with the printed copy, which the class should see.

ILLUSTRATIONS.

J. S. Bach, Sarabande, or Minuet I, from First French Suite.
J. S. Bach, Sarabande, from Second French Suite.
J. S. Bach, Minuet II, or Sarabande, from Third French Suite.
Händel, Courante in F, No. 1, of the "Twelve Easy Pieces."
        (The third period contains ten measures.)
Enke, Op. 8, No. 5, Valse.
Diabelli, Op. 149, Nos. 3, 5, 6, 8, 9, and 13.

Kuhlau, Op. 20, No. 3, Larghetto (middle movement).
Reinecke, Op. 47, No. 1, Andantino (middle movement).
Chopin, Mazurkas 1 or 5, Op. 6 (three periods).

At least two lessons ought to be devoted to this chapter. For the first, the questions as to mode of construction may be general. It will be sufficient in piano music to distinguish between the Trio (third period with a D. C.) and the Afterlude, or Coda, as the latter is similar to the interlude of a Ballad. But where a short Coda is added *after* the *regular third period*, this fact should be specified by the class.

Chapter XVI.

THE DANCE FORM.

COMMON SPECIES.

UNDER the first general heading we will include all styles of composition in which metre, rhythm, and movement constitute the principal characteristic features. Rhythm is the most striking peculiarity of all dance music, as it represents action and motion. With regard to Form, the Dance usually contains two parts, or four periods. The first two periods correspond to our Duplex Model. This is the First Part. The Second Part contains two periods also, but these are in a different key and rhythm. The second period of Part II corresponds to the first period, being similar in style. In other words there are two Ballad Models, in contrast to each other. Each period is repeated. After the repetition of the Second Part, the First Part is to be played again Da Capo, in order to give the necessary prominence to the original key in which the first two periods are written. (In the D. C. do not observe the repetition marks.) Part II has been misnamed Trio; and it will sometimes be necessary to use the word in this sense in order to make ourselves understood. In the previous chapter we found certain short pieces with a third strain in another key (change of signature) and in contrast to the first two periods.

This is a Trio, as Diagram A will show:

Diagram A.

PART 1. In G Major.

Fine.

| :‖ | 1st Period. | :‖: | 2d Period. | :‖ |

Trio in C Major or E♭.

D.C. al Fine.

| :‖ | 3d Period. | :‖ |

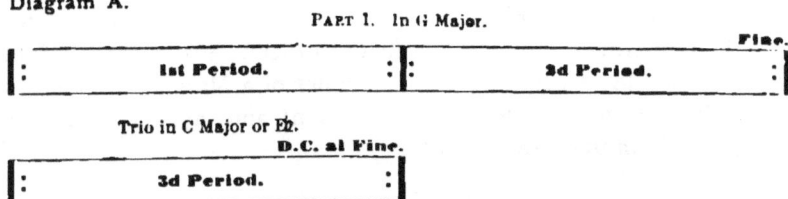

The so-called Trio of the Dance Form corresponds somewhat to that; and when the Trio, or Second Part, is in another key, it is always necessary to repeat the first part, for reasons already given. A brief sketch will illustrate more fully:

Diagram B.

PART I. In G Major.

Fine.

| :‖ | 1st Period. | :‖: | 2d Period. | :‖ |

PART II. In C or E♭.

D.C. al Fine.

| :‖ | 3d Period. | :‖: | 4th Period. | :‖ |

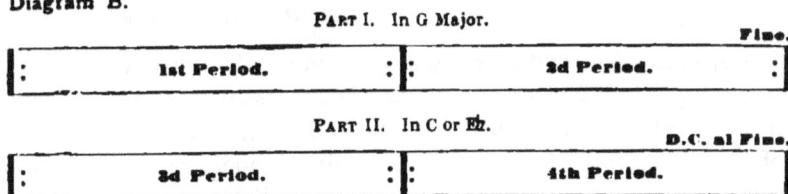

This is the plan of nearly all the common species of Dance Form. To an ordinary listener the Second Part will sound like a new piece of music, and this fact will assist those who are in doubt as to when the Second Part begins.

Nearly all Dances being alike so far as form is concerned, we will make a distinction between Form and Species. When a certain kind of composition depends for its individuality upon metre, rhythm, accent, movement, or mode, we will call it a Species. The Dance form will therefore include different species, such as the March, Minuet, Polacca, and so on, all which have very nearly the same *form*. The analyses of the old Dances, employed by the classical composers of the seventeenth and eighteenth centuries, as well as the more modern ones, will be preceded by brief descriptions and illustrations of the common Dances. (The class should copy into their note-books the following descriptions, excepting the words in parentheses.)

1. COMMON MARCH.

Metre, **4/4**; Rhythm, | ♩ ♫. ♩ ♩ | or | ♩ ♫ ♩ ♩ |; Move-
ment, *Moderato*; Form, two repeated periods of eight measures each,
and a second part, in which the key and rhythm are changed. After
this, the first two periods are repeated in order to end in the original
key. (It would be better to play examples of a March for the class.
to enable *them* to tell the metre, movement, and rhythm, instead of
informing them upon these matters.)

2. FUNERAL MARCH.

Metre, Rhythm, and Form the same as in the common March,
but the Movement is much slower, and the first two periods are in
the minor Mode. Part II is written in major, as typical of the
"freedom of the disembodied spirit."

3. FANTASIA MARCH, OR MARCHE BRILLANTE.

Metre, Rhythm, and accent same as common March, but the Movement is twice as fast—**¢.** The periods are less regular and the construction more free. The "trio" is frequently omitted. Mendelssohn's "Wedding March" contains six periods, besides a short
trumpet introduction, Eingang and Coda. Beethoven's "Turkish
March" contains no trio. It is therefore a single form.

4. SCHOTTISCHE.

Metre, **4/4**; Rhythm, | ♩ ♫ ♩ ♫ | or | ♫.♫.♫ ♩ |; Move-
ment, *Allegretto*; major or minor Mode; regular periods and second
part, like No. 1.

5. POLKA.

Metre, **2/4**; Rhythm, | ♫♫ ♩ | or | ♫♫♫ ♪♪ |; accent on
first three eighths; Movement, *Allegretto*; Form, same as 1, 2, and 4.
A Bohemian Dance of recent origin, and at one time very popular.
(The regular Polka step requires an accent on the first three eighths,
the fourth eighth being silent. But in the music there might be an
unaccented note or two after the third eighth. In this case the accompaniment should stop upon the third eighth, which would preserve the Polka rhythm.)

6. GALLOP.

Metre, $\frac{2}{4}$; Rhythm generally, | ♪♪♪ ♪♪♪ |; Movement, *Vivace* or *Presto;* Form, same as Polka. The Gallop is the fastest of all common Dances.

7. COMMON MAZURKA.

Metre, $\frac{3}{4}$; Rhythm, | ♪♪ ♪ ♪ | or | ♪ ♪ | ; Movement, very moderate. The distinguishing characteristic is the accent upon the second beat of each measure. Form, the same as Nos. 1 and 4.

8. FANTASIA MAZURKA.

Retains the characteristics of No. 7, but the Movement is faster and the construction more elaborate. Some of Chopin's Mazurkas are slow, others fast; but these are ideal Mazurkas, and not for ball-room use. The Mazurka is a Polish national Dance of graceful and courteous movement.

9. COMMON WALTZ.

Metre, $\frac{3}{4}$; Rhythm of the accompaniment, | ♩ ♩ ♩ | ; accent, first of each measure; Movement, *Allegro.* A good Waltz should have a graceful, swinging motion, that is easily recognized. Modern ball-room Waltzes are composed in sets, or numbers, each Set being complete in itself. First there is an Introduction, generally slow; then there are three or four sets of Waltzes and a Finale. Each Set contains two regular periods, which are repeated, and a D. C. or D. S. al ⌒, depending upon the key in which the different periods are written. When a new Set is in a different key, there is a short transition marked Eingang (entrance), which serves to introduce the new key. Frequently a brief Recollection is included in the Finale and marked lento; after which the whole terminates with a short *stretto,*—Presto.

10. VALSE CAPRICE, OR IDEAL WALTZ.

Metre and accent the same, but the Movement is too fast to be danced. The construction is more free, and the Waltz characteristics are less noticeable. (Rubinstein, in his Valse Caprice in E-flat, introduces a period in $\frac{2}{4}$ metre.)

11. THE OLD GERMAN WALTZ.

Metre, $\frac{3}{4}$; Rhythm, $\left| \quad \right|$; Movement, slow. It is more stately and uniform than the common Waltz. This Dance was the signal for departure, and so our German friends call it the "Clear-out Dance." (This is the Grandfather's Dance, which Schumann introduces into his Papillons).

The teacher should perform one or two examples of each of the eleven species just described, after distributing the following questions: 1. Metre; 2. The rhythm of the melody; 3. Rhythm of accompaniment; 4. Movement; 5. Accents; 6. Mode (one or both); 7. Construction (number of periods); 8. Species (form-name).

A period is to be counted but once, no matter how many times it may occur; *e. g.*, if a Funeral March were played, the answer to the seventh question would be "two periods in minor and two in major." The first questions, if correctly answered, will determine the style of each selection, whether a Polka, Gallop, Mazurka, or what not. The class may consult their memoranda made at the beginning of this chapter. The teacher should be provided with a volume of common Dance tunes, containing such as have been mentioned. Any March, like Scotson Clark's "Jacobins," will answer the purpose. Most of the music of this class is rather poor in quality, but this is a necessary evil, and one that will soon disappear, as far as the class is concerned. Two or three lessons should be devoted to this chapter, with the same questions distributed differently.

ILLUSTRATIONS.

Marche des Jacobins, Scotson Clark.

March, No. 15, from the Grateful Tasks, Gurlitt.

March and Mazurka, Walton Perkins.

Mazurka, Chopin, Op. 67, No. 2, or Op. 6, No. 5.

Polka, F. Bold, Op. 37.

Une Perle, (Bluette), Fr. Behr, may be played as an illustration of Polka.

The Finale to Reinecke's Op. 127, No. 4 (Waltz-Rondo).

Nos. 3, 5 and 6, from Op. 8, Enke, are good illustrations.

The old German Waltz may be found in the Schubert Dances, Op. 33. (See Compendium.)

Afterwards more difficult selections may be played, as: Polka de la Reine, Op. 95, and Marche Brillante, Op. 132, by Raff. A Gallop

Bravura, by Schulhoff or Ketterer. A Waltz or Mazurka, by Chopin. The March from Beethoven's " Ruins of Athens." The Second Mazurka, by Godard (in B-flat).

NOTE.—Unless otherwise directed, the class is never to be informed of what they are to hear; but the Species, Form, and character of the pieces must be discovered by them.

Chapter XVII.

THE DANCE FORM—CONTINUED.

ROCCOCO (OR OLD CLASSICAL) SPECIES.

AS the old Dances of the fifteenth, sixteenth, and seventeenth centuries are being revived by living composers, it may be well to state that the word Roccoco (or Rococo) is a mere indication of this fact, and applies to any of the old dances. Thus " Suite a la Rococo" means a collection of pieces written in the antique style. The "Roccoco" by Orth is a real Gavotte in the old style—not a mere March, or Schottische, called Gavotte.

The Form of the Roccoco Dances is usually different from that of either the common species, or the modern classical species hereinafter mentioned. The Sarabande is frequently a Ballad Dance (two periods), or a primary form of three periods. (See Diagrams C and D.) Corelli, Kuhnau, Scarlatti, Händel, and Mattheson usually wrote their Sarabandes as Ballad Dances, and then repeated the two periods with simple variations (Doubles). The Sarabandes of Bach contain a primary form of three periods, as we have seen. The signature in these cases is not changed, and the so-called Trio (Part II) does not appear. The change of tone-color is effected by means of temporary transitions to the related keys. Where the last period ends in the principal key, there is no Da Capo. (See Diagrams C and D.)

The Corrente, Gigue, Musette, Chaconne, and Tambourin have two, three, and sometimes four periods, but not the differently constructed Part II, with change of signature and D. C.

The Gavotte, Loure, and Bourrée were usually written with four periods and two parts, either according to Diagram E or F. The latter, with the change of mode for Part II, and the Da Capo, was more common. For instance, Bourrée I (two periods) in A minor; Bourrée II (same length) in A major. Or the order may appear reversed, tonic major being followed by tonic minor, as in the case of Bach's G major Gavotte, which has a Musette in G minor as Part II.

The Minuet was composed according to Diagrams C, D, or E; the Da Capo was seldom included and the signature did not change.

Diagram C.

Same Signature.

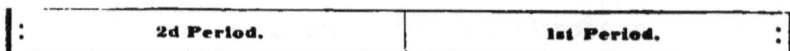

Diagram D.

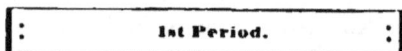

Same Signature.

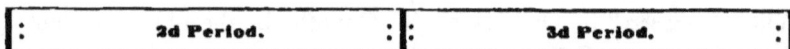

Diagram E.

PART I.

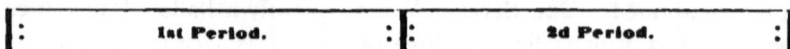

PART II. Same Key.

Diagram F.

PART I. In G Major.

Fine.

PART II. In G Minor.

D.C. al Fine.

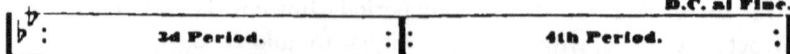

The following technical descriptions are intended principally to aid the student in recognizing the various species of the old Dance Form, and to assist in their practical performance. The questions should be: Metre, Rhythm, Movement, and Accent.

1. MINUET (*French*, MENUET; *Italian*, MENUETTO).

Measure, ⅜; Movement, *Andantino* or *Moderato;* Rhythm, mostly quarters and eighths; slight accent on the third quarter. The Minuet is an old French Dance. According to Washington Irving it was derived from the Pavan, the old Peacock Dance.

2. GAVOTTE.

Metre, $\frac{4}{4}$; Movement, *Allegro Moderato;* Rhythm generally,

♩ ♩ | ♩ ♩ ♩ ♩ | or ♩ ♫ | ♩ ♫ ♩ ♩ | ; accent, first and third metrical divisions. The main feature of a Gavotte is that each period commences upon the last half, and ends upon the first half of a measure. The rhythm is even and the movement measured. This dance may contain three or four short periods, but the style does not change unless joined to a Musette as Part II.

3. MUSETTE.

During the time of Scarlatti and J. S. Bach it was customary to introduce a Musette into the Gavotte as Part II, and if the Gavotte was in major, the Musette would be in tonic minor, and *vice versa.* After the Musette, the Gavotte is repeated, D. C. (See Diagram F.) The Metre, Rhythm, accent, metrical divisions and Movement of the Musette are the same as in the Gavotte. The characteristic of the former is, that it is founded upon a Pedal-note, or Drone bass, which is continued throughout the entire Musette. This drone bass is in imitation of the bagpipe, or old Musette.*

4. SARABANDE.

Metre, $\frac{3}{2}$ or $\frac{3}{4}$; Rhythm, | ♩ ♩ 𝄽 ♩ | ; accent on second beat;

Movement, slow; Mode, generally minor. Sarabandes are sometimes

---

* There are some old Musettes in triple measure, but these are of rare occurrence and not joined to a Gavotte.

written with Doubles, or Variations. It is the slowest and one of the oldest of all the Dances, and follows the Corrente in the old Suites. It was originally a Spanish Dance, having been introduced into Paris by the famous dancing master, Sarabanda.

5. CHACONNE.

Metre, $\frac{3}{4}$; Rhythm, | ♩ · ♪ ♩ | or | ♩ ♫♫ | ; Movement, moderately fast. The Chaconne commences upon the second beat, and is founded upon a species of Ground Bass, or certain harmonic figures which are frequently repeated. The following section from Händel will illustrate this point:

Ex. 135.

Owing to these frequent repetitions the periods in a Chaconne are more or less irregular. Observe the following for example:

Ex. 136.

The complete period ends upon the seventeenth measure in the continuation of this extract. The Chaconne was once a part of the Suite.

6. TAMBOURIN.

The Tambourin is an old French Dance introduced into the opera in the time of Rameau. The Metre is usually ¢, and the Movement much faster than the Gavotte, though the Rhythm is similar. The Tambourin was danced with an accompaniment of one or more Tambourines, and usually founded upon a Pedal-note, which continues throughout. This dance will be found principally in the French Suites.

7. BOURRÉE.

Metre, ♩/♩ **4/4** or **𝄵** ; Rhythm, [musical notation] or [musical notation]

[musical notation] . The periods commence upon the fourth quarter of a measure and terminate upon the third. Movement, *Allegro.* The fourth beat is slightly accented, especially where it indicates the commencement of a phrase or period. (This corresponds to an unwritten law of musical phrasing.) The Bourrée is similar to the Gavotte; but the latter is slower and begins upon the third beat, whereas the Bourrée begins upon the fourth. The old Rigaudon resembles the Bourrée, as does the Loure. This also commences upon the fourth beat, but is rather more stately and has more of this rhythm: [musical notation]

[musical notation] , and in the last [musical notation] . The Bourrée was frequently included in the Suite, or Partita, in place of the Gavotte.

A number of authors of the present day have written Bourrées and misnamed them Gavottes, evidently not aware of the distinction between the two species.

8. CORRENTE—COURANTE.

Metre, **3/4**; Movement, *Allegretto.* The Rhythm is not uniform, though nearly all Correntes commence upon the last eighth note in a measure. It is an old style of Dance, rather lively in character, but less characteristic than the other styles, and consequently more difficult to recognize. In the Suites and Partitas of Bach the Corrente follows the Allemande. (See Diagram D or E.)

9. GIGUE, OR GIGA.

Metre, **6/8, 9/8, 12/8, 12/16,** or **4/4**, with triplets; Rhythm in triplets or groups of three notes to a beat, thus: **6/8** [musical notation] or **4/4** [musical notation]

[musical notation] ; Movement, *Presto.* The character of the Gigue is very lively and sometimes humorous, closely resembling the Irish Jig. According to Von Bülow (who is certainly high authority), the Gigue was named after the old Italian giga, a species of violin. The Gigue was the Finale, or last number, in old Suites and Partitas.

ILLUSTRATIONS.

Ed. Peters, No. 202 (6 French Suites, Bach).

Dances by A. and D. Scarlatti, Couperin, Rameau, Lully, Purcell, and Händel.

Chaconne in *F*, Händel.

" Le Tambourin " by Rameau (in *E*-minor).

Loure from Bach's third 'Cello Suite.

Gavotte in *G*-major and *G*-minor from Gluck's "Iphegenia in Aulis."

The questions will be: 1. Metre; 2. Movement; 3. Rhythm; 4. Modes; 5. Accents (including phrases beginning upon the fractional part of a measure); 6. Construction (according to the Diagrams); 7. Species (name of the Dance).

The words " Da Capo " may be used to describe the repetition of Part I after Part II. Pieces having but two different periods are to be called Ballad Dances.

As a review of this chapter select from the Compendium a few modern Suites a la Roccoco.

Chapter XVIII.

THE DANCE FORM—Concluded.

MODERN CLASSICAL SPECIES.

THE Polonaise, Tarantella, Bolero, Saltarello, as we are accustomed to hear them, are not Roccoco Dances. Hence we cannot base our description of these comparatively modern dances upon the works of the predecessors or contemporaries of Händel and Bach, but must be governed by the compositions of later composers. This will account for the difference in style and construction between the Roccoco and the Modern Classical Dances. The form is generally similar to Diagram B, especially where the dance is written as an independent work. The Military Polonaise by Chopin corresponds o this, though the first period of Part II is repeated three times. Where these dance movements occur in a Suite, or other cyclical form, they are more condensed, and in these cases the different species will be found to correspond to our Diagrams, A, C, or D.

We include the Minuet in both chapters; for though it is a rococo dance, its character has been materially changed since Boccherini, **Haydn,** and Mozart adopted it as a regular movement in their Sonatas and Chamber Music. Those masters added so much grace and charm to the old Dance that it was at one period as much in vogue as are Gavottes at the present time, and this new style has become the standard. The metre is the only feature that survived this metamorphosis. The rhythm became more varied, though seldom deviating from the even quarters and eighths which add somewhat to the grace of the movement. The various periods were made to commence upon the third quarter of a measure, which gives to this part of the measure more accent than it had previously received. Boccherini retained more of the old slow movement, whereas Haydn and Mozart quickened it considerably, and it is now almost Allegro. Another peculiarity of the Modern Minuet is the second part (commonly called "Trio"). This is usually written upon some other tonal foundation, as the Subdominant, Dominant, or Major third below the original key. Part I is then repeated, Da Capo.

In the Minuets of Boccherini, notably the favorite one in *A*, the stately figures of the old dance are still present; but in the Minuets of Mozart and the later ones of Hadyn, not to mention those of Beethoven, we no longer see the sweeping train and powdered wig, the silken knee breeches, broidered waist-coat and depending rapier, but rather the apotheosis of these; a reminiscence of the old scene, becoming a purely musical embodiment.

The technical descriptions now follow. (The metre, rhythm, movement, accent, etc., are to be apprehended by the class, after hearing a fragment of each species). The rhythm of both theme and accompaniment must be ascertained when the Polonaise and Bolero are considered.

1. POLONAISE, OR POLACCA.

Metre, $\frac{3}{4}$; Rhythm of theme in syncopation, either | ♪ ♩ ♫ |

or | ♪ ♩ ♫ ♫ | (In either case the accent falls upon the

second eighth note.)   Rhythm of the accompaniment, ♩ ♩ ♩

♩ ♩ ♩ ♩ ♩   Movement, *Allegretto*.   The peculiar Cadence

♩ ♩ ♪ ♪   or   ♫♫ ♩ ♪   is also to be observed.

The Polonaise was originally a Polish court dance, and, like all court dances, rather slow and majestic.   During the present century they have nearly all been quickened in movement.   The Polacca is synonymous with Polonaise, the principal characteristic of both being the syncopated rhythm of the theme.   (We meet with an occasional short Polonaise in old Suites; but since then it has undergone a greater transformation than did the Minuet.   The modern Polonaise is a very different piece of music.)

2. BOLERO.*

This is a Spanish National Dance, somewhat similar to the Polonaise, but less majestic and more animating.   Metre, $\frac{3}{4}$; Movement about (♩ = 88).   The Rhythm is peculiar.   In the accompaniment

we have this: | ♫ ♫ ♫♫♫♫ | or this: | ♫♫♫ ♫♫♫♫ |

which is marked by castanets.   The Rhythm of the theme is this:

| ♩ ♩.♫ ♩.♫ | ♫♫ ♫ ♫♫ ♫ | etc.   This triplet may

occur in the upper part against the two even sixteenths of the accompaniment, or as we have written it.

This peculiarly Spanish rhythm (3 and 2) is the most characteristic feature of the Bolero.   The Op. 19, of Chopin, is an excellent example of this species of Dance.   We quote the first measure, which should be played in connection with a measure or two of the uneven rhythm:

Ex. 137.

The Bolero is similar to the Cachoucha, and in Spain it is a Pantomime in honor of Cupid.

3. TARANTELLA.

Metre, $\frac{6}{8}$; Rhythm ♫♫ ♫♫ and ♩ ♪♩ ♪; two regular accents; Movement, *Prestissimo*. The motion is something of a whirl, owing to the preponderance of the former rhythm. The Tarantella is an old Italian Dance—the swiftest of all terpsichorean movements. The violent exercise of dancing the Tarantella is (according to popular superstition) supposed to act as an antidote to the poisonous bite of the tarantula.

This dance contains a Trio, or second subject, in which the style changes, but is usually written without pauses. Another characteristic of the Tarantella is the strong contrasts between piano and forte, or rather, the sudden and violent accents in the midst of a soft passage. These correspond to the legendary character of the dance.

4. SALTARELLO.

Metre, $\frac{6}{8}$; Movement, *Presto*. Rhythm, ♩ ♪ ♫♫. The accents are not so strongly marked as in the Tarantella, and the rhythm is more uneven. Otherwise they are similar.

5. CZÁRDÁS, OR CSÁRDÁS.

An Hungarian National Dance of peculiar construction. It contains two models. First, a slow movement (usually in minor), called Lassan. The second part is much faster—*Allegro*. This is called the Friska. The rhythm is mostly syncopated, and the metre is almost invariably $\frac{2}{4}$ or $\frac{4}{4}$. Several of Liszt's Hungarian Rhapsodies are elaborations of the Czárdás, and the well-known Divertissement a la Hongroise, in *G*-minor, Op. 54, by Schubert, owes its charm and novelty principally to a National Hungarian dance tune upon which it was founded. The first Andante corresponds to the Lassan. This is repeated after the un poco piu mosso. The Friska does not commence until after the Funeral March. The only indication is *Allegretto*, and this peculiar rhythm in the melody:

Ex. 138.

This occurs thrice, each time with different rhythm in the accompaniment. The entire composition is a faithful representation of Hungarian Music, and the Coda is especially beautiful.

6. MINUET.

Metre, $\frac{3}{4}$; Movement, *Allegretto;* Rhythm of the accompaniment,

♩ ♩ ‖ ♩ ♩ ♩. The Minuet commences upon the third beat, which is accented; therefore the accents are *one* and *three*. Form, same as Diagram B. Haydn quickened the movement somewhat, and it is now almost *Allegro.*

7. HABANERA, OR AVANERA.

Metre, $\frac{2}{4}$; Movement, *Allegro;* Rhythm of the accompaniment,

♫. ♫. The rhythm of the theme is sometimes in syncopation ♫♫ ♫, and usually contains the Spanish rhythm of the Bolero, thus: ♫♫ ♫ interspersed with this ♫♫ ♫

The Habanera is a Cuban Dance, and its extremely vivacious character, together with the charming rhythmical conceits, have combined to make it popular in the old world and the new.

Gottschalk's "Ojos Criollos" is a good example of this dance:

Ex. 139.

(There are other Dances, such as Galliard, Romanesque, the Brawl, Fandango, Farandole, Kermesse, Sword Dance, Pomponnette, Passacaglio, etc., but as these are either obsolete, or not so characteristic, they have not been described.)

The "Alla Polacca," "Alla Marcia," etc., or Tempo di Polacca, Tempo di Marcia, etc., are used by composers either as a modification of the regular style, or to indicate in a general way a Species which might not otherwise be perceptible at first sight.

Alla Menuetto signifies, in Minuet style, or after the fashion of a Minuet. Tempo di Bolero means, in the movement of a Bolero. Both terms are used synonymously, and usually have the same meaning when applied to any of the dances. Pieces so marked will be found to deviate more or less from the regular form. For instance, a movement headed Alla Menuetto will contain no regular Trio and Da Capo, and the construction will vary somewhat from the strict Minuet form; *i. e.*, the periods will be more extended and the rhythm more varied.

Subjoined is a list of compositions as illustrations of the different species of the Dance Form described in this chapter.

ILLUSTRATIONS FOR MODERN CLASSICAL DANCES.

Polonaise. Polaccas and Polonaises from the Sonatinas. Afterwards some such selection as the Polacca Brillante, by Bohm.
Bolero. Moszkowski, Op. 12. No. 5 (from the Spanish Dances, two or four hands).
    Raff, Op. 111, or Chopin, Op. 19.
Tarantella. Rheinberger, Op. 13, in *B*-flat (four hands).
    Tarantellas, Gottschalk, Chopin, or Liszt.
Saltarello. Löschhorn or S. B. Mills. Finale to Mendelssohn's Italian Symphony (four hands). This is interspersed with fragments of the Tarantella.
Czárdás. J. Löw, Czárdás Album, Op. 473.
    MacDowell, Op. 24, No. 4.
Minuet. From the Oxford Symphony, Haydn. From Mozart's *E*-flat Symphony, arranged by Schulhoff. From Sonatina No. 2, Op. 47, Reinecke.
Habanera. Perles du Madrid (Habanera) Bachmann.
    Habanera from "Carmen" (Bizet), arranged by Lange, Op. 267.
    Ojos Criollos (four hands), Gottschall.
    La Gallina (four hands), Gottschalk.

QUESTIONS.

1. Metre; 2. Movement; 3. Rhythm of Accompaniment; 4. Rhythm of Theme; 5. Modes; 6. Accents (same as before); 7. Construction; 8. Species; 9. Regular or irregular, *a la*.

It is necessary to observe all the details, not alone for cultivation of the hearing faculties, but as a means of determining the character of the piece, and its proper performance.

(See last paragraph in previous chapter.)

There is some diversity of opinion with regard to the movements of these dances, but as it is necessary to have some standard in actual performance, an approximate indication for each species will be given:

Gavotte. $\left(\downarrow = 120 \right)$ to $\left(\downarrow = 144 \right)$. The Gavotte is now played alla breve (¢), sometimes as fast as $\left(\stackrel{\downarrow}{=} 120 \right)$, which represents considerable technic, and very little Gavotte.

Musette. The same; sometimes a few degrees slower.

Sarabande. The slowest of all Dances. $\frac{3}{4}$ metre, $\left(\downarrow = 88 \right)$ $\frac{3}{2}$ $\left(\downarrow = 88 \right)$ or $\left(\downarrow = 76 \right)$.

Chaconne. *Moderato* or *Allegro*, $\left(\downarrow = 120 \right)$ to $\left(\downarrow = 132 \right)$.

Tambourin. About twice as fast as the old Gavotte movement, $\left(\downarrow = 110 \right)$ ¢.

Bourrée. Faster than the Loure or Gavotte, ¢ $\left(\stackrel{\downarrow}{=} 88 \right)$ to $\left(\stackrel{\downarrow}{=} 104 \right)$

Corrente. $\frac{3}{4}$ $\left(\downarrow = 120 \right)$ to $\left(\downarrow = 132 \right)$.

Gigue. Presto, $\frac{4}{4}$ $\left(\downarrow = 144 \right)$ $\frac{6}{8}$ $\left(\downarrow. = 144 \right)$ $\frac{12}{8}$ $\left(\downarrow. = 144 \right)$ Sometimes $\left(\downarrow. = 160 \right)$

Minuet. Old, $\left(\downarrow = 104 \right)$ Haydn, Mozart, and Dussek, $\left(\downarrow = 132 \right)$ Since the year 1810, $\left(\downarrow. = 76 \right)$ This is equal to $\left(\downarrow = 228 \right)$

Polonaise. This was known in the time of Händel, but it bears little resemblance to the modern Polonaise. For those composed during the eighteenth century we would fix the movement at about $\left(\downarrow = 100 \right)$; for those of the present century, $\left(\downarrow = 120 \text{ to } 136 \right)$

Bolero. $\left(\downarrow = 88 \right)$ to $\left(\downarrow = 96 \right)$ The movement of the Bolero is variable, owing to its peculiar Pantomimic character.

Tarantella. From $\left(\downarrow. = 180 \right)$ to $\left(\downarrow. = 100 \right)$ This last is one beat to a measure.

Saltarello. $\frac{6}{8}$ metre, about $\left(\downarrow. = 160 \right)$

Czárdás. It is not well to fix the movement of this, but the contrasts between the Lassan and the Friska should be consider
able (say 30 degrees).

The performer must understand that these movements are only
approximate, and be governed by the Epoch to which the piece
belongs. The character also has some influence upon the movement, aside from the epoch. Some of Beethoven's Minuets, for ex
ample, are to be played in a different movement from others, but the
author would recommend a difference of not more than ten degrees.

PART V.

Chapter XIX.

PRELUDE AND INTRODUCTION. INTERMEZZO.

PRELUDE AND INTRODUCTION.

WE will describe Prelude as a short preliminary passage or movement, of irregular construction; something which comes before the principal form, but without forecasting what follows. Introduction may also be short and of irregular construction, but it is made up out of certain characteristic sounds from the principal form, and must foreshadow what follows, at least in an indirect manner.

The Prelude merely invites attention, but does not intimate what the subject is to be; the Introduction not only invites attention but gives somewhat of a synopsis, epitome, or intimation of the main work, after the fashion of a descriptive play-bill.

Another peculiarity of the Prelude (and frequently of the Introduction also) is, that it is less symmetrical; the construction according to phrases and sections is not so noticeable nor so proportionate. It is also less tuneful.   Here is a short Prelude to a song:

MEYERBEER.

Ex. 140.

After these three measures the voice part enters.   All that the Prelude does in the way of introduction is, to determine the key and mode, the metre, and form of accompaniment. The melody is like this:

Ex. 141.

no hint of which is contained in the Prelude. The Prelude to Bach's First Fugue (among the 48) is a good example:

Ex. 142.

This gives no intimation of what follows. Songs, such as "Goodnight, Farewell," "The Erl King," and "Adelaide," have a short period before the vocal part commences, which is in each case an Introduction. In the "Adelaide" song Beethoven takes the leading motive and abridges it into five measures.

The illustrations mentioned below are to be played, that the pupils may distinguish the Prelude from Introduction:

From "Album Classique," extract from Händel, No. 12. (Play only the movement in ¼ metre, omitting Courante.)

The first eleven measures of Mozart's Fantasie in *D*-minor, before the theme commences. Also, "18 easy Preludes by J. S. Bach" (Augener & Co., No. 8020).

The first part of Rubinstein's Tarantella is an Introduction, though he afterwards uses it as an Intermezzo.

Such Introductions as these are good illustrations: "Traviata," arranged as a Fantasie, by J. Ascher; Feu Follet, by Prudent.

The first four measures of Mendelssohn's Barcarolle in *A*, from "Lieder ohne Worte," have the character of an Introduction, which is used at the end as a Recollection.

The preliminary matter to the "Valse Lente," by Delibes, is an Introduction.

The class should understand, in the case of regular Introductions, where the leading motive is taken from. In the Traviata fantasia the first three notes of the Cavatina "Ah fors e lui" are used as a motive and written in canonic style. This makes it an Introduction.

The first twelve measures of Raff's "Cachoucha Caprice" form an Introduction.

Mendelssohn's Songs Without Words, Nos. 1, 6, 9, 12, 15, 16, and 18 have short Preludes before the songs commence.

Sometimes the preliminary matter is of such character that one cannot tell whether it be a Prelude or Introduction, unless the entire composition be played. In such cases play the principal form, or at least the different Subjects first, and the Intrada afterwards. But, as a rule, the distinction can be made at once. The Introduction to "Sweet Bye and Bye," by S. G. Pratt, is a good exemplification, as every one is familiar with the melody, and can easily recognize the thematic prognostications.

Include the previous questions and add the last, Prelude or Introduction.

The author is aware that these distinctions between Prelude and Introduction have not heretofore been made. But the definition of the words, as well as the musical instances hereinafter quoted, seem to call for a distinction between the two words, especially in Musical Analysis.

INTERMEZZO.[*]

In describing the Intermezzo as part of a form, not as a complete form in itself, we may say it is an Interlude. It plays the same part in a Rondo, or similar composition, that the Interlude does between the verses of a ballad. It relieves monotony by creating a slight diversion. For this reason the Intermezzo is generally of irregular construction, having less of proportionate phrases, and not being so melodious as the regular period. The Intermezzo may consist of scale passages, of a melodic figure in sequence, of responsive phrases or of transitional matter. It may also contain any number of measures, and generally leads back to the principal theme. The Intermezzo in Kuhlau's Sonatina, Op. 20, No. 1, commences upon the last of the sixteenth measure and continues for nineteen measures. Then the principal theme is resumed. This Intermezzo is repeated at the close. So in the last movement of Op. 55, same book. It is a Scherzo in Rondo form, and after the principal theme ends upon the sixteenth measure an Intermezzo begins and terminates upon the essential seventh chord, twenty-eighth measure.

From the Rondo to Op. 59, No. 1, Kuhlau, we may cite another

---

[*] The Intermezzo was originally what we now call *entr'acte*, or pieces played between the acts of an Opera or Drama.

instance. This commences upon the last of the sixteenth measure. It is made up of antiphonal phrases and imitations, thus:

Ex. 143.

This is continued for seventeen measures, when the principal theme recurs with variations. Rondos containing Intermezzo may be found in the Sonatinas of Clementi, Ops. 36, 37, and 38; in the Dussek Sonatinas, Op. 20, and in those of Reinecke, Ops. 47, 98, 127, and 136. Such illustrations should be performed until the class is capable of recognizing the Intermezzo at once.

NOTE—There is, as is well known, a style of composition called Intermezzo; but even this is intended to be played between other pieces.

Chapter XX.

UNEVEN PHRASES. UNITED PERIODS.

UNEVEN PHRASES.

A FEW instances will be given in which the phrases contain an unequal number of measures. The rule is, that a phrase shall contain two long or four short measures, but as the great composers have frequently violated our rules, we will now observe the exceptions. In the annexed example the phrases contain three full measures, which is a characteristic of the piece:

Ex. 144.

In this instance the three-measure phrases have a very serious
character. The last note of each phrase is marked by the composer
with a fermata, as a somewhat striking punctuation of the motive,
and the phrase which corresponds to it. These uneven phrases are
continued throughout the piece, except during the Intermezzo. Various circumstances may give rise to this peculiarity.

First—The content of the motive may require three measures for
its completion, as is the case in Ex. 144.

Second—The third measure may be added as an Echo, as in this
instance :

Ex. 145.

The piano echoes the second measure of the voice part merely on
account of the poetic sentiment, not because the motive requires
three measures for its (musical) completion. The second phrase is
similar, but in the second section we hear but four measures, owing
to the Echo being omitted from the piano part.

Third—The next example, from the first Sonata of Beethoven,
dedicated to Haydn, is still different, owing to a different cause :

Ex. 146.

This occurs in the elaboration where considerable liberty is taken
with the leading motive, which in the first Division contains but two
measures :

Ex. 147.

In the above instance the three-measure phrase serves to relieve the
monotony of even phrases, and it also places the motive in a different
light.

The following pieces contain, in certain places, three-measure phrases, and should be played from beginning to end until the class can recognize the uneven phrases:

Turkish March, from Beethoven's " Ruins of Athens," and Minuetto, from Haydn's " Oxford" Symphony. As the uneven phrases are in the Trio, it will not be necessary to repeat the first two periods. These last three-measure phrases are in antiphonal style and easy to recognize. Play the Menuetto first and the March afterward.

The first two periods of the Menuetto from Mozart's second G-minor Symphony will afford another example.*

The " Little Hungarian Melody," by Behr, contains (in second period) two sections of five measures each. A similar instance occurs in the Presto of Haydn's Symphony, No. 11, Ed. Litolff.

These illustrations may be repeated in order to bring out other answers than those pertaining to this chapter. Rhythm, Form, Accent, Mode, etc., are always useful questions.

UNITED PERIODS.

There are numerous instances in which one period begins simultaneously with the ending of another. Two regular periods may thus contain fifteen or thirty-one measures, and in examining the music the student would be inclined to consider the United Period as an uneven one, owing to the odd number of measures. Such instances we will call by the above name. Here is a practical example from Kuhlau, Op. 20, No. 1:

Ex. 148.

Only the last four measures of the second subject are here quoted, and this ends at 8. At the same time the second subject ends, the Conclusion begins. This is indicated by the figure 8 (which refers to the period just ended) and the figure 1, which belongs to the first measure of the Conclusion, beginning upon the same note as the ending of the other period. The period ending at 8 is entirely complete, as is the one commencing at 8 or 1. For the student's benefit we will write a fragment of this in score:

Ex. 149.

The wind instruments make a regular cadence and end upon the eighth measure with a full period, of which but the seventh and the eighth are quoted. As these instruments end here, the stringed instruments come in simultaneously with the Conclusion, which also has eight measures. (See original Sonatina, first movement, second and third periods, from seventeenth measure to the double bar.) Therefore, though the periods are complete, we find but thirty-one measures in the first division, owing to the Second Subject and Conclusion being united. A similar instance occurs in the same movement, at the fifty-fourth measure, and where the Finale of four measures begins simultaneously with the ending of the Recollection.

ILLUSTRATIONS.

The first movement from Reinecke's Sonatina, Op. 127, No. 5, besides the one by Kuhlau already mentioned, and Op. 55, No. 5, same composer. The first and second subjects of the first movement are joined together into an United Period. United Periods occur more frequently in concerted music than in solos. Other examples of this will be given in connection with Extended Period.

Chapter XXI.

CODA. EXTENDED PERIOD. CURTAILED PERIOD.

CODA.

THE Italian word Coda means tail. Whatever is added to a composition beyond its natural termination is called Coda. When a period or form has been concluded, and then goes on beyond this point, the continuation becomes the Coda. The Postlude to a song affords a good illustration of the character and object of the Coda. After the singer has concluded the last verse the accompanist usually plays a few chords, or short finale, in order to indicate or emphasize the termination of the song. The object of the Coda is frequently different from that of the Postlude (according to this primary definition), but they always resemble each other in this, that both are added after a natural or actual termination.

We will present an example of the Postlude first, as the illustration is more plain. It is from a song entitled "After Years," by A. Schultz:

Ex. 150.

For - get me not.

After the vocal part makes its final cadence upon *D*-minor (a), the accompaniment begins the Postlude and conducts the piece back to the original major key. Observe that the Postlude is entirely separated from the complete cadence of the vocal part (a).

The simplest examples of Coda are merely intended, like the Postlude to a Ballad, to indicate the final ending of a form or movement, especially where the last period has previously been repeated. In this sense the Coda will constitute the most elementary and primitive deviation from, or enlargement of, the Ballad Model of two equal periods.

The teacher may now perform the second movement* to Kuhlau's Sonatina, Op. 55, No. 2, and every time a period is completed the class should mention the fact. Explain that the movement contains a Coda, which must come after a completed period. Pupils should say "Coda" when the Coda begins, and at the close tell the number of measures it contains.

A similar example may be taken from Op. 55, No. 4, same composer. This will be found in the slow movement, where the second period ends with a half cadence, which causes the first period to be repeated.

The next illustration may be the "Alla Menuetto" from Clementi's Sonatina, Op. 36, No. 2. The Coda in this is not so easily recognized. The same explanations should be made and the same questions propounded. There are three periods to this movement, the first occurring twice. After these, the Coda begins, and contains four measures.

Examples of more extended Codas may be found in the following:

"Alla Polacca," from Op. 55, No. 4, and Menuetto, Op. 55, No. 6, Kuhlau.

Rondo from Op. 20, No. 3, Dussek.

Last six and one-half measures of Rondo from Diabelli's Op. 168, No. 3, and last five measures of Andantino, same work.

The Transitional Prelude by Beethoven also has a Coda.

EXTENDED PERIOD.

The second deviation from the ballad model consists in extending a period beyond its prescribed limits. This is done—

First—By means of a half cadence where the full cadence would naturally be expected;

Second—By the aid of an avoided cadence, which prolongs the regular close;

Third—By a repetition after the cadence should have occurred, or through the introduction of a Passage;

---

* This is merely marked "Cantabile," but it is to be played rather slowly.

Fourth—By leading the melody in such manner that it is carried beyond the common length of the period before it terminates;

Fifth—By the introduction of an Echo.

The class must understand that a period is not reached until the music is brought to a state of repose or completion by an authentic or full cadence. There must be a satisfactory ending, or complete cadence, as in the case of poetry.

The Extended Period forms one of the principal advantages in favor of classical over common music; for while popular music represents only brief periods of motion and repose by its short and monotonous cadences, classical music represents longer and more important periods of thought and action, and fewer periods of repose and inaction. Common music is a mere kaleidoscope that exhibits to the outward senses a variety of pleasing colors; classical music is more like a panorama, which gradually unfolds to the intellectual sensibilities a complete scene or series of emotional images.

A simple example of Extended Period occurs here:

Ex. 151. CLEMENTI.

This period, which would naturally contain eight measures, is extended to twelve by means of the half cadence in the eighth measure (see 8). The period is not complete until after the transition to C major, where the complete cadence occurs (see 12).

Attention must now be called to the distinction which is here made between the extension of a period, as above illustrated, and the Coda, which is not an *extension*, but an *addition* to a period already closed. Coda takes place after a period has been concluded and the two are thus isolated. Extended period is continuous and connected, and forms a complete, integral whole. The nine-measure periods in Delibes' "*Valse lente*" come under this heading, though the extension consists in merely throwing in an arpeggio of one additional measure.

An instance similar to Ex. 151 occurs in the Andante to Clementi's Op. 36, No. 4, after the regular period. The second period begins with isolated phrases; then follows a sequence which we would expect to end upon F in the twenty-fourth measure; but here the composer goes to the *D*-minor chord by an avoided cadence, and finally ends upon the dominant, F, in the twenty-sixth measure. The extension therefore consists of two measures. The last five measures form a Coda (not an Extended Period), after the repeated period, which ends upon the tonic in the forty-second measure. Play this, and the other movement, until the class recognizes the Extended Periods and Coda.

The next example, though written in the classical style, is comparatively easy to analyze. It is the Adagio from Kuhlau's Op. 20, No. 2, one of his best Sonatinas. The first period ends upon the sixteenth measure, and is perfectly regular. The second period commences upon the seventeenth measure, and contains four phrases; but the twenty-fourth measure, instead of being a cadence upon *A*-flat major (which would have closed the period there), stops upon the essential seventh chord to correspond to the twentieth measure. This causes the cadence to fall upon the twenty-fifth measure, though the same idea is continued until the first of the twenty-sixth measure. The *G*-major chord on the first of the twenty-sixth measure is recognized as the dominant to *C*-minor; therefore the period commencing at measure seventeen is not complete until the thirtieth measure. Measures twenty-six, twenty-seven, twenty-eight and twenty-nine form a brief Intermezzo of four measures, leading back to the principal period. But as the perfect cadence takes place upon the thirtieth measure we may say that the Extended Period contains thirteen measures, by means of retaining the dominant seventh chord where the cadence would otherwise have occurred upon the tonic, as here:

Ex. 152.

Compare this to the twenty-fourth measure of the printed copy. Considering what follows, this is not so good as the original. After the Extended Period, we hear the first double period again, and then a brief Coda, to make the termination more satisfactory. Pupils should understand this analysis of the periodic construction of the movement, even though it be necessary to repeat the Adagio several times.

The Larghetto from Op. 20, No. 3, same composer, will afford another good illustration of this matter.* The second period, commencing with short, responsive phrases between treble and bass, contains an avoided cadence in the eighth measure, by which means the period is extended to the beginning of the eleventh measure, where the principal strain recurs. This, like the first, constitutes a regular period, with repeat. After the second ending the composer has employed a more elaborate Coda of eleven measures, which is easily recognized. (Play the entire movement, and include among the questions, Intermezzo, Coda, and Extended Period.)

CURTAILED PERIOD.

By these words we wish to indicate a period cut short of its natural length, or left before it is finished by the usual number of measures. This will occur only after the curtailed period has been previously heard in a complete form, except in the case of Introductions. Here is a simple illustration :

Ex. 153.   BEETHOVEN. Op. 16.

This is the Introduction to "Adelaide," which should be compared to the first period of the vocal melody. The voice part enters at the end of our quotation. This is compressed into five measures. The Adagio to Beethoven's Op. 13 contains two Curtailed Periods, the first of seven, the second of six measures.

* A remarkable instance of Extended Period occurs in the second movement of Raff's song, Op. 98, No. 9, where the entire movement is one long Extended Period of thirty-five measures.

In order to further illustrate the peculiarity of a Curtailed Period we will quote a complete period, and then the curtailment, from Beethoven's Op. 7.:

Ex. 154.

This is a Recollection, in form of a Curtailed Period. Observe the difference between the third measure in each example, and how the last is brought to a close within the limits of a section. Other instances of more extended Codas will be cited hereafter.

Illustrations for this chapter, besides those mentioned :

Sonatina, Reinecke, Op. 47, Nos. 1 and 2.*

The Op. 11, No. 1, of Strelezki, is a good example, as it contains a Prelude, Regular and Extended Periods, Intermezzo, and Coda. It also contains three-measure phrases.

In the Minuet, Op. 27, No. 2, Beethoven, the second period is extended.

The Theme of "Nel cor piu," with variations, by Beethoven, affords a singular instance of Curtailed Periods or Extended Sections. The first period is regular, but the next is curtailed to six measures, and the last chord is marked with a fermata. Following this is another curtailed period of six measures.

The favorite Minuet, by Boccherini, affords an example of Extended Period. This occurs in the consequent period, and results in this way : After giving four measures of the second period the composer does not repeat merely the last section of the first period, but writes the entire first period over again. This results in twelve measures instead of eight. It would be well for the class to analyze it in this manner.

The questions are : 1. Metre (and special accents if any); 2. Movement; 3. Rhythm of theme and accompaniment; 4. Number of Periods; 5. Form (single or double); 6. Style; 7. Prelude or Introduction; 8. Intermezzo; 9. Coda, or Extended Period; 10. Curtailed Period, or Uneven Phrases; 11. Modes.

---

* The first Period in Enke's Barcarolle, Op. 8, No. 1, is slightly curtailed every time it occurs.

Chapter XXII.

DISPERSED HARMONIES. ABRUPT TRANSITIONS.

DISPERSED HARMONIES.

EVERY chord has as many open as close positions. These are produced by inverting the order:

Close Positions—C e g, e g C, g C e.

Open Positions—C g e, e C g, g e C.

Ex. 155.

Compare the letter combinations with examples in notation. Require pupils to write several concords in open positions; after which play Ex. 155. The open positions at (b) are produced by inverting the middle note of each chord at (a) an octave higher. At present it will be sufficient for the class to understand that Ex. 155 merely consists of the C-major chord in its close and open positions. The latter are known as dispersed harmonies.

Formerly the positions at (a) were mostly for harpsichord and piano music, while the chords at (b) were the natural result of vocal part-music for mixed voices, the male voices being an octave lower than the female. But since the enlargement of the piano key-board the dispersed form of harmony has become the rule rather than the exception.

A motive which would have occurred to Mozart as at (a), would appear to Rubinstein as at (b):

Ex. 156.

The original contralto and tenor parts (in quarter notes) appear at (b) a tenth, instead of a third apart, while the upper part at (a) is duplicated in the upper octave. The class should name modes and positions (open or close) in Ex. 157:

Ex. 157.

They should recognize that the first two chords are mere re-arrangements of the *A*-minor triad, and that all the positions are open. This might be played in close position, and it would be well to give several illustrations, like the Introduction to Gottschalk's "Last Hope," etc.

ABRUPT AND DISTANT TRANSITIONS.

Certain abrupt progressions will be here introduced, in order that the class may know something of their cause and effect when they hear transitions which go beyond the circle of related keys. Some transitions are of an elevating, others of a depressing, character. But a transition always represents a corresponding change, either of scene or sentiment. A slight change in tonality, such as a natural transition (Ex. 151) indicates but a slightly different view of the same subject; whereas a sudden change to a remote key serves to alter the entire scene, or to present a totally different aspect of the prevailing sentiment. Here is a brief example for the class to analyze auricularly:

Ex. 158.

In the first measure there is a dominant seventh chord leading to *D*-minor, and in the second measure we hear a diminished, followed by a corresponding dominant seventh. Play the example slowly, that each chord may be named.

Several examples, such as the King's Prayer in the first part of "Lohengrin," should be performed.

Beethoven wrote a peculiar Prelude, which consists of a series of repeated modulations through the entire circle of keys, beginning and ending in C-major. This is a most excellent piece to play for the class. It is Op. 39, No. 2, and may be found in Album Classique, Vol. 391, Edition Litolff. It will be sufficient for the pupils to recognize the transitions, and the fact that nearly all the modulations are to major. The means employed are too varied to admit of detailed analysis by an elementary class.

Aside from listening to the Prelude, every student of music is recommended to study its construction thoroughly. Not only are the transitions skilfully planned, but the entire Prelude is developed from this simple motive:

Ex. 159.

which should be traced out in its progress through the various voice-parts.

ILLUSTRATIONS.

Warum, Schumann.
Au Matin, Godard, Op. 83.
Chant sans Paroles, Tschaikowsky, Op. 2, No. 3.
Walther's Prize Song, from "Meistersinger," Wagner-Bendel.

PART VI.

Chapter XXIII.

CHARACTERISTIC STYLES.

**1. LYRIC. 2. THEMATIC. 3. HARMONIC. 4. ANTIPHONAL.
5. CANONIC. 6. FUGAL. 7. BRAVURA.**

AN important and noticeable difference exists between each of
the above characteristic styles, and it is desirable that the
student should understand and be able to recognize these distinctions.

1. *Lyric Style.* Originally a short poem to be sung with the lyre
(as accompaniment). Songs, Songs Without Words, Andantes and
Adagios from Sonatas; Romances and Serenades are in lyric style.
The term is applied to any piece or part of a piece in which a plainly
outlined, distinct melody is the chief feature. The more vocal the
melody, the more nearly it approaches the lyric style. Schumann's
Op. 124 is a pure lyric.

2. *Thematic Style.* This is more artificial, and the melodic
feature is less prominent. As all music, even purely harmonic progressions, must have melody, this needs qualification. If we select
this chord succession, for example:

Ex. 160.

we find a brief melodic progression in the contralto part, and a less
noticeable one in the other parts; while by giving the bass simply
the root to each chord, we have a pronounced and somewhat bold
melody in that part:

Ex. 161.

going down by thirds and up by fourths. Ex. 160 contains as little of melody as possible, being a purely harmonic design.

In **Thematic** music the design is more ornate, as:

Ex. 162.

But even in this the ear will seize upon the melodic design (harmonic and concealed though it be), as at (a); or even the one in syncopation at (b):

Ex. 163.

However, the Ex. 162 is a thematic one, and may be taken as a fair specimen. The other, and perhaps more important, feature of thematic music consists in its sequence-like, or resultant development, not according to the natural tend and flow of the motive, but rather in compliance with canonic law. (The author does not refer to mechanically constructed music, but to those written and unwritten principles which must govern every good composer.) The canon, for example, always has one or two melodies, yet it is constructed artificially. Canon means law (or rule), and the Subject of a canon becomes the law of procedure: thus, this motive is, in strict canon, to be imitated identically by the answering voice after the interval of a measure, as at (b):

Ex. 164.

The Response (b) now becomes the law, and the first voice in the continuation of the canonic theme must be governed by the second voice as at (c). The response to (c) may be seen at (d):

Ex. 165.

Here the first voice must again be in accordance with the part
below. Compare (d) with (e), and (e) with (f). In this way the
canonic theme becomes continuous, or, as it has appropriately been
termed, *endless*. Bach's Thirty Inventions; Toccatas; nearly all
Etudes (such as No. 1 in *C*, by J. B. Cramer), and certain parts
of Sonatas, to be mentioned hereafter, are in Thematic style.

3. *Harmonic Style.* Vocal or instrumental compositions with full
harmony, in which the value of the notes is the same (or nearly so)
in the different parts. Hymn tunes are in the Harmonic style. Here
is a brief example from Weber:

Ex. 166.   etc.

The harmonic tone-color in this style is not merely complemental, as
in the accompaniment to a ballad, but more or less influential in its
effect, as the chords, being heard simultaneously, are more readily
comprehended and compared.

4. *Antiphonal Style.* An antiphonal phrase or section is a response, somewhat different from the original phrase or section which
is responded to, and separated from it by an interval more or less
extended. In the time of Willaert and Tallis the Antiphonal church
style was in full vogue, and carried to a high state of perfection. It
consisted in one choir responding to another, differently situated, or
the response of the choir to the intonation of the priest. In instrumental music the motives and responses are shorter than in the
ecclesiastical style, otherwise we could not disassociate them, as is
intended. Here is an example:

BEETHOVEN. Op. 7.

Ex. 167.   ff   pp

This is repeated during the next four measures in *B*-flat minor. The

Antiphonal style must not be confused with Echo, Sequence, Repetition, nor with Imitation. This style is fragmentary, and requires a decided change in tone-quality, as well as a frequent *ad libitum* style of performance. Antiphonal passages or figures belong to different instruments which naturally possess a different tone-quality; hence, on the piano the *timbre* should be altered accordingly. Imagine, for example, the two *ff* chords (Ex. 167) played by the horns, trumpets, trombones and tuba; and then the response by violins pizzicati, or by flutes, oboes and clarinets, light staccato. Here follows an example which requires an *ad libitum* style of performance:

Ex. 168. Larghetto from Op. 20, No. 2, KULLAK.

The first measure is to be played slowly and persuasively, leaving the tones rather reluctantly. The response in the second measure is a decided rejection, and is to be played *pesante*, the movement being slightly accelerated. The composer's directions, *staccato assai*, indicate an emphatic, rather than a pizzicato, staccato.

The "Ghasel," in Reinecke's Sonatina, Op. 127 (b), No. 4, is exclusively in Antiphonal style. This is more obvious in the four-hand arrangement.

5. *Canonic Style.* This includes not alone canons, but pieces in which any of the various kinds of Imitation form a prominent part. Bach's Inventions are in canonic as well as thematic style, though not regular canons; because the Imitations are both free and interrupted. Strict canons are mostly two-voiced, and consist of a continuous melody, which is reproduced by the other voice-part after the expiration of one, two or more measures. This has already been briefly explained. (See Ex. 164 and 165.) Vocal Rounds are a species of canon, though the melody is shorter (usually eight measures), owing to the fact that Rounds are for three, four, and five voices. "Hark! the merry birds are singing," "Farewell, dear," and that humorous one, "The Previous Question," are illustrations of this. Previous to the time of Bach and Händel canons were so much in

vogue that almost all compositions were canonic, and composers became so skilful in the manufacture of Polyphonic canons that a modern musician could scarcely decipher them. Strict canons are not written at the present time, except as lessons, but the canonic principle is so important that the author advises every music student to study canons, and understand their construction.

6. *Fugal Style.* The fugue resembles the canon, with this distinction: In fugue the response to the subject is made either a perfect fourth or fifth above or below (tonic being answered by dominant, and *vice versa*). The continuation of the subject, after the response begins, is called Counter-subject, and this is not imitated, as in canon, but is so conceived that it will serve as accompaniment to the subject or response either above or below, by simply transposing it from dominant to tonic, or from tonic to dominant. After the response has finished its motive, the third voice enters with the original subject, an octave above or below, while the second voice sings the counter-subject as accompaniment or companion to this. In like manner the fourth voice will enter with the original subject. From this it will be observed that the melody is not continuous, as in canon (only the short subject being imitated), and that the answering voices come in upon the dominant and tonic, if the subject was in the tonic, and upon the tonic and dominant if the subject was first heard in the dominant. In canon there is no counter-subject; but in a fugue the counter-subject plays an important part.* We cannot enter into the various kinds of fugue in this book, nor can we do more than present an outline of the prominent features of fugal construction, so that the class will recognize a fugue when they hear one.

7. *Bravura Style.* This has become associated by common consent with the modern brilliant and showy style of performance, especially in piano-forte music. The bravura style has gradually grown with the improvements in piano-forte manufacture, and even in the time of Beethoven it was considerably developed by Steibelt, Hummel, Clementi, and Kalkbrenner, though Beethoven himself wrote comparatively few bravura pieces. In the present century Thalberg was for some time the ideal bravura pianist; but in a short time the versatile and magical Liszt stripped him even of this distinction. The greater part of Liszt's piano-forte works represent the bravura style in its highest state of development and perfection, combining,

---

* See Illustration of Counter-subject in the Key to this Analysis, Chapter XXXVI.

as it does, the most intricate feats of digital execution with thorough musicianship and poetic inspiration. This style is easily recognized on account of its brilliant, sparkling, or *grandioso* character. Enlargement and extension are two of the most prominent features of the bravura method. A single trill, as at (a):

Ex. 169.

would appear in some such form as at (b):

(From RUBINSTEIN.)

Ex. 170.

This results in a triple, instead of a single trill, as at (a). Or a diminished chord, which is simple in design, as at (a):

Ex. 171.

appears in bravura dress as at (b) or (c) in the following:

Ex. 172. (From LISZT.)

Presto.

These played rapidly through a compass of six or seven octaves produce something of a meteoric effect, and are almost as easily analyzed as the original figure, Ex. 171.

ILLUSTRATIONS FOR THIS CHAPTER.

1. *Lyric.* Chanson sans Paroles, Tschaikowsky, Op. 2, No. 3.
   Canzonetta in *E*-flat, Seeboeck.
   Schlummerlied, Op. 124, Schumann.
   Largo from Op. 2, No. 2, Beethoven.
   Op. 38, No. 1, Mendelssohn.

2. *Thematic.*   No. 9, of the 12 easy pieces by Händel.

Bach Inventions, Nos. 1, 4, and 13.

First subject, last movement, Op. 27, No. 2, Beethoven.

Toccata in *A*, Paradisi.

Album Leaf No. 3, Op. 7, Kirchner.

Preludes 14 and 16, Op. 28, Chopin.

Petite Etude (on a motive by Mills), Goldbeck.

3. *Harmonic.*   Op. 78, No. 4, St. Heller.

First two periods of Mendelssohn's Wedding March.

Prelude No. 7 (the little one), Chopin.

Military Polonaise, Op. 40, No. 1, Chopin.   (This is nearly all in Harmonic style, except the first period of the Trio, which is a martial lyric.)

Grillen, Op. 12, No. 4, Schumann.

4. *Antiphonal.*   The Dialog (last of No. 10), Schumann's "Papillons."   (The Dialog is occasionally interrupted by sounds from the ball-room.)

Introduction, in *D*-minor, to Sonata, Op. 40, No. 3, Clementi. (The last half of the three-measure phrases is in antiphonal style.)   Also the Andante from his second Sonata, Op. 47, measures 13, 14, and 15 constitute an antiphonal phrase.   Also measures 16, 17, and 18.   The three-measure phrases are divided in the middle (or nearly so) by the responses.

The Duetto from Mendelssohn's "Lieder ohne Worte," Op. 38, No. 6, will prove a good selection, as here the antiphonal passages are not so isolated and fragmentary as those already quoted.   After the prelude the lady sings her opening sentence (a section), which is immediately responded to by the baritone, who is more serious in his sentiments.   This is continued until the two voices in unison unite in singing the gentleman's melody.

5. *Canonic.*   M. Clementi, Op. 40, No. 1, third movement of Sonata in *G* (No. 2 Cotta, No. 9 Peters).   (This movement is specially recommended for the illustration of this style.   We can also make good use of the entire sonata hereafter.)   It is a strict two-voiced canon, in Menuetto Style.   The first two periods are in strict style (*per moto retto*); Part two is in contrary or reversed imitation (*per moto contrario*).   See explanation in Key.

Play also the third number from Schumann's "Papillons." Repeat the last period, where the masks pass each other, as this is a canon.

Scherzo in canon form, Jadassohn. This is a harmonized canon. (In the other illustrations there are no complemental parts.) It would be well to have sung for the class the duet in canon by Marzials, "Friendship," for two voices.

6. *Fugal.* From J. S. Bach's 48 Preludes and Fugues (the Well-tempered clavichord), Nos. 6, 11, and 31. Also "The Art of Fugue," containing fourteen fugues, all written upon one subject. (This book also contains canons with every contrapuntal device imaginable.)

Preludes and Fugues, Op. 16, Clara Schumann.

Five Fugues, for four hands, from the Clavier Suites, Händel, *Peters, Leipzig.*

Fugue in *G*-minor, Op. 5, No. 3, Rheinberger.

Six pieces in Fugal Form, Rheinberger.

Fughetta, Schumann, Op. 68.

(The subject of each fugue should be played separately for the class. Also the counter-subject, when it is characteristic and in contrast to the subject.)

7. *Bravura.* Fragments from the following Concerti: Hummel, Op. 85. Beethoven, Op. 37. Von Weber, Op. 32 or 79. Mendelssohn, Op. 25. Schumann, Op. 54. Reinecke, Op. 72. Henselt, Op. 16. Liszt, in *E*-flat (the one with the warning motive). Grieg, Op. 16. Saint-Saëns, in *G*-minor, or Scherzo, Op. 4. Brahms.

Polka de la Reine, Op. 95, Raff.

Two Polish Dances, Op. 40, Z. Scharwenka.

Magic-Fire Scene from "Walküre," arranged by L. Brassin.

Waldesrauschen, Polonaise in *E*, or second Hungarian Rhapsody, by Liszt.

Toccata di Concert, Op. 36, Dupont.

Tarantella, Nicodé.

March Characteristique, Schubert-Tausig.

Silver-Spring, Wm. Mason.

Also the following from Chopin come under this heading: Prelude, Op. 28, No. 18. Rondo, Op. 16. Variations (La ci darem la mano), Op. 2. Polonaise, Op. 40, No. 1. The Fantasie, or any of the Scherzi. In fact, nearly all of this master's compositions are in bravura style.

GENERAL QUESTIONS (AS TO STYLE).

1. Lyric. 2. Thematic. 3. Harmonic. 4. Antiphonal. 5. Canonic. 6. Fugal. 7. Bravura. 8. Form-Name (whether Rondo, Minuet, Polonaise, or what).

NOTE—A certain selection might contain two or more of the above styles, in which case the fact is to be mentioned by the class. The illustrations are to be performed miscellaneously, not in the order enumerated.

Chapter XXIV.

INTERMEDIATE DETAILS.

EINGANG, SECOND SUBJECT, EPISODE, TERMINATION, RECOLLECTION, STRETTO, SEQUENCE, PASSAGE, CADENZA.

THE two following chapters are devoted exclusively to the intermediate parts and details of the Rondo and other forms, and not to any species or form as a whole. To illustrate these will require a considerable variety of compositions; but for the present the details are to be understood and considered separately.

EINGANG.

This term has been used by modern composers to indicate the entrance to a new key. The author has adopted this term to signify an irregular short passage of a transitional nature when the object of the transition is to establish a particular key, either for the Second Subject or Episode. This distinction seems necessary, because many transitions occur in modern music which do not aim at any particular key, but merely represent a changing scene or sentiment. Therefore such passages will be indicated simply, Transitions; but where the object is plainly to establish a certain tonality, in order that a particular part of the work may be heard in that key, we will use the word Eingang. This will be better understood by referring to the pieces which have been analyzed in this chapter.

SECOND THEME, OR SECOND SUBJECT.

This refers to a period in contrast to the first subject, and should be sufficiently changed from the first subject to constitute a change of style. Second Subject has often been confused with Episode, not alone by music students, but by writers upon this subject. The Second Subject *must* be related in some recognizable manner to the principal subject; must be taken from some phase of the leading motive, or be a natural offspring from the parent motive. Here is a good illustration of this point :

Ex. 173.   BEETHOVEN.

At (a) we have the first phrase, or motive, of the First Subject ; at (b) may be seen the first phrase of the Second Subject. Very little analytical knowledge is required to detect the resemblance between the two examples. One is an ascending, the other a descending chord.

EPISODE.

"A separate incident; an incidental narrative or digression." The word should have this, its proper meaning, or none at all. But it has been used by musical writers with a recklessness scarcely understandable. All high class composers have employed adventitious matter in their works, the effect of which is to give greater variety to the rest of the piece. Or the sentiment may be such that an apparently foreign passage is perfectly natural and appropriate. Therefore we will apply the word Episode only to such passages as deviate from the subject matter, or digress from the principal theme.

TERMINATION.

In regular Sonata pieces the word Conclusion is applied to the last and shortest of the three subjects from which the Sonata is constructed. But in such cases the Conclusion is not merely a motive subject of the first division of the Sonata movement, but is also separated from the preceding subject in the manner of a Coda. The nature of the Conclusion, therefore, and the generally accepted definition of Coda, as referring to an afterthought, make it undesirable to use these terms synonymously. Yet there are many instances in

which the latter part of a movement is neither Conclusion nor Coda;
and to designate such instances the author has thought best to use
the word Termination. This necessitates no contradiction of meaning, as we apply it merely to the last part of certain movements.
What we wish to designate is the last part of a movement, after the
cadence to the last period; where the natural ending of the movement is joined to the Termination almost imperceptibly, and in a
restless or impatient manner. In such cases the Termination is
more like an united period, and is an extension or continuation of the
movement, but without being an afterthought, as is the Coda. Observe the Coda to Beethoven's Op. 49, No. 2, last movement beginning thus:

Ex. 174.

The movement naturally concludes itself at (a); but the Coda commences at (b). This is an afterthought, though it is built upon the
principal motive, and affords an excellent instance of what a Coda
should be. The last eight measures of Beethoven's first Sonata in
F-minor, Prestissimo movement, is not a Coda, but a Termination, or
Stretto. In the principal editions this is called second conclusion
("close II"), a syllogism which we do not wish to apply.

The Coda, according to this definition, is usually to be performed
a little more slowly, or even *ad libitum*; whereas, the Termination
partakes somewhat of the nature of a Stretto, and is to be played
crescendo, or *accelerando*.

RECOLLECTION.

We apply this term to the last part of any movement, when a
fragment of the principal subject is employed in an isolated manner,
somewhat resembling a short Coda. Here is an example from the
Rondo to Beethoven's Op. 13, which occurs at the end of the Termination:

Ex. 175.

This is an imitation of the motive of the Rondo, being major instead
of minor, and is to be played somewhat slower. The motive from
which this was taken is this:

Ex. 176.

The preparatory note (sixth-eighth note) is omitted from the first example and the mode is changed; otherwise they are identical (compare Ex. 176 with 175). Other instances will be mentioned. The above Recollection is followed by a device which we will now mention. That is the

STRETTO.

This word has for some time been applied to the performance of passages of an exciting, hurried nature, where the time of performance is lessened by increasing the movement, and thus bringing the notes nearer together. Stretto is also used in Fugue, when the response commences before the conclusion of the subject. In the former case the compression consists in performing the passage in a lesser space of time; in the latter case the number of measures is lessened by introducing the response before it would otherwise occur. Our application is more like the first definition, and will be applied to the last few measures of a movement which require an accelerated speed. This is frequently indicated by the composer, but sometimes the hurried character of the passage is so apparent to a musical nature that no further indication is given beyond what the notes divulge. Here is a simple illustration :

Ex. 177.

The Recollection here is to be played *ad libitum*, a little slower than the preceding and following Allegro. The Stretto begins at once upon the fourth measure of our quotation, and is to be hurried through to the end, *Molto cresc.* This is from the Rondo to a Sonatina already quoted. A still better illustration is what follows the Recollection quoted in Ex. 175:

Ex. 178.

This can scarcely be played too quickly or too loudly.

SEQUENCE.

"The natural order of following; a consequent succession." The musical definition is the same. Any group or figure which is repeated upon successive degrees of the scale. *a b c* being the model, the Sequence would be, *g a b, f g a*, etc., descending; *b c d, c d e*, etc., ascending. This is a Melodic Sequence.

A Harmonic Sequence consists of a succession of chords, all in the same position, like the opening of the last movement to Beethoven's Op. 2, No. 3. Or it may consist of a certain resolution of a discord being repeated in transition.

Following are examples of the Melodic and Harmonic Sequences just described:

Ex. 179.

The Sequence consists of the repetition of the melodic figure of the first measure. Each succeeding group is similar to the first, or a different shade of the same color.

Ex. 180.

At (a) we have a Sequence of diminished seventh chords resolved to their tonic minors. The fifth is omitted from each diminished chord, and the position of each minor triad is the same, 1, 5, 3, counting from the bass up.

At (b) the Sequence consists of an avoided cadence in each case. Some of the resolutions are to major and some to minor, but there is as much similarity as the tonality admits.

1 is the model, and 2, 3 and 4 are sequences. The Sequence is discontinued at the chord marked ✕. Sequence occurs in almost every musical composition, and should terminate at the end of a phrase, section, or period.*   There is no rhythmic sequence, because rhythm can only represent motion without direction.   It lacks color, yet supplies what color lacks.

When a Melodic or Harmonic Sequence exceeds the limits of a period it becomes what is called

PASSAGE.

This is usually non-melodious, and without the rhythmic proportion which belongs to a well-defined period.   The Passage is built upon arpeggio, or broken chords, harmonic sequence, or imitative scale groups:

MOZART SYMPHONY XXIII.

Ex. 181.

By continuing this a little farther the listener will unconsciously seize upon the design, and be led by it to a realm in which phrases and sections are unknown, or until this fancy-flight has fulfilled its mission.   The Passage is an important factor, especially in lengthy works.   This subject will be recurred to hereafter, and other examples given.

CADENZA.

An ornamental figure, or series of figures, introduced at the end of a period, but usually before the cadence takes place.   The Cadenza resembles the Passage, though it is less important, and generally founded upon one harmony; whereas, the harmonic basis of the

* The Eighth Etude from Bertini's Op. 32 is a good example of Sequence.

Passage almost continually changes. Here is a simple Cadenza, which has often been used:

Ex. 182.

This may be continued throughout the entire compass of an instrument; or the chord of *C*-major might be held below while the Cadenza is playing. Here is a short Cadenza, which is a good elementary illustration:

KUHLAU.

Ex. 183.

Observe that no melodic phrases appear in the Cadenza, and that it is isolated from, and independent of what follows.

Cadenza's have been written three and four pages in length, to be played at a certain point in the Concertos of the great masters. See No. 351, Breitkopf and Härtel. But it is not advisable to more than mention the fact here.

ILLUSTRATIONS.

Rondo Album, 2123, Ed. Peters.
Songs Without Words, Mendelssohn, Nos. 1, 2 and 9.
Musette from Pabst (Op. 12) or Morley.
One or two of the previous selections may be repeated.

QUESTIONS.

1. Prelude or Introduction; 2. Eingang or Transition; 3. Sequence; 4. Passage or Cadenza; 5. Coda or Termination; 6. Number of Periods; 7. Styles (Lyric, Thematic, etc.); 8. Recollection or Stretto.

Chapter XXV.

INTERMEDIATE DETAILS—Concluded.

ECHO, ANTICIPATION, REPETITION, PARENTHESIS, PEDAL-POINT.

THE Echo is an acoustical phenomenon, and consists in the re-verberation of any sound back to the place whence it originated. The Echo is always softer than the original sound, and frequently seems to be an octave higher, though in reality the pitch is the same. We apply the term not alone to pieces of this name (as they are few in number), but more especially to isolated, intermediate instances in which a certain phrase, or part of a phrase, is repeated an octave higher. The principal parts must be suspended in order that the Echo, which is soft, may be heard, and it is thus isolated from its antecedent and consequent. Otherwise it would become canonic imitation.* Here is a simple illustration of an Echo:

Ex. 184.

This has something of antiphonal style, being played by a different instrument in orchestral music. Echo must not be confused with Sequence, which is the repetition of a certain figure by the *same voice-part*, upon *different* degrees of the scale; nor with Repetition, which is the exact repetition of a group or figure by the same voice-part upon the *same* degrees of the scale.

Echo must also be disassociated from Canonic Imitation, in which a different voice-part imitates a melody above or below, but without interrupting the principal theme. Here is an example of each for comparison:

---

* Bach and other Organ composers have written pieces named " Echo "; but the echo effects in these pieces were produced upon another manual.

Ex. 185.

(The dynamical marks refer to the style of performance. The parallel lines indicate an Organ tone of equal power throughout.) 1 is a Sequence; 2, Repetition; 3, Canonic Imitation; 4 (the upper part), an Echo.*

The Echo should always be performed more softly than the original passage which it echoes, whereas the canonic imitation is accented, especially when it occurs below. The ascending sequence is played ‾‾◁‾‾ ; the descending Sequence is played ▷‾‾‾ , and the repetition ‾‾‾‾‾‾ .

ANTICIPATION.

The author applies this term to a short prefatory or intermediate passage of an impatient character, which seems to anticipate the following principal strain. In this case Anticipation is similar to the principal motive, of which it is anticipatory. The Anticipation may be either in form of a sequence or repetition. Following is an example from a popular Overture:

HEROLD.

Ex. 186.

The Anticipation consists of the passage marked *cresc.* which leads to the principal theme, *ff*. The resemblance between the two—(a) and (b)—is to be observed. Ex. 186 is by Sequence. Here is one as a Repetition:

Ex. 187.

etc.

---

* Read the description of these, and have class name each as it is played

The **Repetition** at (a) is anticipatory of the first three notes of the principal theme, which are these:

Ex. 188.

The regular strain commences at (b), on the last eighth of the measure, marked with an accent.

Anticipation may also consist of certain rhythmical peculiarities of a theme, repeated in advance. It is intended as an introduction to the following strain which it introduces and anticipates. The Anticipation is generally to be performed accelerando.[*]

PARENTHESIS.

Klindworth and other recent annotators have applied this term to an ornate group of notes inserted parenthetically between two principal melodic notes. The parenthesis may be written in small or large notes, and is of secondary importance—though we should be loth to omit some of Chopin's parenthetical sayings. We will recur to this subject in a future chapter.

PEDAL-POINT.

A simple explanation of this is, that a section or period of changing harmony is accompanied below by a stationary or continuously reiterated fundamental bass. In organ music this stationary fundamental tone is usually held by one of the pedals; hence the names Pedal-note, or Organ-point. In this case the distance between the Pedal-note and the manual parts is such as to ameliorate the dissonance which results from sounding certain harmonies above, that have no apparent relationship to the Pedal-note below. The principal justification of a Pedal-note lies, however, in the unity and tenacity which it imparts to the changeable design above. Here is a primitive illustration:

---

[*] Some similarity exists between the Anticipation and Return; but the latter is reminiscent, rather than anticipatory, and occurs more frequently in the Sonata movement.

Pedal Note.

On the piano it is better to repeat the organ-point, unless the passage is very soft and the organ-point of short duration. Other examples of this will be presented in the illustrations, and also in future analyses. In describing the Musette we had occasion to speak briefly of the Pedal-note which accompanies the Musette, as a Drone bass. But the Musette, as a piece of music, is named after an old instrument of that name (similar to the bagpipe), whose chief peculiarity was that its largest tube was called Drone, because it emitted a low, continuous sound. Therefore Drone bass is only another name for Pedal-note, but of different application. The former should be used in a more limited sense.

ILLUSTRATIONS.

Echo. Raff, "Echo" (Souvenir de Suisse).

Kuhlau, Op. 59, No. 1, first movement.

Beethoven, Op. 49, No. 1, first movement.

(The Echo is in the Second Subject, to be played softer.)

Anticipation. Beethoven, Bagatelle, Op. 33, No. 3.

The opening measures to Chopin's *D*-flat Waltz, Op. 64, No. 1.

Kuhlau, Rondo of Sonatina for four hands, Op. 44, No. 1. (The anticipation occurs after the Intermezzo, and serves as eingang to the second subject in *E*-minor. This occurs several times.)

Parenthesis. Chopin, Op. 32, No. 2, Nocturne. This contains several instances of Parenthesis, which it would be well for the class to discover for themselves.

Pedal-note. Chopin, Mazurka, Op. 17, No. 4. (The repeated period in *A*-major.) Mazurka, Op. 68, No. 3, the Trio.

Beethoven, Op. 13. In the Development there is a Pedal-note of twenty-one measures' duration (on *G*), beginning *PP*.

F. Hiller, Dudelsack.

Le Tambourin, Rameau (*E*-minor).

The selections should be played in miscellaneous order, with the following general questions: Echo (how many measures?). Anticipation (the motive following should be played first). Parenthesis. The mere recognition will suffice here. Pedal-note, or Organ-point. (Drone bass may be applied to the Hiller selection.)

Chapter XXVI.

MISCELLANEOUS SINGLE FORMS.

UNDER this head we will consider a variety of short movements, in which the form does not change. These are:

1. The Spinning Song (Spinnlied).
2. Hunting Song (The Chase).
3. Boat Song (Barcarolle or Gondolied).
4. Cradle Song (Berceuse).
5. Bell Piece, (Carillon).
6. Night Song (Serenade and Romance).
7. Bagatelle.
8. Invention.
9. Toccata.
10. Song Without Words.
11. The Pipers (I Pifferari).
12. Study (Etude).
13. Scherzo (Humoresque or Burlesque).
14. Idyl. (Pastoral.)

The first four may be recognized by the accompaniment alone, which is characteristic.

1. SPINNING SONG.

This has for its principal feature a rapid, figurated accompaniment (usually in ⁶⁄₈ metre), with a Rhythm of twelve sixteenths in a measure. This is the corresponding musical representation of the hum of the spinning-wheel:

Ex. 190.

This quotation is from Schubert's beautiful song " Marguerite at the Spinning-Wheel," the text from Goethe's " Faust."* The melody which this accompanies is supposed to be the song of the spinner.

There are many interesting compositions in this style, some of which will be mentioned at the conclusion of this chapter.

2. HUNTING SONG (*Die Jagd, La Chasse*).

This is usually in ⁶⁄₈ Metre, quick Movement, and animating Rhythm. A distinguishing feature of most hunting pieces is the imitation of the tones sounded by hunting horns during the Chase.

Ex. 191.

These natural, open tones of the horns are frequently used by composers as a motive, as in Ex. 191. The peculiarity of this is not so much in the melody as in the blank fifths of the harmony.

3. BOAT SONG.

A Gondolied, or Barcarolle. Rhythm, ; Metre, ⁶⁄₈ ; Movement, *Allegretto*. Here again the accompaniment plays an important part, with its rocking, boat-like motion. The melody is supposed to be the song of the gondolier, and is usually of an amorous nature.

4. BERCEUSE.

This is the French name for Cradle Song, or Lullaby (in German, Schlummerlied). The Metre may be common, triple or quadruple. The movement is rather slow. The accompaniment suggests, in a

---

* If convenient, it would be well to have this sung for the class.

relative way, the motion of the cradle, while the melody typifies the song of the mother. The gentleness and purity of the sentiment have inspired many beautiful compositions, and these characteristics should belong to all pieces of this style.

Chopin's Berceuse, Op. 57, is founded upon this accompaniment:

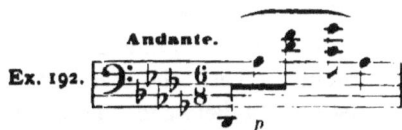

Ex. 192.

which is repeated throughout the entire opus until the beginning of the Recollection.

5. CARILLON.

A composition founded upon, or pertaining to, the chimes of bells. The most distinguishing feature consists of a repetition, or imitation, of some of the well-known bell melodies, which are here quoted:

Ex. 193.

The motive at (b) is employed by Schumann in the Allegro of his Piano Quintette, Op. 44. The others also have been frequently used in instrumental and vocal music.

Campanella also comes under this heading. The word signifies, a small bell. The Campanella Organ Stop is an imitation of little bells, and this is characteristic of the pieces of this name.

The Rondo, by Field, entitled " Midi," will be a good selection, as it is founded upon a Carillon similar to Ex. 193 (a). This occurs in several places, and is always to be brought out prominently, especially where it appears in a lower part. In the Coda the tower clock begins to strike twelve (on a continuous tone), and this is accompanied by the bell melody (a) previously mentioned. The Rondo is very ingenious, and will repay a careful analysis.

6. NOCTURNE (NOTTURNO).

A Night Song, somewhat sombre in tone-color, and usually of a quiet, contemplative nature. The Serenade is similar to the Nocturne, but of a more amorous and complaining nature, soft and persuasive.

Beethoven has written two Serenades in Chamber Music form, but these have more than one movement.*

The Romance is included with the Serenade; in fact, it is not always possible to distinguish between them. But the Romance usually partakes more of the mysterious and romantic. Like the Serenade and Nocturne, it is in lyric style.

7. BAGATELLE.

A trifle; a light composition of an unimportant nature, not in any particular style. These are mentioned here merely on account of their single form. Beethoven wrote twenty-four.

8. INVENTION.

A collection of thirty short pieces in thematic and canonic style, by J. S. Bach, were named Inventions. They are similar to etudes, or free canons, and contain excellent food for the musical student to chew and digest. The two-part Inventions are easiest.

9. TOCCATA.

An ancient style of composition treated in thematic manner somewhat like the Etude. The word signifies, *to touch ;* and it was originally the Introduction, and afterwards the Finale, to a Sonata. It has, however, this characteristic, that certain phrases or figures are repeated ; and, in fact, the construction is mostly by means of repetition and imitation, thus :

Ex. 194.

Observe that the first four groups, 1, are repeated literally at 2. This

---

* The first one, Op. 8, contains five numbers.

scheme is followed throughout, with this addition : that in the repetition of certain sections the theme and counter-theme exchange places and appear inverted.

10. SONG WITHOUT WORDS.

This title was bestowed by Mendelssohn upon forty-eight short lyric pieces composed by himself and his sister Fannie. Stephen Heller has given a characteristic title to most of these pieces. Their chief peculiarity is, a well-defined melody, and a more or less elaborate accompaniment. Even these little pieces show the necessity of analysis, as nearly all the songs contain a prelude or introduction, an intermezzo, cadenza, or episode, extended periods, coda, or stretto. Nearly all these peculiarities call for a different style of performance, and the *song* must be kept distinct from the intermezzo, as well as from the accompaniment.

11. PIFFERARI.

This signifies the Pipers, or Italian street musicians. The music is founded upon a ground bass, which represents the accompanying instrument, such as a bassoon, 'cello or bagpipe, while the melody is sounded from a flute or fiddle. The monotonous accompaniment and the quaint, rustic character of the treble part serve to make pieces of this description easy of recognition. The movement is lively.

12. ETUDE.

An Etude is a study, composed principally of sequences, passages and contrapuntal devices. Etudes are technical rather than poetical; though Moscheles, Henselt, Liszt, Tausig, Chopin, Rubinstein, and Scharwenka have written some of their best concert pieces in this form. The Etudes of Cramer, Bertini, Heller and Löschhorn are also artistic and interesting.

13. SCHERZO.

This form was introduced by Beethoven into his Sonatas and Symphonies, in place of the Menuetto of Haydn and Mozart. The character of the Scherzo is extremely vivacious, and in the hands of Beethoven often droll and humorous. The Scherzi of Mendelssohn are more romantic and have a lighter grace than those of the immortal German composer. The name was used prior to the advent of

Beethoven, but it was he who gave the form its present important position, and imbued it with artistic life and pleasantry. The definition of Scherzo is, playful, merry, jestingly; and many Scherzi are a species of Humoresque or Burlesque. But the nature of the sounds must determine whether the first or last definition is to be applied.

The Humoresque and Burlesque come under this heading, though they are seldom included in large works as is the Scherzo. Many of Haydn's Finales provoke a smile or a laugh from musicians when first they hear them, on account of some odd conceit or grotesque figure. These are humoresques. But with the greater means at the control of recent composers this style of music has become more characteristic and humorous. Several good examples will be mentioned in the list following.

14. IDYL.

Originally a short pastoral poem. In music the application is similar. The nature of the sounds and character of the work must be the guides, not the form or rhythm. A well-conceived Idyl will suggest rural life or scenery by the simplicity, freshness and pastoral character of the music. The Pastoral Rondo by Steibelt is a simple illustration. The Idyl by Pabst, Op. 20, and the Forest Idyls by Jensen partake more of the mysterious, and have less rustic simplicity.

ILLUSTRATIONS.

1. No. 34, Songs Without Words, Mendelssohn; A Spinning Song by Litolff; Liszt's arrangement of the Spinning Song from Wagner's "Flying Dutchman"; Omphale at her Spinning-wheel, by Saint-Saëns.
2. The Hunter's Horn, by Kornatzki, Op. 25; The Chase, by Stephen Heller, Op. 29; The Chase, by Rheinberger, Op. 5; and No. 3 of the "Songs Without Words," Mendelssohn.
3. Chopin, Op. 57; H. Sanderson; Mason, Op. 34; Gottschalk; and the exquisite Schlummerlied of Schumann, Op. 124.
4. Numbers 6, 12 or 29 from the "Songs Without Words"; "On the Sea," by Kuhe, or a Barcarolle from Chopin or Rubinstein.
5. Op. 41, Taubert; "Midi," Rondo by Field; La Campanella, Liszt (arranged from Paganini); "Carillons du Village," Delacour.

6. One of the Field Nocturnes. The No. 11 of Chopin's Nocturnes may be played as a second illustration, also the Nocturne from " Midsummer-night's Dream."

7. The *Bagatelles* of Beethoven are Ops. 33, 119 and 126. Those of the first volume are the most pleasing.

8. An excellent edition of Bach's Inventions has been published by Augener & Co., 8018 and 8019, with explanatory text, an notations and fingering. No. 13, in *A*-minor, first book, is a good example.

9. *Toccata*. No. 15, " Album Classique (from Sonata in *A*), Paradisi; Schumann, Op. 7; Toccata by Seeboeck; one by Clementi (in *B-flat*); one by Bach in connection with the great fugue, and one by Rheinberger in *G*-minor, Op. 12.

10. The 48 by Mendelssohn are divided into eight books. Nos. 1, 3, 8, 12 and 18, from the first three books, may be played at different times. Th. Kullak's edition is best. Rubinstein's " La Melodia," in *F*, may also be included, or, La Pensée, by Blumenthal.

11. Several of these have been written, but the author can recall only the one by Gounod, in *F*, " Les Pifferari," and " Dudelsack," Hiller.

12. The first Etude by J. B. Cramer, in *C* (from his book of 50), is especially recommended for this lesson (Knorr's or Von Bü low's Edition), though any of the famous Etudes, such as were mentioned previously, would be appropriate.

13. *Scherzo*. Chopin, Rubinstein, Mendelssohn, and nearly all great composers have written in this style. Beethoven's best Scherzi, written for Orchestra, may be played upon the piano, but they should afterward be heard in full score to be thoroughly appreciated. The Scherzo from Beethoven's Op. 2, No. 3, will be a good example. This is written in the dance form, with a trio and da capo. The style is that of a musical trialogue. The Humoresque and Burlesque are invariably of a quaint or playful nature, containing sudden contrasts and odd surprises. Nicodé, Op. 28, No. 2; Humoresque in *D*, Em. Moor: Sternberg, Op. 26.

14. *Idyl*. Bargiel, Idyl in *G*; Gade, Idyllen, Op. 34; Thome, " Under the Leaves "; The Shepherd's Pipe, by Gregh.

Under the sixth heading we might mention the Romanza, for though it has no distinctive outward form, musicians can usually recognize it from its character. It will be sufficient to mention the Op. 28, No. 2, by Schumann, and the " Romantic Album," published by Peters, Leipzig.

The illustrations should not be played in the same order as the headings, which correspond to the numbers of the previous catalog. It would be well, however, to call attention to the first four styles, in which the accompaniment plays so prominent a part, as these styles are more easily recognized. After this, the class may learn to name the others after a single hearing.

QUESTIONS.

1. Metre and Movement; 2. Rhythm (especially of the accompaniment); 3. Mode; 4. Prelude or Introduction; 5. Equal or Extended Periods; 6. Coda or Intermezzo; 7. Form; 8. Principal Characteristics (whether the piece contains a ground bass, an imitation of bells, hunting-horns, spinning-wheels, etc.); 9. Style or Character. (Some advanced pupil might make an attempt at qualifying the nature of the piece, whether gay and humorous, tender, meditative and gloomy, or impatient and headlong, as the hunting-song.)

The different harmonic cadences could be included as a question if thought necessary.

Chapter XXVII.

ROMANTIC SINGLE FORMS.

FEU FOLLET. WILL-O'-THE-WISP. FAIRY REVEL.

THE superstitions and legends connected with the Will-o'-the-Wisp (*ignis-fatuus*) are very numerous, and composers have been attracted by the poetic fancies which these phenomena have inspired almost as naturally as the victims in legendary romance were attracted by the transient spectacle of the *fata morgana*, or the hallucinatory charms of Lorelei.

COMPLETE MUSICAL ANALYSIS.

Of a kindred nature are the songs of Schumann, Liszt, and others, entitled " The Nymph of the Rhine," " The Nymph of the Forest," etc. Schubert's great song, " The Erl King," (following the text of Goethe,) is more tragical than the others; but all are associated with the influence of spirits that were believed to represent agencies of good and evil. This belief has had numerous seeming analogies in the phenomena of mind and matter; in vital as well as chemical agencies. Thus the phosphorescent light of the fire-fly or the glow-worm, or of the still stranger chemical phenomenon, *ignis-fatuus*, seen in certain marshy places during a starless night, have acted powerfully upon the imagination of man. And in music there is a certain affinity between all these species of phenomena, whether they are the result of a merely fantastical mirage or the *fata morgana;* a fitful and glinting fire-fly, or the more preternatural lumination of the *ignis-fatuus*, Will-o'-the-Wisp.

Feu follet has generally been translated " Will-o'-the-Wisp"; but one is a vital, the other a chemical, agency. *Ignis-fatuus* is more commonly associated with the evil influence, as may be inferred from the following poem :

> " When night's dark mantle has covered all,
>   I come in fire arrayed.
> Many a victim I've seen fall,
>   Or fly from me dismayed.
> ' Will-o'-the-Wisp ' they trembling cry ;
>   ' Will-o'-the-Wisp, 'tis he ! '
> To mark their shriek, as they sink and die,
>   Is merry sport for me."

The fire-fly and glow-worm are more analogous to the Ariel-like spirit of playfulness and sportive phantasm. The French designation, " feu follet," *i. e.,* " merry fire," gives a better idea of the effect which composers have, as a rule, endeavored to create in their pieces of this name. Their efforts to transcribe the corresponding musical expression of these phenomena, and the legends to which they have given rise, have resulted in a peculiar style of music, in which there is no accented melody, no visible, outward, melodic structure, but a continuous, aerial flow of sounds somewhat resembling this, if it be hummed with the lips entirely closed :

Ex. 195. *pp* Moderato. Legatissimo.

Very softly and without accent.

This is only intended to represent the effect of an indistinct melodic outline.

We have demonstrated that melody is common even to purely harmonic combinations; but in the style of music now under consideration the melodic element is not prominent, and on account of the accents being omitted the music assumes something of a supernal, or dissolvent, character. The effect is often spectral, as of forms or figures emancipated from our laws of gravitation, and suspended in mid-air. The flowing of water (especially where it makes no sound) is frequently suggested by music in a similar manner. The smooth, limpid and ceaseless flow of the current is similar to the continuous, unaccented flow of sounds in the music. The nature of the sounds, the rhythm and the poetic character of the piece must of course express the difference and the distinction between a water course; the mysterious and awe-inspiring sight of an *ignis-fatuus* hanging at midnight over a dank and dreary lowland; the scintillating gleams from the thorax of a glow-worm; or the dainty capers and gambols of a fairy revel. Fairy Fingers, by Mills; Bubbling Spring, by Madam Rivé-King; Perpetual Motion, Von Weber; Dance of Gnomes, Carreño; Feu Follet, Prudent, and The Dance of the Fairies, by Liebling; all have this unaccented feature as of a continuous flow of sounds, or something gently poised above the surface. Another and more common instance is the "Titania," by Wely, especially after the introduction and before the accented melody appears. To have called this Feu Follet would have been quite as appropriate as to name it after the Queen of Fairies, especially as it has but little of the romantic spirit. Both are aerial and mystical subjects, and have a similar corresponding expression in music of this class.

In the "Nymph of the Forest," by Schumann, and even the "Will-o'-the-Wisp," by Cherry, there can be no doubt as to the elementary spirit of evil being represented, even though the words were suppressed and the music alone remained. Whether this malign influence is represented by the fatally beautiful Lorelei, or assumes the guise of an *ignis-fatuus,* we may not always determine

COMPLETE MUSICAL ANALYSIS.

from the music. But the spirit of evil and the mysterious manifestation of this power or essence—these can be embodied and set forth
by the composer with more or less characteristic effect. It will be
comparatively easy for the listener to make a distinction between
compositions of the ignis-fatuus or fata morgana order, and those
which merely represent the harmless coruscations of the *elater noc-
tilucus*, or the mystic, volatile pictures from fairy-land. By way of
distinction, therefore, we will frequently be obliged to associate the
fire-fly with the French *feu follet*, fire-play or merry fire, as typical
of the beneficent or merry spirit; whereas the Will-o'-the-Wisp and
the *fata morgana* naturally represent the evil influence. Instrumental composers have generally taken the former view of these
phenomena, even when they gave the title Will o'-the-Wisp to their
compositions. But the more serious, supernatural view has frequently been adopted, both by vocal and instrumental composers.

An unusual amount of time and space have been devoted to this
somewhat vague subject, not so much for its present importance as
on account of its direct bearing upon the Romantic and Realistic
styles of the present day, which are to be analyzed in Chapters
XLIII, XLIV and XLV. Something of this may be found as far
back as the Opus 31 of Beethoven; then in the Operas " Euryanthe "
and " Oberon "; the overture to " Melusine "; the " Midsummer-
night's Dream " music, and considerable of the music of Liszt, Schumann, Chopin, Wagner, Rubinstein, and other recent composers.

Illustrations for this part of the chapter will be found in the
Compendium, though the pieces already mentioned should be interspersed with the other single forms during this lesson.

PART VII.

Chapter XXVIII.

CANONIC IMITATIONS.

FREE. STRICT. CONTRARY. PARTIAL.

A GENERAL understanding of this subject has been acquired through the illustrations in the previous chapters; but it will be necessary to have at least a slight acquaintance with the four principal species of canonic imitation, as they are extensively employed in the construction and development of high-class music.

1. FREE IMITATION.

In this, the nature of the intervals is not *exactly* preserved by the imitating voice, thus:

Ex. 196.

The nature of the intervals at (a) is: two major seconds (*e* to *d*, and *d* to *c*) and a minor second, *c* to *b* descending.   In the imitation at (b) we hear one major, one minor, and then another major second (whole step).*   This is known theoretically as an imitation in the sixth below, which always results in a Free Imitation.   Let the class analyze the second phrase, and the imitation thereof (c) and (d) (one minor second, and two major seconds are answered by two major seconds and one minor second).

---

* (b) imitates (a); (d) imitates (c).

It is not always necessary that free imitation should bear as close resemblance to the Proposta (subject) as it does in Ex. 196. Even in tonal fugue for example, this motive (a) would be imitated by the Risposta (response) as at (b) :

Ex. 197.

This is done in order to preserve the tonal relationship between dominant and tonic. The interval from the dominant, d, down to the tonic, g, is a fifth, whereas the interval from the tonic down to the dominant is but a fourth; and this discrepancy is obviated by imitating the rhythm, but not the melody, as at +. This results in free imitation, though the response at (b) is a regular tonal one.

2. STRICT IMITATION.

Here the theoretical nature of the intervals in the Risposta must be identical with those of the Proposta. A major second is answered by a major second; a minor second by a minor second; a perfect fifth by a perfect fifth, and so on :

Ex. 198.

The class is to analyze these examples, as previously explained, and tell the interval in which the imitation is made. (Observe the crossing of the voices at (b), Ex. 2.) Imitations may take place in any interval, those in the fourth, fifth, sixth and octave having already been given. Imitations in the prime or octave (1 or 8) are naturally strict. Those in the fourth or fifth are mostly strict, though requiring an occasional sharpened fourth (Ex. 2) or flattened seventh (Ex. 3). Imitations in the second, third, sixth and seventh are free. (As the second inverted becomes a seventh, and the third becomes a tenth, these numbers are generally used synonymously.)

3. CONTRARY IMITATION.

In this species the *direction* of the Risposta is reversed. A descending interval is answered by an ascending one, and *vice versa*.

Ex. 199.

From BACH'S "ART OF FUGUE"

Observe that the ascending fifth is answered by a descending fifth;
and that the descending scale passage becomes in the risposta an
ascending one. The nature of the intervals is almost identical.
Compare (b) with (a).* Contrary imitation represents a difference
of opinion, a dissension, or an opposite view from that of the Proposta. Hence, in music which enters the arena of strife and conflict this species of imitation becomes the exponent of an opposing
principle.

NOTE.—Retrograde Canon is not here included, because in the imitation
of an ascending, or a descending subject, retrograde canon and contrary imitation are identical. But the majority of subjects if taken backwards are not
only difficult to analyze, but still more difficult of recognition by the hearing
faculties.

4. PARTIAL OR INTERRUPTED IMITATION.

This style is of very common occurrence, and enables the composer to be more fancy-free than in the strict style. Only parts of the
leading motive are imitated, and these may be either free or strict.
There is an actual distinction between partial and interrupted imitation, but as this difference is not material, except to the composer,
we will not describe it here. This will be sufficient for the class: to
recognize that only a fragment, not a considerable portion, of the
principal theme is imitated. Following is a brief instance from the
introduction to Beethoven's sixth Bagatelle, Op. 119:

Ex. 200.

etc.

The first figure of five notes (a) is repeated in strict imitation below
(b). Here the imitation is interrupted, because the continuation is
in different style, and does not require, or admit, the responsive ac-

* In nearly all of the Gigues by Bach the Second Part begins with the principal subject
reversed.

companiment below. Whether the Partial Imitations be strict or free, need not be specified by the class at present.

Imitations in augmentation and diminution are of such rare occurrence in modern music that they will not be specialized here.

Little Scherzo in *F*, Theo. Kullak.

Bach's Petite Preludes (Augener & Co. No. 8020). Book I, Nos. 2, 4, 6, 7, 8, 9 and 11, contain partial imitations. The Inventions are also made up of partial imitations.

Pavan in *G*, by Herbert Sharpe. (May be had in the "Artist's Album," White, Smith & Co., or singly.) Partial imitations occur in all but the "trio" and Introduction.

Following is an example from Beethoven's Sonata, Op. 2, No. 2, second part of the Scherzo (in *A*-minor). The principal melody is:

Ex. 201.

This is sketched in simple score in order to show the imitations. The first four descending tones of the clarinet are answered in free imitation by the oboe, a fourth above. Here the imitation is interrupted for two beats to be repeated in the same manner. This is more natural than to suppose that the melody consists of these

notes: Ex. 202. which would make the im-

itations both contrary and awkward.

For strict imitations the first two periods of the Canon from Clementi's *G*-major Sonata may be played, also the "Scherzo in Canon Form" by Jadassohn. The class should distinguish between the old two-voiced canon, and the more modern harmonized canon, containing complemental or *ad libitum* parts, as in the Scherzo-

Canon.   The Trio (per moto contrario) from the Clementi Canon should be played as an illustration of reversed imitation.

The class may also observe the distinction between partial free and partial strict imitation.   The Bach Preludes, 7 and 11, will be good illustrations for this.   In the 7th the imitation is to be found in the third and fourth measures of the bass, and is to be designated. (No. 11 contains partial free and partial contrary imitations.)   The Bach two-part Inventions, Nos. 1, 8 and 13, Book I, should also be analyzed, as they contain excellent examples of free, strict, and partial Imitations.

The questions should first be given to the class collectively, and the distinction between two kinds of imitation combined is to be made when possible.

Chapter XXIX.

OLD CYCLICAL FORMS.

OLD SONATA. SUITE. PARTITA.*

THE Suite, Partita, Sonata, Symphony, Concerto, and nearly all chamber-music, constitute what we may call mixed or combined forms.   Pauer terms them Cyclical Forms, a very good word, if it is not understood in its chronological sense.   But in this chapter we will examine the old Cyclical Forms, as a preliminary step to what follows.

The Suite, Sonata, and Partita were synonymous until the advent of Philip Em. Bach.   Before that time any and all of these terms were applied to a composition containing a collection of dance tunes, or certain dances interspersed with other popular forms of the day. Some commenced with an Overture, some with a Präludium, and others with an Allemande.   An Air, or Fugue, was frequently included in place of the Courante or Gavotte.   The key was the same throughout, with exception of an occasional change to relative or

---

* Partitur and Partition are used in foreign Catalogs to designate a full orchestral score.

tonic minor.   The Suite usually ended with a Gigue.   (The Partita
and old Sonata are included when we speak of Suite.)   Here follow
the contents of a Suite, Partita, and Sonata, by J. S. Bach:

Suite.	*Partita.*	*Sonata.*
1. Allemande.	Overture.	Praludium.
2. Courante.	Grave.	Fuga.
3. Sarabande.	Air.	Adagio.
4. Gavotte.	Gavotte.	Allemande.
5. Polonaise.	Bourrée.	Courante.
6. Bourrée.	Gigue.	Sarabande.
7. Menuetto.		Gigue.
8. Gigue.		

Bach's Orchestral Suite in *D* (arranged for four hands by Mendelssohn) contains but five numbers; but the Overture is somewhat
extended, consisting of a Grave, Vivace and Grave, after the style of
the French Overture.   From the comparative table just given it will
be seen that the three form-names were used synonymously, and
that the old Sonata was merely a collection of dances, occasionally
including an Air and Fugue.   They were, however, excellently written, and should be included in the curriculum of a thorough musical
education.   Couperin, Scarlatti, Lully, Rameau, Mattheson, Purcell,
Händel, and other contemporaries of the great Bach, wrote Suites
and Partitas similar to those whose contents have been quoted.   The
prevailing styles were Italian, French, English, and German.

We will quote a few from the author of the "Messiah," for
though he and Bach were born in the same year, and within a short
distance from each other, they never met; and as Händel lived principally in Italy and England, his Suites very naturally represent the
Italian and English styles.

First Suite.	*Second Suite.*	*Third Suite.*	*Partita, by J. L.* *Krebs* (1713-1780).
1. Prelude.	1. Adagio.	1. Prelude and	1. Preludio.
2. Allemande.	2. Allegro.	Fugue.	2. Fuga.
3. Courante.	3. Adagio.	2. Allemande.	3. Allemande
4. Gigue.	4. Fugue.	3. Courante.	4. Corrente.
		4. Air and five	5. Sarabande.
		Variations.	6. Burleska.
		5. Presto.	7. Menuet. I II,
			and III.
			8. Gigue.

(The Suites, etc., may be procured from any large dealer.)

It would be well to play a few Suites, giving out questions similar to those in Chapter XVII, as most of the numbers are old dances. This will prove a good review of Chapter XVII.

This style has recently been rehabilitated, and the following are worthy of attention: Raff, Suite in *E*-minor, Op. 72; Bargiel, Op. 31; Eug. d'Albert, Op. 1; Suite in *D*, Jadassohn, Op. 36; Pauer, Suite Facile in *C*; Sherwood, W. H., Suite, Op. 5; E. A. MacDowell, Ops. 10 and 14; B. O. Klein, Suite in *G*, Op. 25; Grieg, Op. 40, for String Orchestra.

Chapter XXX.

MIXED FORMS.

POTPOURRI.   THEME AND VARIATIONS.

THE Potpourri is a melange or medley.   It consists of a miscellaneous series of favorite airs following one another without much regard to *unity*, but with as much variety as possible.   Operatic potpourris are numerous and often ingenious in their order of arrangement.   Such Overtures as "Zampa" and "Poet and Peasant" are really Potpourris.   This form is comparatively unimportant, and seldom has a better *raison d'etre* than the gratification of uncultivated tastes.

THEME AND VARIATIONS.

In this form of composition the Theme consists of two regular periods in lyric style, each of which is repeated, like the ballad form. Variations of the theme then follow, the simplest coming first, and the more elaborate afterwards.

We will give, as a preliminary study, the principal means by which Variations are constructed, with an example of each:

Motive from HAYDN.

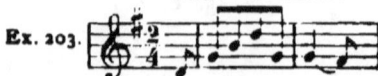

Ex. 203.

The simplest variations of this will consist in altering the value of the notes, thus:

Ex. 204.

Variation 3 is in syncopation. Thus for the same number of notes in the first measure (four) have been used in each example. We may now introduce iterated and reiterated notes:

Ex. 205.

Then change the Metre:

Ex. 206.

All of these are rhythmical and metrical Variations, the melodic notes being the same. Considering the theme as an outline, we may introduce passing tones between the harmonic intervals:

Ex. 207.

Or appoggiaturas may be placed above or below the melodic notes.

Ex. 208.

The accent marks in both examples show the original melodic notes. These are similar to syncopation.

The appoggiaturas can be doubled in number, as were the passing notes in Var. 14. (See Ex. 207.)

Ex. 209.

Arpeggios and broken chords will afford other means of variations of the theme :

Ex. 210.

The 25th Variation is by means of anticipation, an opposite effect to that of syncopation.

Ex. 211.

26, 27, 28 and 29 are more elaborate than the others.   26 contains diatonic passing tones ; 27 has both diatonic and chromatic passing tones ; No. 28 has somewhat the effect of a trill above the theme ; 29 possesses more of the peculiarity of dance rhythm.

Supposing the original harmonization to have been this :

Ex. 212.

We might change the effect materially by using different harmonies, without altering the melody :

Ex. 213.

The melody does not admit much variety in the harmonic treatment, but these examples will serve to illustrate one of the means employed in varying a theme. By changing the key and varying the treatment, still different results may be produced, as here:

Ex. 214.

At 32 the melodic design is considerably altered, but without destroying the resemblance; at 33 the original melody is led in a different direction by ascending a fourth instead of descending a fifth to the key-tone, and then by shortening the value of the long appoggiatura and continuing this downward melody. We may now change the mode, and write as many variations as we choose:

Ex. 215.

A change in the form of accompaniment will give us other variations:

Ex. 216.

The theme is not materially altered here, but the rapid, figurated accompaniment gives us a different style. This may be inverted by playing the theme below:

Ex. 217.

This is somewhat in bravura style, as is the next:

Ex. 218.

This is the same thing, said in a different way. Here is one in the old style, being an embellishment:

Ex. 219.

The melody is concealed by the appoggiaturas. Finally we may employ contrary inversion, and produce thereby a theme apparently new, but really the same in contrary inversion:

Ex. 220.

This is like turning a picture upside down, as in a *mirage*. With exception of metre and rhythm, this is distinctly opposite and contrary to the original motive; the intervals are turned upside down. After the last Variation it is customary to include a coda or finale, as conclusion to the whole.

Mention is here made of the Metempsychosis, by S. G. Pratt, as being the most remarkable "transformation and transmigration of a tune" which has ever come to the author's notice.

These examples will be sufficient to illustrate the principal peculiarities of variations of a theme or motive, so that the class may know them either by sight or sound.

Variations like Nos. 3, 8, 12, 13, 15, 20, 29, 30, 32, 33, 34, 38 and 39 are best.

Further explanation of the esthetic character of different kinds of variations must be left for a future chapter.

ILLUSTRATIONS OF THE POTPOURRI, AND THEME WITH VARIATIONS.

Potpourris by Vilbac, Ascher, Pease, H. Cramer, etc.
Variations, Mozart, Vol. 349, Litolff.
Rondos and variations, Dussek, Vol. 399, Litolff.

Variations, Beethoven, 2 Vols., No. 298 *a* and *b*. Edition Peters.
Variations, Von Weber, Vol. 393, Litolff.
"Sweet bye and bye," with variations, S. G. Pratt.
Gurlitt's Op. 115, "Buy a Broom," humorously treated in the style of classical composers.

IMPERFECT FORMS.

Such a great variety of forms have been employed by composers for various purposes that we cannot pronounce very positively upon the propriety or impropriety of a particular form without first knowing the design (if any) of the composer. The form of a ball-room Waltz, for instance, would, in any other situation, be liable to severe criticism ; but as the principal requirements for such a piece are merely correct rhythmical construction, equal mensural proportion and pleasing variety, it would be hypocritical to judge the dance Waltz according to higher standards.

In the Gipsy Rondo from Haydn's Fifth Trio we have an example of ill-proportioned form. The principal strain is very pleasing. The Intermezzo of ten measures and the return to the principal theme are also correct. The next regular period, which stands in the place of Second Subject, is founded upon a Pedal-note, and consists of a section repeated four times. This is followed by a period in the same key, having the appearance of an accompaniment, and drawn out to the length of a period by the same tedious process of repetition. The fifth strain is in *G*-minor, quite different from the previous matter. This also is constructed by means of repetition. The following period consists of two six-measure sections. Part I then recurs. The seventh period is in *G*-minor. (The Gipsy rhythm is more characteristic here than in any of the other strains.) The eighth period is in *B*-flat major, interspersed with *G*-minor, and returning to the First Part as before. The last seventeen measures form the Coda. The principal faults lie in the number and irrelevancy of the different periods, which seem to have no other object than that of consuming a certain amount of space. The Rondo contains enough material for a comic opera.

The Turkish March, from Mozart's *A*-major Sonata (the one with variations) calls for almost the same animadversions as the Haydn Rondo. Aside from the Coda there are five regular periods (which, however, are too many for so small a piece), and the tonal arrangement is bad. The second subject (first period in *A*-major) is forced into too great prominence by its frequent repetition. The different periods are more relevant than in the Gipsy Rondo, but the harmonization is beggarly, and the Coda is a mere piece of patchwork, ragged and ill-proportioned.

The two favorite Marches by Mendelssohn (from The Midsummer-night's Dream and Athalia) afford another proof of how a composer's poorest works may become the most popular. We will select The Priest's March. No fault can be found with the Prelude, except that it is commonplace. The principal objection is to the unusual number of equal periods (seven in all), and the desultory, unconnected manner in which they follow each other. The tonal structure, the harmonies, and the Coda are something of an improvement upon the two previous selections, but the form is one which young composers should avoid. The Wedding March belongs in the same category. There is too much music for the occasion; and we infer that Liszt experienced the effects of this redundancy in making his arrangement of the March and Elfin Dance, for in the *finale* he gives expression to a very humorous bit of impatience.

The alleged "Farewell to the Piano," by Beethoven, is another instance, though we know not who is responsible for this flimsy piece of bathos.

Innumerable instances might be cited from the works of would-be composers, but these are unworthy of notice.

The Hungarian Rondo, Turkish March, and The Priest's March, should be played as additional illustrations.

Chapter XXXI.

THE RONDO FORM.

THIS is the most natural and important of all the popular mixed forms. The chief peculiarity of all rondos is that the principal theme occurs at least three times; being interspersed with an intermezzo, episode, or second subject, after each of which the first subject recurs. In the Rondo the consequent period (*i. e.*, the second period, similar to, and following, the first period in regular conse quent succession) seldom appears; but the first period or principal theme is either repeated or extended into as complete a strain as possible. (See Ex. 127. The second period is a plain instance of the consequent or twin period. as both are similar in rhythm and melody.) This principal theme is succeeded by an Intermezzo or transitional Eingang. The Principal theme usually follows. Then we have a second theme, in which the style changes. This is not to be confused with the consequent or *second period* of the Ballad or ballad dance, which is a counterpart or duplicate of the pattern pe riod (first period). The Second Subject, as applied to Rondos and Sonata movements, is more of a subsequent than a consequent period, as the rhythm, key and style are changed in the Second Sub ject in order to present a contrast to the First Subject. The second theme is usually a single or extended period, like the first, and sel dom contains the consequent period. The word Subject is applied to a strain or period of dissimilar material, or a different pattern Therefore as the twin periods of the Ballad are similar, and in the same style, we might call the entire melody a Subject, as has been done. But it is really better to reserve the word Subject for its more proper and particular application in the Rondo, Sonata and Song forms.

Note.--The Rondo by Dussek, " Les Adieux," contains a consequent period following the first regular period, but this is an exceptional case.

This is the general construction of the Rondo:

1. Principal theme, consisting of an equal period which is usu ally repeated, with slight modifications.
2. Intermezzo; of irregular construction, less tuneful than the principal theme and leading back to
3. The Principal subject same as before.
4. Second theme, in contrast to the first. In this part the key, or mode, is changed and the rhythm is somewhat altered. The sec ond theme usually constitutes a change of style. At the end of the second theme we usually find an eingang, passage or cadenza lead ing back to the
5. Return of Principal theme.
6. Intermezzo, as before; or an Episode of more adventitious matter.

7. Return of first subject, as before.

8. Coda, Recollection and Stretto, or Termination.* (Sometimes No. 6 is omitted, in which case the first subject is heard three instead of four times, the Coda coming in place of the second Intermezzo.) The Rondo in Kuhlau's Sonatina, Op. 20, No. 1, is constructed in this manner, the Recollection and Stretto being included in the Termination, which begins at the one hundred and thirty-fourth measure. The Recollection and Stretto really constitute a Coda, commencing upon the last of the one hundred and fiftieth measure. The last four measures form the Stretto, and should be played faster.

The construction of the Rondo from Kuhlau's Op. 59, No. 1, is this :

1. Principal subject, sixteen measures.
2. Intermezzo of seventeen measures.
3. Principal theme varied.
4. Eingang, with transition, eight measures.
5. Short second theme in Dominant, eleven measures.
6. Episode in tonic minor.
7. Principal theme, as at first.
8. Intermezzo, same as 2.
9. Theme varied.
10. Second theme in tonic.
11. Coda of six measures, in form of Recollection.

Here is the plan in detail, of the Rondo from Dussek, Op. 20, No. 1 :

1. Principal theme repeated.
2. Intermezzo, eight measures.
3. Principal theme not repeated but extended to fourteen measures.
4. Second theme in tonic minor, preceded by a short Anticipation of four measures.
5. Principal theme.
6. Intermezzo as before.
7. Principal theme extended, as at 3, with the addition of two measures to indicate the final ending.

---

* A distinction is made in this book between Coda and Termination, where the latter is continuous, and of an impatient or exciting character.

The Rondos iu Clementi's Sonatinas are divided into two parts : Part I contains the principal theme, Intermezzo, and return to the principal theme, with a Coda and double bar marked fine, or ⌢| Part II has an extended Second Theme with transitions, and a Cadenza or Passage, ending upon the dominant to the principal key. This is marked D. C. al fine, which terminates the Rondo at the end of Part I. (The Coda should be omitted until after the D. C.)

The Second Movement to Beethoven's Sonatina, Op. 49, No. 1 is a Rondo. The Second Movement to Op. 49, No. 2, is marked "Tempo di Menuetto," but this also is a Rondo with a short inter- mezzo between the repetition of the principal theme; an eingang, second subject, episode in C, and Coda of thirteen measures. The principal subject occurs six times.

The old rondos contained the recurrent theme and digressions ; but the latter were rather additional short themes thrown in between the repetitions of the principal melody. But it is not the purpose here to enter into the development of the Rondo from its earliest in- ception, nor to its subsequent enlargement and elaboration. After the student has become thoroughly familiar with the rondos we have analyzed, there will be no difficulty in analyzing the large Rondo form.

ILLUSTRATIONS.

Turkish Rondo, Steibelt.

Rondos from the Sonatinas of Clementi, Dussek, Reinecke, Seiss, Kuhlau, and Krause.

QUESTIONS.

1. Modes and Movement; 2. Number of times which First Sub- ject occurs; 3. Eingang or Transition (which?); 4. Second Theme (Mode and rhythm of); 5. Sequence and Passage; 6. Cadenza; 7. Number of Periods; 8. Styles; 9. Intermezzo and Episode; 10. Coda or Termination; 11. Recollection and Stretto.

PART VIII.

Chapter XXXII.

—

AURICULAR EXERCISES.

**PITCH, FORCE AND QUALITY OF TONES. STYLE OF PERFORM-
ANCE. NUMBER OF VOICE-PARTS, AND LOCATION OF PRIN-
CIPAL THEMES. PHRASING. ANALYSIS OF THE PARADISI
TOCCATA.**

MUSICAL Pitch refers merely to the length of the string or the
size of the tube which may be employed in the production of
a given tone. Scientifically, each tone is known by the number of
vibrations or pulsations which it makes in a second's time. The
most natural associate or harmonic of any fundamental tone is its
octave, in which the ratio is 2 to 1, 4 to 2, 8 to 4, etc., because the
octave is produced by stopping a pipe, or touching a string exactly
in its center. Thus, if a tube of a certain diameter requires four

feet in length for the production of this tone: Ex. 221.

the octave above would be produced by stopping the tube in the
center (or closing one-half), in which case the vibrations would
traverse a distance of only two instead of four feet, and produce this

tone: Ex. 222. All other intervals have a mathemati-

cally proportionate ratio, which applies to the entire compass of recognizable musical tones. The lowest tone which can be accurately
distinguished as to pitch makes about sixteen vibrations per second;
the highest makes about 5824, being the $\equiv$ according to the German

entablature. Very few can name the absolute pitch of a given tone
but it is a matter of so great importance that the author would
advise music students to practice daily with a view to acquiring this
ability. Begin by carrying in the mind a recollection of this tone.

Ex. 223. Listen to the tone attentively, then sing it, and

remember how the voice is pitched in producing it. After the lapse
of a few minutes try to sing this tone, and prove your ability by
some musical instrument. When you hear a voice, a bell, a whistle,
or even a hand-organ, endeavor to locate the pitch or the key. Once
or twice every day try to sing the once-marked *a* and apply the test.

In reference to musical dynamics we will merely call attention
here to the variations in tone-force, or tone-quantity, which occur in
correct musical performance, and which every listener should observe. Let the class begin by taking note of the six degrees: *pp*,
p, mp, mf, f, ff. The first is very soft; the last very loud. The
other letters show the degrees of force or tone-quantity between *pp*
and *ff*. These signs are understood to refer to the degrees of soft-
ness or loudness throughout a passage or period, or until they are
contradicted. Then there are the three species of accent explained
in Chapter III, which apply only to the note or chord above (or
below) which they may be placed. The *sf* of the Tarantella is still
more forcible than the common accent ∧. Finally we have the still
more important increase and diminish in tone generally indicated
by these symbols: ◁ ▷

The author remembers a performance by Rubinstein of the
Turkish March, from Beethoven's "Ruins of Athens," in which a remarkable crescendo from *pp* to *ff* was made in the first half of the
piece, and a corresponding diminuendo from *ff* to *pp* in the last
half. The effect was so realistic that it required little imagination to
fancy the gradual approach and disappearance of a military band
through the streets of the once glorious city of Pericles! (Beethoven should not be held responsible for the recent attempt of
Michaeli's in this direction.)

In reference to tone-quality, not much need be said at this time.
For the benefit of the inexperienced student the author will make
the rather trite observation that the quality of a tone is its peculiar
color or shade. A musician can recognize the tone-quality of a flute,
oboe, clarinet, horn, trombone, trumpet, violin, harp, or piano, even

though they should all produce the same pitch of tone.   This difference in tone-color is called *timbre*, and even in piano-forte literature
it plays an important role.   The piano is primarily a pulsatalic instrument, but modern pianists have succeeded in subduing and pro-
longing the tones to such an extent that it is now the greatest of all
instruments in completeness of expression.   The violin, viola and
'cello are remarkable instruments, but they lack the facilities of
accompaniment; the organ being almost equal to a full orchestra
has a great variety of tone-color, and a certain majestic grandeu.
which no other instrument possesses : but it is lacking in the accent
of feeling and the more subtle shades of expression which can alone
be produced by means of *touch*.

STYLE OF PERFORMANCE.

In this connection attention is to be called to the marks and signs
of expression, as indicated in the printed copy.   The class should
first hear the difference between Legato and Staccato, and recognize
the fact that in the former style the tones are sustained and connected, one with the other ; in the latter style they are short and de-
tached, and cease to vibrate almost as soon as they are sounded.
After this they may learn to distinguish between the Legatissimo,
the Legato, and the ordinary Non-legato touches.   Also between the
forcible Staccatissimo, which is quite loud ; the light, Pizzicato staccato, which is shorter in duration of sound ; and the Semi-staccato
(slurred), in which a very slight separation of the tones is made.
In this case one-half the value of each note is taken away and
becomes silent, as if a rest of that value were interposed.

PHRASING.

This is chiefly influenced by the Slur.   The slur indicates the
legato, connected style, but it is more specific; for the word legato,
or sostenuto, merely indicates the style as being smooth, whereas
the Slur tells just how many tones are to be connected, and where
the disconnection, or punctuation, is to occur.   A phrase, section, or
period is never to be connected beyond the end of the slur ; but
whether the disconnection is to be slight or considerable depends
upon the length of the last note and the nature of the piece ; *e. g :*

Ex. 224.

(b) Allegro.

Ex. 225.

(c) Andante.

Ex. 226.

If the movement were *Allegro*, this would be played as at (b); but if the movement were *Andante*, the last note of the first Slur would be treated as at (c).

The *b*-flat at (c) should be only slightly separated from the following *c*-sharp; whereas the *b*-flat at (b) is to be made quite staccato. The Slur therefore indicates not only the style, but the punctuation and accent, as the commencement of each slur is to be somewhat accented to indicate the beginning of a phrase or period.

As a farther illustration of this matter of phrasing we will analyze the Toccata in *A* by Paradisi. This will serve a double purpose: 1. To indicate the punctuations and accents; 2. To show how music of this kind is analyzed. Being in thematic style, the constructional divisions are not so apparent as in ordinary cases; and we must be governed to a considerable extent by the nature of the cadences, and the esthetical import, and not always by the mensural proportion of the phrases and periods. This is the first phrase:

Ex. 227.

As the rhythm in sixteenths is continuous through the first period, thereby joining the phrases together, it is well to practice the periods separately, with a slight punctuation at the end of each phrase, thus:

Ex. 228.

Another, and sometimes better mode of phrasing, consists in drawing a slur over the entire period, and omitting the punctuations, making the whole period even and continuous. In this case it will be necessary to slightly accent the beginning of each phrase, but without disconnecting the tones, as here:

Ex. 229.

The accent is here placed under the first note of the second phrase (b).

In view of the fact that the first period is perfectly regular, this phrasing is advised; especially as the ground-bass represents the melodic element during this period, and the punctuations may be placed in this lower part with good effect :

Ex. 230.

In the fourth measure the phrases commence upon the third, in place of the fourth eighth note, and the slurs must be placed accordingly. This plan gives the proper punctuations to the lower part, without interrupting the steady flow of the figures in sixteenths above. The first period is concluded on the first of the eighth measure, after the perfect cadence; but the following Coda is joined to it at once in order to modulate to *B*-major. The transition, and what may be considered the first subject, ends upon the first half of the twelfth measure. The Second Subject (or Second Period) begins on the last half of this measure, with the theme above. This is to be phrased as follows :

Ex. 231.

Meanwhile the Counter-subject below may be played continuously, as though a slur were drawn over measures twelve, thirteen, fourteen, fifteen, and including the *G*-sharp in the sixteenth measure. The counter-subject then passes into the treble part, and the bass has the theme. This is to be played in the same manner, with the understanding that the parts are here Inverted. Measures twenty, twenty-one, twenty-two and twenty-three form an extension of the second period by means of repeating a cadence-figure over and over. From twenty-four this is repeated softly, in the octave below. During twenty-one and twenty-two the left hand part should be played so as to represent the two voices;

Ex. 232.

The upper part is most important, and it should have this effect in the performance:

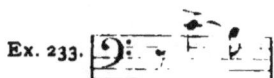

Ex. 233.

From the last of measure twenty-four the phrasing should be:

Ex. 234.

Sustain this last chord its full value, and then separate the tones from what follows. After the double bar, Part II begins with the First Subject in the Dominant. This is similar to Part I. The phrase commencing on the second eighth (from thirty-six) is to be executed in this manner:

Ex. 235.

and the following phrase the same. Each semi-phrase of the sequence in the bass, commencing at the end of forty, is to be phrased in the same manner, in order that the sequence of style may correspond to the sequence of notes. The third eighth is to be made as short as possible. On the last of forty-four the parts are again inverted, and the right hand has the melodic sequence. The slur of the previous eight measures should continue to (and include) the F-sharp on the second half of the measure, thus:

Ex. 236.   etc.

and then the F-sharp must be left quickly, as the following a is the beginning of the sequence-figure previously heard in the bass.

(Compare the theme in the bass with the inversion above, forty to forty-eight.) The cadence-figure from forty-eight is similar to the closing of Part I, but changed from *E*-major to *F*-sharp minor. The first subject in the original key recurs on the last of fifty-six. The previous period is to be brought to a close and disconnected somewhat from this recurring subject, which should be distinctly accented to indicate its return. After this the ear will follow the design without any special accent to aid it. The remainder is similar to the first part, but transposed from dominant to tonic.

This Toccata should be played in strict movement from beginning to end, except the very slight pause between Parts I and II. In the Litolff Edition the phrasing is almost wholly incorrect, and even the dynamical signs are misplaced.

The deviations from a regular movement are also to be observed. These are indicated by Crescendo and Accelerando (the latter is more proper) when the movement is to be gradually quickened; and by Rallentando, Ritenuto or Morendo, when the movement is to be slackened.

The abbreviations, *rall.*, *rit.*, etc., are frequently confusing. Rallentando and Ritardando indicate a gradual slackening of the movement; whereas Ritenuto signifies that the movement should at once be slower, but without a gradual retard. Ritenuto and Ritardando should therefore be written out in full. Morendo indicates a gradual diminution of both tone and movement.

Some compositions require an almost strict and uniform movement throughout, especially music of an intellectual character, concertos, and most of the old thematic works. The majority of Beethoven's sonatas and songs require frequent, though generally slight, deviations from the indicated movement. Chopin, Schumann, and Rubinstein allow still more latitude in the tempo of certain of their works. Mendelssohn, though he came after Beethoven, seldom varied from the fixed movement. The tendency of the present day is to indulge in too much of the *rubato* style, which is a dangerous privilege if used by one who has not the stamp of genius.

The fermata (⌒) is also of importance, as indicating a pause in the movement, a change of form, or a decided punctuation mark. The terms, *Allegretto, con brio, dolente, pomposo, strepitoso,* etc., indicate different styles of performance, which are certainly not more difficult for the listener to describe than for the performer to express.

NUMBER OF VOICE-PARTS.

Pupils should learn to distinguish the number of parts in a piece of music, at least from one to five, for each part in a trio or quartette, for example, may have a melody of its own, and one of equal importance, as here :

Ex. 237.

The second part comes in upon the third beat of the first measure, and the bass enters upon the same beat in the second measure. Each voice-part is individual and equally important. (Play this for class and have them analyze it by telling the metre, number of parts employed, and where they enter.)

The first two sections of Gottschalk's "Last Hope" and the first part of the Chopin "Berceuse" are good examples.

LOCATION OF THE PRINCIPAL THEME.

Some practice is necessary in order to determine at once whether the principal melody is in the contralto, tenor or bass part. The following examples will illustrate this.

(These are to be played separately for the class, that they may locate the theme wherever it may appear.)

Ex. 238.

When the theme appears in any of the lower parts it may be slightly accented. The soprano melody is omitted here because it is so easily recognized. Before mentioning the illustrations we will recapitulate the main features of this chapter, as showing the points of interest and instruction in a well-written composition.

---

* Some pupils are inclined to consider a tenor melody like that at (c), as a bass melody, because it is below the treble parts.

1. The pitch, power and quality of the tones.

2. The details of style, such as legato, staccato, accents of rhythm and of expression, the punctuations, accelerando and rallentando, the character of the piece as indicated by its title, or such terms as *friska, maestoso, dolente,* etc.

3. The number of voice-parts, and

4. The location of the chief melody.

ILLUSTRATIONS FOR THIS LESSON.

1. Album leaf, Op. 12, No. 7, Grieg.

2. Romanesque, Op. 15, No. 1, L. Pabst.

3. Gavotte and Musette from Bach's Third English Suite.

4. Spring Flower (in *D*), N. W. Gade.

5. The Mill, Op. 17, No. 3, A. Jensen.

6. Berceuse in *A*-flat, E. Nevin.

(1) In listening to No. 1, the class is to mention the dynamic character (piano); the non-legato of the first measure; the appoggiatura and light staccato, followed by the accent on the second beat in such measures as two, three and six; also the pedal-note of the first period. In the second period the tenor melody, the sustained bass, and the syncopated accompaniment above, should all be remarked upon; also the dynamical marks ⬍ and the bell note in the third and fourth measures. This is a ballad model.

(2) The Romanesque will require close attention. The first period is piano, the second, forte. The theme is accompanied partly by three harmonic parts, and partly by a counter theme in the tenor. The dynamic marks ⬍ and ⬍ play an important part, and all these features should be distinguished by the class. The style is legato, and the phrasing is distinctly marked by the composer. The legato and staccato of the second period should likewise be mentioned, and the ritenuto at the end of the sections and periods. The piece requires very little accent in the first period. The character is meditative, neither gay nor sad.

(3) The style here is mostly legato (except in isolated cases). In the first period a loud phrase is in each case followed by a soft one. (In the *musette* repeat the pedal-note often enough to make it perceptible to the listener.) Include Modes as a question. For this number Litolff's Edition is best, No. 389.

(4) The legato melody, staccato accompaniment, and sustained bass are the most prominent features. The style is cheerful and

mostly soft, with frequent ——————— and ——————— and an occasional ritenuto. The arpeggio accompaniment of the second period is also to be noticed. Enough has been said in this connection to indicate the objects of this chapter and the nature of the questions.

Give the class to understand that this is but the beginning of the art of listening to classical music.

Chapter XXXIII.

THE SMALL SONATA FORM, IN MAJOR MODE.

THE Sonata form is so important, and frequently so complex, that we will begin with the Sonatina. From this the transition to regular Sonata form will be more natural and systematic.

There are usually three complete movements or pieces in the Sonatina. These are:

1. The Allegro (or Sonata Movement).
2. The Slow Movement, or Song.
3. The Finale, which is generally a Rondo or other vivacious movement.

With the second and third movements we are already familiar, therefore the first movement now claims our attention. This is the most important, and the most difficult to analyze.

The Sonata Movement has three divisions and three subdivisions.

First Division—From the commencement to the double-bar.

Second Division—From the double-bar to the end of the Development.

Third Division—From the return of the Principal Subject to the end of the movement.

The subdivisions refer principally to the first and last divisions thus:

The First Division contains the three motives from which the entire Sonata is constructed. These are known as: First or Principal Subject; Second subject; and Conclusion or Close. These may be briefly described as follows: FIRST SUBJECT of about one period in the Tonic SECOND SUBJECT about the same length, but in the Dominant, and in contrast to the first. CONCLUSION, shorter than the other two Subjects. This is also in the dominant, and ends at the double bar. These three Subjects comprise the First Division. which is repeated. D. C.

The Second Division commences after the double bar, and consists of the working out of some of the principal subjects of the first part. This part is called the Elaboration, the Development, and also the Free Fantasia, as here the composer is fancy-free. The Elaboration is also a relief to the formality and regularity of the other divisions, on account of the greater freedom, not only of outline and form, but with the periodic construction and the natural melodic flow.

From the end of the Elaboration the Third Division commences. It is called the Return or Reprise, as the first division is here repeated, with the following distinctions: The First Subject appears as before, in the tonic; but the Second Subject and Conclusion are transposed from the dominant to the tonic. Frequently a few measures are added to the Conclusion to emphasize the final ending of the movement.

As the Principal Subject appears first, we need not describe it here.

The Second Subject is not so easily recognized by inexperienced students. Therefore these distinctions will be of assistance to all such:

1. It must appear in the dominant* (fifth), when the piece is in major.
2. It must be sufficiently contrasted to the first subject to constitute a change of style.
3. And yet it must bear some resemblance to some part of the first subject.
4. The second subject cannot begin until the first subject has concluded at least one period.

The principal subject to a Sonata seldom contains the consequent period following the first period; but the first period is extended, or

---

* Dominant here signifies, in the key of the dominant being somewhat different from the signification of that word in tonal fugue.

so conceived that it forms a complete theme. Otherwise it would have too much of the Ballad-Dance character. When the first subject is in *thematic* style, the second subject should be, as a rule, *lyric*, and *vice versa*. The Conclusion, also, is in the key of the dominant, and usually consists of some fragment of the first or second subjects slightly altered or developed into a motive. In Sonatinas, and many Sonatas, the Conclusion corresponds to our definition of Coda; but it is not called by this name, as very frequently the Conclusion is treated as a third subject and as a motive in the Development. These three divisions correspond to what Mr. Dannreuther calls the "Exposition, Illustration, and Repetition." The Exposition is the announcement or citation of the three principal subjects in the first division; the Illustration is the Development, second division; and the Repetition indicates the Reprise, or third division, in which the original order is restored, and the principal key-tone prevails so as to leave its final impression.

The Tonality. In the first division the principal subject is the only subdivision in the original key; the other two subdivisions are in the Dominant or some other related key. But in the Reprise the principal key prevails during the repetition of all three principal subjects. According to this system the principal key more than predominates over the other tonalities, which is natural enough. But perhaps Mozart (and others after him) had in mind a more equal distribution of the connecting keys when he introduced the principal theme after the Development, in the key of the Subdominant; returning to the original tonic for the repetition of the Second theme and Conclusion. This is more nearly an equalization of the amount of periods in the tonic, as against those in connecting keys. Of related keys the Dominant is the most important, especially in the first and second parts. The Supertonic and Mediant come next, though they both produce, naturally, a different tone-color from the major tonic and dominant. The Submediant is the most closely related to the tonic and naturally alternates with it, notwithstanding the difference in mode. The transition to the Subdominant is retrospective, and very frequently retrogressive. Therefore it is not naturally adapted to the first two divisions. (See Chapters VII and XV.)

DEVELOPMENT.

Before analyzing a Sonatina Movement entire it is desirable that the class shall have an understanding of musical Development, at least in its simple application. It consists in selecting any part of a principal theme and working it out in a manner different from the original. Take, for example, this from Mozart:

Ex. 239.

Motive.   2d Phrase.

The first or second measure of either the motive or second phrase may be selected for development.

The simplest method is that of Sequence:

Ex. 240.

Compare these with (a) and (b), Ex. 239. The second phrase of the original may be treated in the same manner.

Ex. 241.

These are more or less artificial, as they do not follow the natural melodic flow.

Another method is to change the mode, and lead the melody in a different direction from that of the original:

Ex. 242.

By comparing these with each of the four measures of Ex. 239, and understanding the figure from which the development proceeds, and wherein it is different from that figure, the student will be enabled to readily comprehend the first instances of development which we will quote. These will naturally lead to other and more complicated examples of this important subject.

We will now select a favorite Sonatina, and proceed with the analysis and explanation of each division and subdivision. From Kuhlau, Op. 20, No. 1:

Ex. 243.

This is the first section of the Principal subject in *C*. After eight measures this motive is repeated in a different form, with the accompaniment above, and in order to lead to the key of the dominant. In the fifteenth measure *f*-sharp in the bass causes a transition to *G*-major. On the seventeenth measure commences the

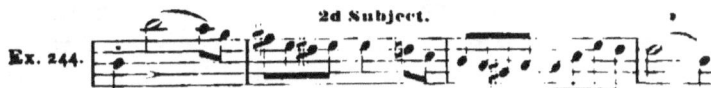

Ex. 244.

This is in the key of the Dominant, and affords considerable contrast to the first subject. There is also a noticeable resemblance between this and the first subject, especially here:

Ex. 245.

(a) is from the seventh measure of the first subject, (b) is the twenty-third measure,† and belongs to the second subject.

The Conclusion begins simultaneously with the ending of the second subject (twenty-fourth measure), and constitutes an united period, illustrated in Ex. 149. This is in thematic style, and consists of a scale passage founded upon the *G*-major chord. The repeated notes of the twenty-fifth and twenty-seventh measures are a reminiscence of the last of the second measure (See Ex. 243):

Ex. 246.

But this is still more analogous to the first motive:

Ex. 247.

The accented notes here constitute what there is of melodic outline, which is very plainly this:

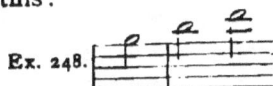

Ex. 248.

---

*The remainder of this Subject was quoted in Chapter XX, Ex 148.
† Number each measure continuously, from 1 to 80.

and is identical with the first part of the leading motive, thus:

Ex. 249.

Compare Ex. 248 with 249. (It will be instructive to observe the striking analogy between the motives of each of the three movements. The Andante is almost identical, excepting key and rhythm. The *outline* of the first section of the Rondo is the original theme reversed):

Ex. 250.

The Conclusion runs into a short Cadenza, leading back from the double bar to the repetition of this division. The Development is brief—eighteen measures—and commences immediately after the double bar. A small fragment of the principal subject is the basis

of this development. Observe these two notes: Ex. 251.

from the fourth measure, and how they are repeated in sequence in the development, as here (a):

Ex. 252.

etc.

At (b) we hear another reminiscence of the first subject in the three repeated notes staccato. (See second measure of the original.) In

the thirty-eighth measure there is a grupetto: Ex. 253.

which occurs twice in the second subject, and may therefore be attributed to that. Measure thirty-nine (counted from the beginning) is the commencement of a Passage, in which fragments of the Conclusion and of the First Subject are elaborated. Notice the scale figures in the bass (such as measures forty-one and forty-two), and the three repeated notes following. The Passage may be said to continue to the Reprise, measure fifty, but measures forty-six, forty-seven, forty-eight and forty-nine are, strictly speaking, in the form of a Cadenza. The Reprise commences at the fiftieth measure, and is identical with the original First Subject, both being in the tonic, C. As the Second Subject is to be heard in this last division in the tonic, instead of the dominant, the transition to G-major is not included here. Compare measures fifteen and sixteen with sixty-four and sixty-five. The second theme begins at sixty-six, and is transposed literally from dominant to tonic. The Conclusion is joined to the second subject and constitutes an united period as in the first division. The scale figures terminate upon the tonic at seventy-nine, and two full chords are included to emphasize the final ending of the movement. (Compare measures thirty and thirty-one with seventy-nine and eighty.)*

It is important that this analysis should be read carefully, and the examples and comparisons attentively studied. The mere formal outline will not be sufficient for the class to understand, but every detail must be appreciated, and the relationship of certain motives and parts of motives with kindred passages should be observed.

We will now select a Sonatina by Reinecke for analysis. This is more modern than the one from Kuhlau (who was a friend and companion of Beethoven), and it is also more artistically conceived.

Here is the motive of the principal subject:

REINECKE. Op. 47, No. 2.

Ex. 254.

Allegro moderato.

The main feature of this is the ascending melody—f-sharp, g, g-sharp, a, which is still more noticeable in measures ten, eleven and twelve. Before leaving the motive, attention is called to the little arpeggio figure in the last of the first and second measures. The first four measures constitute a curtailed Period. The first subject begins again in the fifth measure and becomes an Extended Period, with Transitional matter. In strict designation the period is not brought to a close until the entrance of the Second Subject.

On the last quarter of measure sixteen the Second Subject begins. Here the key, rhythm and form of accompaniment are changed in contrast to the first subject. But the unity of design may be espied by analyzing these first four measures of the Second Subject (seventeen, eighteen, nineteen and twenty):

Ex. 255.

---

*The second movement, Andante, is a simple Ballad, and the third movement, a Rondo, has been analyzed in Chapter XXXI.

The ascending melody is still present, though the chromatic tones
are here excluded. Notice, also, the arpeggio figure in the nine-
teenth measure above, and its relationship to those of the first subject. This is merely in different rhythm and a little more extended.
The first period of this second theme is closed at twenty-four. Then
the second period begins, accompanied at first by an interrupted
canonic imitation and afterwards (from twenty-nine to thirty-seven)
by a regular canon. Simultaneously with the ending of the second
subject at thirty-seven, the Conclusion begins. This is an almost
exact transposition of the first four measures of the principal theme.
The first division ends here at the double bar. Both endings should
be numbered forty-one, as one is omitted when the other is played.
The Development commences upon the last half of forty-one (second ending) with the motive of the first subject as text. The difference between this and the original first theme should be noticed
by comparing the two. During forty-four, forty-five and forty-six
the theme takes a still different turn, and at forty-seven the arpeggio
figure becomes more prominent. This is repeated in different keys,
and finally ends on the dominant, fifty-three.

Two peculiarities of this Development, which make it different
from the natural course of the first theme, are: the mode is minor
in place of major, and the melody is in the contralto, being somewhat concealed by the soprano. This is also true of the phrase beginning upon the last of forty-eight. In the other cases the rhythm
$\left(\begin{array}{ccc} | & & | \\ \flat & \bar{\flat}\flat & \flat \end{array} \right)$, rather than the melody, is imitated. At fifty-four the Reprise, or third division, occurs. We have here an Extended Period
of eleven measures, with the first Curtailed Period omitted. This
leads to the second subject, now in the tonic. Everything here is
transposed from dominant (*A*) to tonic (*D*), including the canon,
which concludes the second subject at eighty-four. The last five
measures constitute the Conclusion, in the style of a recollection.

The class may now attempt an analysis of the first Sonatina
from the same book, Reinecke, Op. 47, No. 1. This should first be
done from the notes, and a general synopsis like this may be of assistance:

1. Principal subject in tonic, frequently repeated, with alterations.
2. Passage or Transition to the Dominant.
3. Second subject in the Dominant, constituting a change of style.
4. Conclusion at the end of the second theme, shorter than the other
    subjects, and resembling a Coda.

5. Development commencing after the double bar, and continuing until the return of the principal subject as at first.

6. The second theme transposed from Dominant to Tonic, but otherwise the same.

7. Conclusion, also in the Tonic, with perhaps a few measures added as final ending.

The resemblance of the different Subjects to some part of the principal theme must be pointed out, also the original passage from which the motive for the Development is taken. The Principal theme may contain any amount of measures, and frequently it has two periods, besides the transitional matter, which comes just before the second theme.

The first movement of the Sonatina Op. 47, No. 1, is to be played for the class after they have examined and analyzed it. The outline and main features are here presented for comparison: The Principal subject is the first of the piece, Allegro, but the first six measures are somewhat prefatory, and the most natural continuation of the motive is that beginning at *P* last of the sixth measure. The thirteenth, fourteenth, fifteenth and sixteenth measures are the same as nine, ten, eleven and twelve, changed from major to minor. The Transition begins at eighteen, constituting an extended period. At twenty-two the key is established as that of the dominant *G*, and from here there is a Cadenza of six measures, leading to the Second Subject. This commences upon the dominant seventh chord in the the key of *G* (at twenty-eight), and is rather more lyric than the Principal subject. The repetition of this (from thirty-six) is an extended period of thirteen instead of eight measures. The Conclusion begins upon the second eighth of the forty-ninth measure. This is in Thematic style, and extends to the double bar. The Development is in the relative minor of the dominant. It is founded upon and developed from the motive of the Conclusion. Simultaneously with ending of the (curtailed) seven-measure period at sixty-three, the bass gives out the introductory period of the first subject, unaccompanied. Then it is taken up in regular form with accompaniment above, and continued by the upper part. This motive from the first subject next appears in the bass in the key of the dominant. After a section of this, the theme is transferred to the upper part, as before. From eighty-seven a fragment of the original first subject is treated canonically, and this runs into a short transitional passage leading back to the Principal subject, or the Reprise.

ninety-five.   This is the same as at first, with exception of the prefatory period, part of which is curtailed in the end of the Development.   The Cadenza is slightly altered in order to lead to the Tonic,
in place of the Dominant, as before.   The Second theme recurs (in
C) after the rallentando, one hundred and fourteen. This is an exact
transposition of the second theme from *G* to *C*. The Conclusion (one
hundred and thirty-five) is also the same as far as one hundred and
forty-one, where a few additional measures are added as Termination.

For illustrations, play those already analyzed, by way of em-
phasis :
   Reinecke, Op. 47, No. 1 and No. 2, first movements only.
   Krause, Op. 1, No. 1.
   Kuhlau, Op. 20, No. 1, first movement.
   Clementi, Op. 36, No. 6, first movement.
   Seiss, Op. 8, No. 1.

The questions should be like these : First Subject, Transition or
Passage ; Second Subject; Conclusion ; Development, what motives
developed; The Return of the First Subject; Return of Second
Subject ; Return of Conclusion.   Style (whether Lyric, Thematic,
Harmonic, Antiphonal, or Canonic).   Cadenza, if any, is also to be
mentioned.

Chapter XXXIV.

THE SMALL SONATA FORM, IN MINOR MODE.

THE outline and form of a Sonata movement in Minor are not
materially different from a movement in Major ; but the tonal
arrangement differs considerably.   The first subject being in tonic
minor (the minor key represented by the signature), the second subject appears in the relative major (also same signature).   The Conclusion is naturally in the relative major also ; though it frequently
contains a transition to the dominant of the key-tone, for the repeat.
No rule is prescribed for the tonality or key-relationship of the

Elaboration, therefore we will pass that at present. The return of the principal theme is in tonic minor as before. The return of the second theme is in tonic major (as a rule). The Conclusion usually terminates in the tonic minor (key-tone), though it frequently begins in the tonic major. To make this more plain we will include a sketch of the keys for a Sonatina movement in *A*-minor :

First subject in *A*-minor (tonic).

Second subject in *C*-major (relative major).

Conclusion also in *C*-major, with, perhaps, a transition to the dominant chord of the key-tone, *E*, g-sharp, *b*.

After the Development, the Principal theme recurs as before in *A*-minor. The second subject recurs in the tonic major (*A*), and the Conclusion the same. The dominant chord being the same in *A*-minor that it is in *A*-major, the composer may avail himself of this fact and return to the key-tone, *A*-minor, whenever he chooses. The last few measures are in *A*-minor.

The class should transpose this sketch into other keys. Thus in *G*-minor the keys would be : *G*-minor, *B*-flat major, *G*-minor again, *G*-major, and finally *G*-minor.

The same unity of design (or conception) between the different subjects is observed, whether the piece be in major or minor, and the same mode of developing certain motives from the first, second or third subjects is also applicable in both modes. In truth, the key-relationships and the modes are the only distinguishable features between a sonata movement in major and one in minor.

We will analyze two small Sonatinas by Reinecke, Op. 127, a (Op. 127, b, is the same for four hands):

Op. 127 No. 5.

Ex. 256.

This is the first section of the principal theme in *G*-minor. At the end of our quotation the theme is transferred to the bass, and the period is extended to eleven measures. The second subject commences at 12. This is in *B*-flat, the relative major. In place of Conclusion there is an Extended period, with a transition for the D. C. The Development commences after the second ending, and contains ten measures. It is upon the first motive, somewhat altered and repeated in sequence and transition. The Reprise commences at 34, and is like the first. The Second subject, from 45, is in tonic

major, and here the composer has changed the signature from two
flats (*G*-minor) to one sharp (*G*-major). The Second subject stops
upon a half cadence (55 and 56), which leads to the following Coda
in form of a Recollection in *G*-minor. This is marked *Piu lento.*

The outline of Op. 127, No. 6, is this: Principal subject in *A*-
minor, eight measures. Second subject in *C*-major, eight measures.
As the transition to the dominant major, *E*, is not perfected until the
18th measure, we may look upon these three isolated measures (17,
18, 19) as an extension of the period for a transitional purpose. The
Development commences at 19 (third measure of the second ending).
The Principal motive is used first, then we hear a brief reminiscence
of the Second subject. From 27 a fragment of the first subject is
developed, and especially the rhythm 🎵.* The Reprise begins at
35, and is the same. The Second subject appears at 43 in *A*-minor,
in place of *A*-major. This is frequently done, as the dominating
chord is the same in both modes. The Coda of two measures ends
in *A*-major, as if to re-assure us that the minor key was not chosen
on account of any serious plaintiveness in the sentiment of the
piece.

This chapter will be concluded with an analysis of the Sonatina
in *G*-minor, Op. 49, No. 1, by Beethoven.

The Principal subject extends from 1 to 15 inclusively. The last
two measures are transitional. The Second subject begins at 16, in
the relative major, according to the prescribed plan. This is continued to the first of the 29th measure. The last four measures, from
this point to the double bar, constitute a short Conclusion, founded
upon a fragment of the Second subject, also in relative major.

The Development commences upon the fourth eighth note, as do
all the motives in this movement. This is an easily recognized
elaboration of fragments of the Second motive. The Reprise takes
place at 66. This is the same as at first, with exception of the theme
being transferred to the bass from 74, and the necessary difference
in transition just before the recurrence of the Second subject. This
is now in tonic minor, tonic major being reserved for the final ending, as in our last analyzed Sonatina. The Conclusion begins at 99,

---

* Frequently the last of the second division contains a few measures separated from the
regular development, and somewhat anticipatory of the Principal theme. This has been
called Return. The distinction between this and Anticipation is very slight, and will appear
hereafter.

the fragment of the Second subject being in the bass. The last eight measures constitute a Coda, founded upon a pedal-note (G).

NOTE.—The original annotators of Beethoven's Sonatas term these last eight measures "Appendix," which is only another name for Coda.

The illustrations for this chapter are:

Reinecke, Op. 127, Nos. 5 and 6.

Beethoven, Op. 49, No. 1.

Löschhorn, Op. 187, No. 1, in A-minor.

The first movement of Beethoven's Op. 49, No. 2 in G major), may be included, but without telling the class it is in the major mode. They will probably discover the fact. The Second subject in this is easily recognized, being in the dominant, and isolated from the previous period. The Conclusion does not occur until the 49th measure.

QUESTIONS.

1. Principal Subject: Mode and extent, whether regular, repeated, or extended period.
2. Transition, or Passage.
3. Second Subject (mode and extent).
4. Conclusion (mode and extent).
5. Development (of what motives).
6. Return of Principal subject. Mode.
7. Return of Second subject. Mode.
8. Return of Conclusion.
9. Coda, if any. Final mode.
10. Style (Lyric, Thematic, Harmonic, Canonic, Antiphonal). This question should be applied to each subject, and to the Development.

If the answers are at first correct, the repetition of the first division may be omitted.

Chapter XXXV.

IRREGULAR PERIODIC CONSTRUCTION.
CONTINUED THESIS.   APOTHEOSIS.
LISZT'S WALDESRAUSCHEN.

MENTION has been made, under Periodic Construction (Chapter XIII), of the effect of a continued Thesis, without the consequent Antithesis. The simplest illustration of this is to be found in certain introductory movements, where the composer does not wish to create an impression of a regularly constructed period, but rather to leave us in *anticipation* of the regular period, which comes after the Prelude or Introduction. The Intrada to the Priest's March from "Athalia" is an illustration. This consists of a brief fanfare by drums and trumpets upon the Dominant seventh harmony, and without any resolving cadence. The amount of measures in such instances is of no particular consequence. A better illustration may be cited from Raff's popular Cachoucha Caprice, Op. 79. Here we have thirteen measures of irregular construction, containing a mere hint as to what follows, and yet sufficiently suggestive to excite our interest. This is founded mostly upon a secondary seventh chord, serving as a subdominant harmony. Observe that no antithesis occurs, and that the last chord leaves an impression analogous to that of the half cadence.

The next example occurs in the Termination, after the ear has been satiated with regular periods.

A very simple instance will be presented first; and to make the matter plain we will quote the original subject, with its antecedent and consequent phrases, and then the Continued Thesis, as it occurs in the Termination :

Ex. 257.

In the first example (b) is the antithesis of (a), and (d) of (c). In the second example the thesis (a) is continued at (b), (c) and (d). The phrases (a), (b) and (c) are alike; merely repeated upon different intervals of the same chord. (Compare the two examples by phrases.) Observe also the changes in harmony at 1; and that in example 2 the tonic chord is continued throughout. This style is especially adapted to the last of a movement, after the music has been brought to a satisfactory conclusion. The Termination here contains twelve measures; but before the last chord is sounded the ear has ceased to anticipate the constructional divisions, and no one could name the number of measures in the Termination unless counted separately, whereas, any musician will tell you the exact number of measures in the first example without counting them individually. Experienced orchestral performers seldom count eight or sixteen measures in popular music, because they know intuitively when the period ends. This, however, cannot be done with music of irregular construction, as, for example, the Continuation of Thesis. The Stretto (last eleven measures) to Cherubini's "Lodoiska" Overture, and the last six measures of Liszt's "Waldesrauschen" are similar, though more artistic examples of a final period without resolution or consequent phrases, being in the nature of a repetition or continuation.

Hundreds of instances like these might be quoted. But we will proceed to show examples of this kind which occur intermediately. The first Intermezzo in Rubinstein's Tarantella, Op. 6, may be cited. This occurs sixteen measures before the Intermezzo in ⅞ metre, which, with the latter, constitutes thirty-seven measures without antithesis. All this is founded upon a dominant pedal-note without resolution. The resolution takes place after the ⅞ metre is resumed. The first four measures here, preceding the principal subject, are of the same nature, but much more brief. After sixteen measures of the *Piu Allegro* we have a somewhat Extended Thesis upon the tonic harmony. This commences eight measures before the ⅞, and embraces seventeen measures. Throughout the opus there is considerable expression of suspense and vain desire. This is the usual esthetic effect of a prolonged Thesis, and in the works of Beethoven and Schubert we meet many instances. The uninterrupted melodies of Wagner are a still farther expression of this effect. Take, for example, the Improvisation of Bendel upon Walther's Prize Song from "Die Meistersinger." The entire first page (twenty-eight measures) is one unresolved prologue, without cadence or consequent! It is skilful in conception and exalted in effect. Observe particularly how the theme is drawn out, and the cadence postponed! In its higher application the Continued Thesis is an attempted psychological expression of, or yearning for, the Infinite; the soul's longing to be emancipated from its vicious and narrow surroundings, and explore the vastness of ethereal space.

The Fantasia in *D*-minor by Mozart will furnish us two instances where the effect is different. The first occurs where the principal theme is introduced in *A*-minor, as here:

Ex. 258.

After leaving the extended section thus incomplete, there is a cadenza, Presto, ascending and descending, and then a brief intermezzo. When a second cadenza is introduced the principle theme is brought back to *D*-minor. This period of ten measures (just before the Apotheosis in *D*-major) ends upon a half cadence. Both instances are merely illustrations of the oft-repeated adage, "All is vanity" The entire first part (*i. e.*, the Prelude, Air and Fantaisie * in *D*-minor) is an expression of vain desire and longing, as far as the half cadence already mentioned. The Second Part in *D*-major is as bright and positive as may be, and becomes something of an Apotheosis of Part I.

Our last quotation is from Schumann's Romance in *F*-sharp major. After the repeated first period there is a syncopated theme and counter-theme below, accompanied by the richest harmonic tone-colors, and this is led on through doubt and gloom for eight measures :

Op. 28, No. 2.

Ex. 259.

In the eighth measure we emerge from the darkness, and in the tenth measure the first theme is resumed, but still without a cadence until the last of the eleventh measure. The next cadence does not occur until the commencement of the Coda. The entire Romance is a plaintive and negative sentiment almost from beginning to end ; the coda being as free from positiveness or contentment as was the first period.

We will close this chapter with a critical review of the Waldesrauschen Etude by Liszt. The English translation, "Murmuring Woods," is too much like a bare statement of fact, and not properly suggestive.† The music represents a forest scene, where all is silence, save the rustling of leaves and the songs of birds. It is not, however, a representation of these, but an expression of the sentiments which a lover of nature would experience under these influences.

We are not to undertake the analysis of this fancy-sketch as an exemplification of our formulas as to cadence-periods, first and second subject, melodic construction, etc., but rather as the antithesis of these fundamental principles. The whole Etude is constructed upon these two phrases :

---

* An examination of this First Part will reveal the characteristics of a Fantaisie more fully than a worded description.

† " Woodland Murmurs " is, perhaps, better.

Ex. 260.

One peculiarity of these is, the consequent phrase (b) has the appearance of an antecedent, and the antecedent phrase (a) seems to be a consequent. These two phases of the subject (one descending, the other ascending) are to be specially observed on account of their subsequent employment. The third phrase is a repetition of the first, with the addition of a few short appoggiaturas; but the last measure of the fourth phrase (commenced in *D*-flat) is concluded in *F*-sharp minor, with the signature of four sharps. No close is effected here, however; but, on the contrary, the first measure of the fourth phrase becomes a thesis, which is carried higher and higher through four measures of sequence until it reaches *C*-sharp. This is succeeded by a consequent phrase of three measures descending. Then the original tonality is resumed, but still no periodic cadence. After the *D*-flat signature is restored the theme passes into the upper parts, and the same thing is repeated, with the melody slightly altered, an interrupted counter-theme below, and different accompaniment.

After the sharp signature is introduced the second time we hear a fragment of the subject in the bass against the melodic sequence above. In the two measures just before the signature is changed to one flat, the previous figure of the bass is in augmentation—the eighths becoming quarters. In the 27th measure (numbering the preludatory measure, 1) the *b*-flat in the bass becomes a subdominant pedal-note, and above this our composer twines the dominant and tonic harmonies of *G*-minor with peculiar and strange effect. Upon the first of the 29th measure the resolution of a perfect Cadence takes place; and this is particularly mentioned as being the first complete Cadence which has thus far occurred. We then hear a measure (*legerissimo*) where all is again silent save the rustling of leaves. Observe that no melodic outline here appears, and consequently no accent is to be indulged. In the 30th measure a semi-phrase of the melody is heard, as of some forest songster calling to its mate. Then another almost inaudible measure of tree-top murmurs, and the bird resumes its song, which is answered in the 34th measure. Observe how the two original phrases (a) and (b) are treated as theme and counter-theme in this woodland duet. At 37 an abrupt transition is effected into *A*-major, and similar melodies are wafted as from some distant part of the wood. When the signature is altered to *C*-major (46), the sounds become gradually louder and more animating, while the duet is continued upon the two phases of the subject. The wind increases in force, the branches bend to and fro, birds have ceased their songs, and the tall pines " Lash their lithe limbs, and call to each other through the majestic gloom." (In some editions the signature of *D*-flat is resumed three measures too soon.) In the 72d measure we see the first material deviation from the subject, but this is very slight, and the next measure is plainly taken from the motive. The double-handed trill at 80 and 81 may be considered as an enlarged shake upon *G*-sharp, and what follows is a two-part Cadenza leading to the full cadence after the pause. The remainder is Coda, in form of a Recollection of the first part, and here the sounds gradually die away, and so vanish.

It is evident from our imperfect review of this opus that it contains no second subject; no consequent period ; not even a regular melodic period, such as we usually find. But, on the contrary, the nine pages are conceived and constructed out of the first two phrases, considered as two motives. These are woven together by means of sequence, avoided antithesis and abrupt transitions into something of an endless melody, revealing consummate knowledge, tact and artistic fancy.

NOTE.—The movement of this etude is indicated by the word *Vivace ;* but this is not to be applied as it would be to a Gavotte or March brillante, for that would destroy the intended effect, even if it could be properly executed in such a quick movement. The word *Vivace* applies to the twenty-four sixteenths of the accompaniment, this being a characteristic and continuous feature of the piece. If quarter notes are taken as a standard, the movement should be not faster than Allegretto.

ILLUSTRATIONS FOR CHAPTER XXXV.

(Besides those analyzed) :
Improvisation upon Walther's Prize Song, Bendel.
Berceuse, Op. 57, Chopin.
First Allegro, from the Scotch Symphony, Op. 56, Mendelssohn.
Waldesrauschen, Liszt.
(The Berceuse is an elaboration of the short subject contained in the first four measures after the Prelude.)

PART IX.

Chapter XXXVI.

ABBREVIATED SYMBOLS, AND KEY TO THIS ANALYSIS.

EXPLANATION OF THE SAME.

FOR purposes of convenience and brevity the author has designed an abbreviated Key, to be used by the student in examining music analytically. The letters, figures, or combination of letters and figures, are designed to suggest that particular style or device, detail or part of a composition which it is desirable to observe. The Key to these Symbolical letters and numbers will be found on parallel lines to the Abbreviations, and an explanation of the whole is afterwards given.

This system will likewise serve in recalling to mind many important details heretofore mentioned, which might otherwise be forgotten or neglected.

As these abbreviations are to be employed in *examining*, not in listening to music, we have omitted all such references as to tonal and metrical signature, movement, motives beginning upon the fractional part of a measure, and the signs of expression, like *legato*, *staccato*, *piano*, *forte*, etc. These, though they are not to be overlooked, need not be included in the analysis. In most cases the letters are initial, and accordingly suggestive of the *Key*, as, for example, P. U., which indicates that *two periods are united at a certain point*. An exception to this principle is observable in the first of the symbols. A refers to the first subject, as being the first part of every regular movement. The Principal Theme is therefore indi-

cated initially by the first letter of the alphabet.   The Second Subject is indicated in a similar manner by the initial B.

The abbreviated Symbols, together with the corresponding
Key, here follow:

ABBREVIATIONS AND KEY TO ANALYSIS.

A.	First Subject.
A 1.	First half of First Subject.
A 2.	Second half of First Subject.
A. B.	First and Second Subjects combined.
An.	Anticipation.
Ap.	Apotheosis.
Aux. T.	Auxiliary Theme.
B.	Second Subject.
B 1.	First half of Second Subject.
B 2.	Second half of Second Subject.
B. M.	Bell Motive, or Chime.
Ca.	Cadenza.
C. F.	Change of Form.
Co.	Coda.
Con.	Conclusion.
C. S.	Counter-subject.
D. A.	Development of First Subject.
D. B.	Development of Second Subject.
D. Con.	Development of Conclusion.
Dev.	Development.
D. S.	Dual Subject.
Ec.	Echo.
Eg.	Eingang.
Ep.	Episode.
F. C.	Concerto Form.
F. D.	Dance Form.
F. M.	Mixed Form.
F. O.	Overture Form.
F. Rh.	Rhapsodical Form.
F. Ro.	Rondo Form.

F. Sl.   Single Form.
F. Son. Sonata Form.
F. Sym. Symphonic Form.
F. U.   Uninterrupted Form.

G. B.   Ground Bass.

H. H.   Hunting Horn Motive.
H. S.   Harmonic Style.

I. C.   Imitation, Contrary.
I. F.   Imitation, Free.
I. P.   Imitation, Partial.
I. S.   Imitation, Strict.
In.   Introduction.
Inv.   Inversion.
I. R.   Imitation of Rhythm.
Iz.   Intermezzo.

K. A.   Cadence, Avoided.
K. C.   Cadence, Complete.
K. F.   Cadence, Full.
K. H.   Cadence, Half.
K. P.   Cadence, Plagal.

L. M.   Leit-Motiv.

M. P.   Preliminary Motive.
M. T.   Middle Theme.

P. C.   Period, Curtailed.
P. E.   Period, Extended.
P. R.   Period, Regular.
P. U.   Period, United.
Par.   Parenthesis.
Pas.   Passage.
Po.   Postlude.
P. N.   Pedal-Note.
Pre.   Prelude.

Rec.   Recollection.

Recit.	Recitative.
Ref.	Refrain.
Rep.	Repetition.
Ret.	Return.

S. A.	Style, Antiphonal.
S. C.	Style, Canonic.
S. F.	Style, Fugal.
S. L.	Style, Lyric.
S. T.	Style, Thematic.
Se.	Sequence.
St.	Stretto.

T. Aug.	Theme in Augmentation.
T. Dim.	Theme in Diminution.
T. C.	Thesis continued.
Ta.	Theme above.
Tb.	Theme below.
Tm.	Theme in the middle.
Ts.	Theme in Syncopation.
Tv.	Theme Varied.
Ter.	Termination.
Tr.	Transition.

U. P.	Uneven Phrases.
U. S.	Uneven Sections.

EXPLANATION OF THE KEY TO ANALYSIS.

A. *Refers to the First Subject or Principal Theme.* This continues until a Transition, Intermezzo, or Second Subject is introduced.

A 1, A 2. *Natural Analytical Divisions of the First Motive or Subject.*

A 1 applies especially to the first motive when it is used in the Development. But should the phrase numbered 2 appear as a text in the Development, it should be marked D. A. 2. If any other part of a principal subject than the chief motive is developed it is to be marked D. A. 2 or D. B. 2.

A. B. *First and Second Subjects combined.* This Combination is not liable to occur outside of the Development. It refers to the simultaneous employment of both subjects, either in canonic, antiphonal, or thematic style. Such instances seldom occur in small works. In large works two, or even three subjects may appear simultaneously, or in juxtaposition.

An. A few measures, of an impatient character which seem to anticipate the following strain. (Explained in Chapter XXV.)

Ap. *Apotheosis.* Something of a final idealization or triumph; as in the third movement to the characteristic **Sonata** by Beethoven, or the Finale to his *C*-minor Symphony. (See Chapter XXXV.)

Aux. T. A secondary or subsidiary theme in Overtures or Symphonies.

B. *Second Subject.* Must be in contrast to the first theme, and constitute a change of style. In the Sonata movement it comes after the first subject, usually preceded by a passage or transition. In the Rondo the Second Subject comes after the Intermezzo, and usually after the second appearance of the Principal theme. (See Chapter XXIV, Second Subject.)

B 1, B 2. To be understood similarly to A 1 and A 2. These symbols are to be used only when the first or second part of the second subject appears as a text in the Development; otherwise the numbers are to be omitted

B. M. To be used to indicate a bell melody or a Carillon. The peculiar manner of playing a bell melody renders this necessary in the Analysis. (See "Midi," by Field, Chapter XXVI.)

Ca. *Cadenza.* Described in Chapter XXIV. More or less ornamental and unaccompanied.

C. F. *Change of Form.* This should be applied only to a change of movement, or to a different piece of music, as from the Dance to the Rondo form, etc.*

Co. *Coda.* What is added after the natural ending of a period or movement. (Already explained.) In fugue the word Coda is applied to a brief appendix added to the end of the subject, or response, in order to modulate to the dominant, or back to the tonic.

Con. *Conclusion.* The third and shortest subject in the first division to a Sonata movement. In other forms it is called Coda.

C. S. *Counter-Subject.* or Counter-Theme. Not to be confused with Second Subject, as it is a secondary melody which *accompanies* a principal subject as simultaneous counterpoint. The counter-subject must be so conceived that it may be inverted, and accompany the principal theme above as well as below, thus:

---

* Change of style is usually better than change of form. The form seldom changes in a movement.

Ex. 262.

D. A. *Development of First Subject.*
D. B. *Development of Second Subject.*
D. Con. *Development of Conclusion.*

> These refer to the Development, Illustration, or Elaboration of any of the subjects or parts of subjects in a Sonata, Overture, or Symphony. (See Chapters XXXI, XXXIII, and XXXV.) A farther distinction is sometimes to be made, as when a *certain part* of a subject is developed. In that case the marks would be D. A. 1, D. A. 2, D. B. 1, D. B. 2, or D. Con.

D. S. *Dual Subject.* Whenever the principal subject contains two different parts, or two opposite phases, it is to be indicated by the letters D. S. (In this case A may be omitted.) The first movements to Beethoven's Op. 7, and Op. 31, Nos. 1 and 2, have Dual Subjects, also the Concerto in *B*-flat, Op. 19. The Dual Subject is designed to represent something more than a mere two-fold theme: it applies to a subject which naturally divides itself into two parts, each part being typical of a different sentiment. It may sometimes be difficult to distinguish between this and the Preliminary motive, but the actual instances quoted will, if properly examined, show the distinction which is to be made in this system.

Ec. *Echo.* (Described in Chapter XXV.)

Eg. *Eingang.* A few measures of transition or entrance to any key in which a certain subject is to be heard.

Ep. *Episode.* (Explained in Chapter XXIV.)

F. C. *Concerto Form.* (See Chapter XLII.)

F. D. *Dance Form.* This also includes the Ballad Dance, because this style is either repeated with some embellishments, or included in the Cyclical Forms.

F. M. *Mixed or Cyclical Forms.* This refers to Suite, Partita, Medley, Potpourri, common Operatic Overture, and Theme with Variations.

F. O. *Overture Form.* Similar to Sonata form, but with two instead of three divisions, the Development usually being omitted and the principal themes being more extended. (See Chapter XLII.)

F. Rh. *Rhapsodical Form.* (See Compendium.)

F. Ro. *Rondo Form.* (See Rondo.)

F. Sl. *Single Form.* (See Chapters XXVI and XXVII.)

F. Son. *Sonata Form.* Indicates any movement or opus written according
to the classical formula as to outline and construction.

F. Sym. *Symphonic Form.* (See Chapters XLII, XLIV, and XLV.)

F. U. *Uninterrupted Form.* (See Chapters XLIV and XLV.)

G. B. *Ground-Bass.* The accompaniment to Gounod's "Pifferari" is an
example:

Ex. 263.

This is continued throughout the piece. The finale to Herold's
Overture, "Zampa," contains a ground-bass, where the ascending and descending scale passage occurs in the violin parts.
There was a style of music in vogue during the time of Purcell,
called a Ground. The accompaniment consisted of a series of
natural harmonies (similar to the complete Cadence), which
were repeated throughout the piece to a changing melody
above. The Grounds were principally vocal; but the compound, Ground-bass is to be understood in the same manner.

H. H. *Hunting-Horn Motive.* (See Hunting Song, Chapter XXVI.)

H. S. *Harmonic Style.* (See Chapter XXIII.)

I. C. *Imitation, Contrary.* ⎫
I. F. *Imitation, Free.* ⎪
I. P. *Imitation, Partial.* ⎬ (See Chapter XXVIII.)
I. S. *Imitation, Strict.* ⎭

In. *Introduction.* Must foreshadow what follows. (See Chapter XIX.)

Inv. Refers to the Inversion of a theme or counter-subject, an octave
above or below. The placing of an upper part below, or a lower
part above. A melody transferred to some other voice-part.
(See Ex. 262.)

I. R. *Imitation of the Rhythmic Device.* This may be done upon a
monotone, as when the rhythm is imitated by a drum in
orchestral music:

Ex. 264.

Iz. *Intermezzo.* See *Rondo.* (Von Bülow applies this word to the
Menuetto in Beethoven's Op. 27, No. 2, because it comes
between the two principal movements.)

K. A. *Cadence, Avoided.*
K. F. *Cadence, Full, or Authentic.*
K. H. *Cadence, Half, or Incomplete.* ⎫ (See Chapter IX.)
K. C. *Cadence, Complete, or Perfect.* ⎬
K. P. *Cadence, Plagal, or Amen.* ⎭

L. M. *Leit-Motiv.* Characteristic Motive. (See "Culprit Fay," Chapter XLV.)

M. P. *Preliminary Motive.* This has more of the introductory character than the Dual Subject, and comes before the most important or Principal theme. Following are examples: Hummel, Op. 13; the first measure and a half before the regular hallelujah motive. Von Weber, Sonata, Op. 24; the first four measures. Schubert; first eight measures in the *B*-minor Symphony. Beethoven, Concerto in *E*-flat, Op. 73; the Introduction between Orchestra and Piano. Haydn, Oxford Symphony; after the Adagio, the first four measures before the principal subject. This preparatory section has something of a dual character, but it is preliminary to the main subject. Two of Mendelssohn's overtures contain Preliminary motives, namely, the Midsummer Night's Dream and Ruy Blas.

M. T. *Middle Theme.* Usually a third subject in a Finale, and constitutes a change of form. (See Paine Symphony, Chapter XLV.)

P. C. *Period, Curtailed.* ⎫
P. E. *Period, Extended.* ⎬ (See Chapters XX and XXI.)
P. R. *Period, Regular.* ⎬
P. U. *Period, United.* ⎭

Par. *Parenthesis.* A parenthetical group. (Chapter XXV.)

Pas. *Passage.* (See Chapter XXIV.)

Po. *Postlude*, to be applied to the final Coda in Vocal Music.

P. N. *Pedal-Note*, Drone Bass. (See Chapter XXV.)

Pre. *Prelude.* An introductory part to a principal Theme or movement, but not a prognostication. The Prelude to Mozart's Fantaisie in *D*-minor is an instance.

Rec. *Recollection.* (See Chapter XXIV.)

Recit. *Recitative.* To be understood in the same sense as vocal recitative. Should be performed in an *ad libitum*, declamatory manner. The Introduction to Liszt's second Hungarian Rhapsody is a Recitative. Examples may also be found in the works of Chopin: Op. 28, Preludes 2 and 4, and Op. 25, No. 7, Bass solo. Also, Op. 31, No. 2, Beethoven, first of the Reprise (after the Development).

Ref. *A subsidiary Theme in Waltzes and certain single forms.* The Refrain is a burden, frequently in the style of a lament. See Refrain in the Ball Scenes by Nicodé, Op. 26.

Rep. *Repetition.* (See Chapter XXV.)

Ret. *Returning to a Principal Theme.* Where the object is plainly to return to a main subject. Similar to Anticipation, but more transitional. The Reprise, or third division, is to be indicated by the letters A, B, Con., as in the first division. The distinction between this and the appearance of a principal theme in the development is to be indicated by the combinations: **D. A., D. B.**, etc.

S. A. *Style, Antiphonal.* ⎫
S. C. *Style, Canonic.* ⎪
S. F. *Style, Fugal.* ⎬ (See Chapter XXIII.)
S. L. *Style, Lyric.* ⎪
S. T. *Style, Thematic.* ⎭

Se. *Sequence.* (See Chapter XXIV.)

St. *Stretto.* (See Rondo Form.)

Ta. ⎫ Indicates the location of the theme, whether *above, below*, or in
Tb. ⎬ the *middle*. This is sometimes essential, and will be men-
Tm. ⎭ tioned again.

T. Aug. ⎫ These are to indicate a principal theme, either in notes of greater
T. Dim. ⎭ or less value than the original arrangement.

T. C. *Thesis Continued.* (See Chapters XII, XIII and XXXV.)

Ts. *Theme in Syncopation.* (See Chapter XXX, Ex. 204, Var. 3.)

Tv. *Theme Varied.* Distinction must be made between this and Thematic development, as thus far described. (See Mozart's Sonata in *A*, No. 12 Peters, and Chopin, Op. 73.)

Ter. The last part of a movement, corresponding to coda, but composed of more adventitious matter, and joined to the preceding without interruption. (See Chapter XXIV.)

Tr. *Transition.* Modulation, or the Transposition of certain motives or subjects.

U. P. *Uneven Phrases.* Refers to three, or six-measure phrases, instances of which were quoted in Chapter XX, which see; also Compendium.

U. S. *Uneven Sections.* These usually contain five measures. See Hungarian Dances by Brahms, or Behr.

In order to make a complete analysis of certain compositions, it will be necessary to employ this entire catalog of reference marks.

From this Key it is apparent that there are more than one hun
dred characteristic features included in the outline and among the
details of a well-written musical composition. These are not imag
inary points of distinction, but important constituent elements, many
of which have existed since the time of Graziani and Frohberger.
The author's task has been merely to adopt such terms as seemed
appropriate, to reject such as were inappropriate or ambiguous (how
ever general they may have become), and to apply new terms and
symbols to those features and details which form the essential minu
tiæ of high-class music. To systematize these almost innumerable
points of distinction has been the chief difficulty, and the attention
of the teacher is thus called to this matter because of its great importance in all didactic works. The Application of the Key to analysis
will be shown in the following chapter.

Chapter XXXVII.

ANALYSIS OF THE SONATA FORM.

APPLICATION OF THE KEY TO ANALYSIS.

FOR the first complete analysis we will select the *G*-major Sonata,
Op. 40, No. 1, of Clementi. (No. 2, Cotta, fingered and metronomized by Moscheles. In Peters' select edition this Sonata is No. 9.)
Clementi lived through an important transition period in music,
having been born in the year 1752 and died 1832. He played
in friendly contest with Mozart, who highly complimented the Ital
ian's improvisations and performance. Beethoven also held Clementi
in great esteem for his interesting style and correct forms.

The first movement should be numbered consecutively from the
first full measure to the end of the movement.

The first section of the Principal Theme is this:

Ex. 265.

This should be examined attentively, and then performed until its
character is well established in the mind. The most important part
of the motive is this:

Ex. 266.

(A 1), for the composer repeats it in the bass as a partial imitation,
which should accordingly be played as loudly as the upper part; not
as a mere chord accompaniment. See measures 1 and 2. (The bass
here is to be marked I. P.) This is repeated, and then the same is
continued in a figurated style, with accompaniment of triplets. Observe the similarity between (a) from the first period, and (b) from
the second period, thus:

Ex. 267.

The principal tones are *d* and *g*, as they fall upon the accented parts
of the measure; *b* in the second measure is included at (a) in the
triplet, together with the other passing tones, *c* and *a*.

Another analogous comparison is between the first figure in the
last of the 8th measure, and the first three notes of the motive after
the grupetto:

Ex. 268.

This is a curtailed period, ending with the arpeggio chord upon
D, to be marked in the beginning of 15, P. C. Upon the fourth
quarter of the 15th measure the principal theme recurs, slightly
varied, Tv. The partial canonic imitation in the bass at once
follows, as before, though only the melodic outline is used below.
See 16 and 20. The second phrase of the theme is also varied, the
melodic notes being somewhat concealed, but marked by the com-

---

* The numbers refer to the measures.

poser with accented staccato marks. The transition commences at
the 23d measure, Tr. Observe the *c*-sharp, and also the fact that the
transition is built upon a fragment of the first motive, as may be seen
from example :

Ex. 269.

These should be marked A 1, as this is a species of thematic devel
opment. From the last of the 26th measure (all the motives begin
upon the last quarter) we have a descending melody in the harmonic
minor form. This affords a rather plaintive view of the subject,
though the motive afterwards appears in brighter colors. These ten
measures, from 26 to 36, are played upon a pedal-note. (Mark in
the bass P. N.) This first subdivision comes to a conclusion at the
end of the trill, 36, all this being included in the Principal theme, or
first subdivision. The Second Subject commences with the grupetto,
"*Dolce*," and is in the key of the dominant, thus :

Ex. 270.

dolce.   37   38   39   40

The similarity between this and the first subject (especially the second phrase) is so remarkable that no particular analysis of the intervals is necessary. It represents merely a milder phase of the same
bright and confident sentiment. The pedal-note accompanying the
first eight measures is to be marked; also the variation of the
theme :

Ex. 271.

Tv.   41

Compare this with 37. From 48 there is a bell-like melody, or rather
the outline of two melodies, thus :

Ex. 272.

48   50

The lower melody at (a) is taken from the motive of the second sub

ject.   At (b) the two are combined, and the harmonic sequence
(tonic, subdominant and dominant) compressed into half the time
which it occupied at first.   To this is added the measured trill below,
in form of a pedal-note.   This design is inverted at 54, and the figure
outlined at 48 and 49 is placed below and becomes a ground-bass
(G. B.).   Upon this ground-work appears a fragment of the second
subject, like sparkling dew drops upon a bending rose bough.   The
passage beginning on the second quarter at 60 is the Termination of
the Second Subject in Thematic Style.   From the last of 62 a fragment of principal theme appears somewhat figurated, in the relative
minor.   This is accompanied by the partial imitation in the bass, as
heretofore.   (All these details are to be marked by the class when
mentioned here, as a correct performance of this or similar works is
not possible without an understanding of the many constituent elements which must form a homogeneous whole.)

The Second Subject comes to an end with an Authentic Cadence
(K. F.) at 70.   Upon the last of this measure is the entrance of the
Conclusion (Con.), which is more of a lyric than either of the other
subjects.   It is taken directly from the last of the first subject, being
major, instead of minor, and of course the continuation is different.
The Conclusion is eleven measures in length, and owing to its more
decided lyric nature it should be played *smorzando* from 71 to 78.
From the latter point the movement is to be increased back to the
Allegro vivace.   The first division ends here, 90.

The Development starts with a scale passage from the Conclu-
(D. Con.).   Compare 82 with 78.   This passes through *G*-minor (82,
83), *C*-minor (84, 85), and into *A*-minor, before any melodic design
appears, 90.   This is similar to the harmonic minor motive in the
last of the Principal subject, 27 and 28.   Observe that this melodic
design in *A*-minor does not stop upon *b* (91, second quarter), according to its natural tend, but continues on diatonically to *g-sharp*
and ends upon *a*, 92.   This is thematic development simply illustrated.   The descending scale melody is repeated in *D*-minor, 96, 97,
98, and then this figure passes hrough *G*-minor into *E*-flat major,
101 (Tv.).   Here a graceful bit of melody appears in the upper
part (taken from the chord figure previously quoted), and this is
responded to by a stormy, scolding answer in the bass, 103.   The
descending chord motive re-appears at 104, in *F*-minor (having been
forced away from *E*-flat by the bass) :

Ex. 273.

This is followed by the response in the bass, as stormy as before. From 103 to 110 is to be marked S. A. The descending chromatic progression in the bass is to be played louder than the melodic figure above, to which the bass responds. From 106 the interruption of the treble melody by the bass is to be noticed, and how the upper voice is finally silenced by the more powerful, fate-like motive below (see 109, 110). After the pause a fragment of the Principal motive appears in *F*-sharp minor. This is repeated in *B*-minor, and extended to a section. The development is continued in like manner, and from the last of 129 there is a phrase of Anticipation (marked by the composer, *cresc.*), which leads naturally to the Reprise, *ff*. Everything is here the same as at first, except the slight alteration in treatment at 136. The transition (143) begins sooner than it did in the first division, owing to an abridgment of the continuation of the theme. The melody in harmonic minor beginning at 150, last quarter, is the same as before, transposed from *D* to *G*-minor, in anticipation of the return to the tonic for the second subject. 150 is to be marked Tr. After the brief Cadenza, 159, the second theme recurs, this time in the tonic, and is an exact transposition. The Conclusion (last of 193) is also in the tonic, and identical with that of the first division until we come to measure 204. Here is a brief Recollection (Rec.), followed by a stretto of three measures (St.).

Here ends our analysis of the most important movement. The other movements, Adagio, Canon, and Finale, we will briefly analyze when we consider the entire Sonata, and the relationship of the different movements.

BRIEF ANALYSIS OF SONATA NO. 5, IN *C*, BY HAYDN,[*] FIRST MOVEMENT ONLY.

Principal Subject commencing thus:

Ex. 274.

---

[*] This Sonata, like many others composed during the same period, was manufactured according to the prescribed formula, consequently the form is correct, but the music is in significant.

continues for thirty-five measures. Second Subject in the dominant begins like this:

Ex. 275.

and continues for twenty-seven measures, ending with a perfect cadence upon *G*. The Conclusion begins at the fourth quarter of
measure 62. It has almost the same rhythm as the first subject:

Ex. 276.

This is likewise in the dominant.   The three subjects are so similar
in melodic and rhythmic construction that the student might find
more difficulty in designating them than if they were more strongly
contrasted.   The tonality of the different subdivisions, and the perfect cadence just before the Conclusion, afford considerable assistance
in such cases. The Elaboration consists in working out the different
parts of the first subject.   This continues for thirty-six measures,
and ends upon the dominant seventh harmony.   The Reprise is the
same, with the customary transpositions from dominant to tonic.
The Conclusion is slightly extended in the final ending of the
movement.

ANALYSIS OF THE OUTLINES OF A SONATA IN *D*, NO. 7, BY
HAYDN.

This is an improvement upon the one in *C*. It commences with
this sprightly motive:

Ex. 277.

This is sixteen measures in length. The motive of the Second
subject is this:

Ex. 278.

consisting of nineteen measures. Immediately following the ca
dence of the Second subject, the Conclusion begins, as here :

Ex. 279.

This also is in the key of the dominant, and has six measures. The
Elaboration commences with a fragment of the first subject inverted
the subject being below, the counter-subject above. The third di
vision is similar, with usual transpositions.

Analysis of the Outlines of a Sonata Movement in C, by Mozart. (No. 15, Peters, No. 7, Litolff.)

Principal subject with this motive, twelve measures :

Ex. 280.

Second subject (after a prelude of one measure) :

Ex. 281.

This continues thirteen measures. The last three measures before
the double bar constitute the Conclusion :

Ex. 282.

The Development contains but thirteen measures, during which the
figure of the Conclusion is briefly elaborated. The return of the
first subject is thrown into the subdominant and slightly extended.
The Second subject and Conclusion appear in the tonic,* and are
otherwise identical with the first division.

The class should make a more thorough analysis of the last two
Sonatas, using the abbreviations wherever they are required. Both
teacher and pupil must, of course, be familiar with the Key.

The Haydn, Clementi and Mozart Sonatas should then be played,
giving out as many questions as can be answered by the class.

---

* This is a more equal distribution of Keys than we have previously observed

Chapter XXXVIII.

THE ENTIRE SONATA.

FURTHER APPLICATION OF THE KEY TO ANALYSIS.

WE will here review and analyze the various movements of a Sonata, both separately and as a homogeneous, united whole. As the first movement is more or less turbulent, strifeful, or disputatious, the second movement is quiet, hopeful, or retrospective. If the Allegro is stormy, the Adagio depicts a cessation of the storm elements. But a lull in a storm does not always bring sunshine. So the Adagio may breathe of peace and contentment, of love, of hope, of regret, or even of sorrow and despair. Our first examples of the Adagio were in simple ballad model, of two equal periods. Then we had the addition of a short Coda; next, a briefly extended period; finally an intermezzo, episode, or a third subject.

We will now resume our examination of the Clementi Sonata in *G*, after the first movement.

The Adagio.

The Key of the Allegro is changed from *G* to *E*-major (a somewhat unusual choice, which here necessitates a pause between the two movements). The connection between the first and second, and especially the third and fourth measures here:

Ex. 283.

and the second measure of the Allegro is intimate. Also compare the fifth measure of the Adagio with 46 and 47 of the Allegro. From measure 10 the theme appears slightly varied, and in Syncopation (Tv., Ts.). The principal subject closes at 18; P. E. The Second begins at 19 *ff*, in the relative minor, *B*. Observe the unity of design between these two phrases:

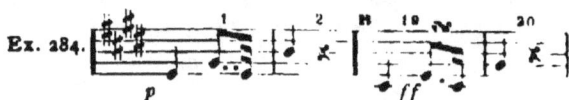

Ex. 284.

We have omitted the arpeggio group between *c*-sharp and *e* at 19, to show the principal melodic design. The first is in *E*-major, and quite soft; the second is in *C*-sharp minor, and *ff*. The Second subject is continued in ornamental style, with numerous fioriture in the form of grupetti, appoggiature and parenthetical scale passages. On the last half of 26 there is a melodic sequence (Se.) somewhat resembling the mordent. The sequence should be analyzed in this way

Ex. 285.

in order to show more distinctly the melodic outline. The Second Subject is concluded at 33. The Parenthesis leads back to the Principal subject (34) as before. At 51 the Second subject is joined to the First, constituting an United Period (P. U.). The second subject here appears in tonic minor, and is otherwise altered in the continuation. From 66 (the return to *E*) we have the beginning of a more extended Coda than we have previously analyzed. At 70 the sequence appears in Antiphonal style. From 74 to 77 may be considered a Cadenza on a pedal-point. The regular cadence is postponed by means of the avoided cadence (77 and 79), as though the composer were loth to quit this peaceful scene.

The Canon.

The third movement is the Canon, in Minuet style, with which we are familiar. It is bright and chatty, and presents no difficulties in the analysis. It is to be indicated, S. C., I. S.

The connection between the motives is so apparent that a few citations will suffice. The ascending melody, *g*, *a*, *b*, is directly from the first subject of the Allegro. The motive of the Second period is almost identical with the chord figure so frequently quoted in the previous chapter:

Ex. 286.

The last four measures beginning *pp* are also founded upon this brief chord melody, *a, f*-sharp, *d*. These four measures form a Coda to the first period. The second period (not the second subject) ends upon *f*-sharp in the bass, just before the return of the first period. This is similar to the first, except the transition back to the tonic. The last four measures form the Coda.

The Middle part (Canon II) is in contrary imitation, and the mode is changed to *G*-minor and *B*-flat major. The second voice follows the first after an interval of three beats, but in contrary movement, I. C. The first period ends in *B*-flat major, the second in *G*-minor. The first two periods in *G*-major then recur as in a D. C.

The Fourth Movement (Finale).

The form of this is what might be called a Scherzo in Rondo form. The motive is here given:

Ex. 287.

There are several features to be noticed in this motive:

1. The last three notes of the first measure, *d, b, g.*
2. The descending fifth, *a* to *d.*
3. The diatonic figure *d, e, f*-sharp, *g.*

The peculiar turn which the first of the melody takes in going from *c* to *e* (in place of *c* to *d*, as heretofore), thus:

Ex. 288.

The first period ends on the first quarter of measure 9 (calling the first six notes 1); it is then repeated with slight variations in the theme. These will be noticed here, as tending to show the possibilities of thematic development, and variation. Example 289 shows the original melody, and simultaneously the variations:

Ex. 289.

Both are written together for convenience of reference. The lower part shows the original (2), and the upper part represents the same melody as it appears in the repetition, measures 9, 10 and 11 The 11th and 12th measures present a similar case:

Ex. 290.

The plain melodic outline is this:

Ex. 291.

which is preserved in both parts of Ex. 290. Either (a) or (b) will therefore represent the melody at (c), and may appear in thematic development, or in a variation of the theme, as above.

The first repeated period is regular, and should be so indicated (P. R.). Upon the last half of 17 a short Intermezzo commences and leads back to the principal theme, 23. After eight measures this terminates on the first of 31. A transitional Passage begins here simultaneously with the ending of the principal theme, thus forming an United Period. The sequence of fourths in the bass (as theme) is also to be indicated, Se. At the end of the transition the Second Subject is introduced, 43. This commences, like the first subject, upon the second quarter of the measure; hence it should be played in this manner:

Ex. 292.

Like the Sonata movement, this second theme is in the dominant. It forms a regular period, and terminates at 59.

Before dismissing this subject, attention is directed to these notes, heretofore mentioned in connection with the first subject:

Ex. 293.

Compare this to the first four notes of the principal motive Also observe the free imitation in the upper part at 53. The rhythm and the melodic character of this resembles the last of the second measure also:

Ex. 294.

From 59 there is a recurrence of the transitional passage at 31, but leading in a different direction. The descending fourth appears first in the highest part, then in the tenor, and finally in the bass. This may be marked Repetition, as the accompanying figure remains unaltered. At 62 the counter-subject is transferred to the bass and the melodic notes of the bass at 61 are given to the treble part. Mark this Inv. At 67 a reminiscence of the first movement is heard in these sounds:

Ex. 295.

This familiar outline is embellished during the six following measures; but the peculiar halting, Spanish character of the rhythm renders this less noticeable to an inexperienced listener. From 75 there is a slight development of fragments from the principal theme, the *d, e, g, f*-sharp being several times repeated. Observe the strict imitation in the fourth below at 82. Upon the second quarter of the 85th measure the Principal theme recurs for the second time. (The Thesis is continued until this theme recurs, T. C.) This is repeated after the short Intermezzo, as before, and ends at 108.

The Middle Theme, commencing in *G*-minor, is of peculiar construction. It is too elaborate, and bears too strong a resemblance to the chief motive to be considered an Episode; yet it contains some episodical features. To call it Coda would be to imply that the tail is longer than the body. We have therefore termed it a Middle Theme, as the Principal subject comes again at the termination of the Middle Theme. The motive of this minor middle theme is this:

Ex. 296.

This is taken directly from the principal motive, the mode being changed from *G*-major to tonic minor. The slurs are included to show the divisions of the motive, not to indicate the phrasing. The last half (b) is an inversion (contrary) of the first half (a). The inversion is employed in the development almost as much as the original figure, being frequently varied as at 2 and 3 in this example:

Ex. 297.

This should be observed closely.

The melodic figure by the oboe, Ex. 298:

Ex. 298.

is responded to by the clarinet, Ex. 299:

Ex. 299.

This is to be marked S. A. The first period, ending at 118, is slightly extended (ten measures). The second period is extended to twelve measures. From the last of 130 the Middle Theme is repeated, ending upon *D*-minor as before, 152. From this point there is a thematic development of the motive quoted in Ex. 296. The first is transitional, and from the last of 156 this idea is carried out by a contrary canon between the contralto and soprano. The soprano melody from the last of 160, with the counter-subject in the tenor, is inverted from the last of 162. The soprano takes the counter-subject, the tenor takes the contralto pedal-note (*c*), and the theme passes into the contralto part. (All these details are important, and must be observed.) The four-note motive is now extended to eight notes, 164, 165, and first half of 166. The response above is to be indicated S. A. The response to the second phrase of the bass commences (in the middle-upper part) before the bass has concluded its phrase, 169, 170. The same motive afterwards appears in chromatic form, 172-3. After the antiphonal phrases in *ad libitum* style, the first of the middle theme is repeated, with some alterations in the melodic and thematic continuation. From the last of 202 there is a simultaneous melodic and harmonic sequence, the same motive appearing in this development.*

These peculiarities are to be observed and indicated. After the change in signature (210) the principal subject of the rondo appears in Augmentation, as may be seen by comparing *a* with *b*:

---

* The word Development is here used as a mere statement of fact. It does not refer to a particular part of the movement, as in the regular Sonata movement, but to the development or elaboration of a motive, wherever it may occur.

Ex. 300.

The first occupies three fourths of a measure; the second occupies
one measure and a half. Consequently the original first period,
which was *eight* measures in length, will here require *sixteen* measures for its completion. At the end of this, 226, the Passage occurs
again; this time more in the style of an Intermezzo. This includes
the eight measures of episodical matter from 237.

The Coda, containing twenty-one measures, begins at 245, with
an imitation of the first motive. Measures 260, 261, and 262 (from
the second quarter) constitute a brief Recollection, thus:

Ex. 301.

The stretto is very brief, containing but three measures (St.).

As a further illustration of the connection and unity between the
various movements of a Sonata, the motive of each of the three
movements to Mozart's Sonata in *C*, will be quoted:

Ex. 302.

Each of these motives is founded upon the intervals of a broken
chord, either ascending or descending. There are other reminiscences and kindred passages in the Romance and the Finale; but
the above examples will suffice in this place to show the unity of
design. (The quarters of the Romance about the same as the halves
of the Allegro.)

* This also serves as Finale to the *F*-major Sonata, founded upon a chord motive.

The Adagio and Finale to the Clementi Sonata should now be played for the class, that they may recognize as many as possible of the details mentioned.

QUESTIONS.

1. Rhythm of the melody of the first subject.
2. Rhythm of the accompaniment
3. Periods in the first subject (forty-two measures).
4. Number and length of periods in second subject.
5. Rhythm of the accompaniment.
6. Imitations.
7. Style of each of the three subjects.
8. Sequence and Passage.
9. Modes and Tonality.
10. Inversion and Syncopation.
11. Coda, or Termination.

(Other details are to be mentioned, if observed.)

PART X.

Chapter XXXIX.

THE ORIGIN AND DEVELOPMENT OF THE SONATA FORM.

THE Sonata Form, as we have found it in the first and sometimes in other movements of the Modern Sonata, has been the embodiment of so much high-class music that compositions written in this form only, were dignified with the name Classical.   During the last half of the 18th century the Sonata Form was so thoroughly established as to become the great test of productive musicianship. Indeed, it has exercised a powerful influence upon the plastic nature of music.   We have become acquainted with the outlines and many of the details of this form, at least sufficiently so to enable us to appreciate its growth and development.

This inquiry will prove as instructive as it is curious.   In truth, we could not intelligently pass in review the periods during which the Sonata Form reached its perfect state of development, and final disuse, without knowing the origin and development of this remarkable musical embodiment.

Two circumstances materially retarded the progress of musical composition until after the productive period of Palestrina.   These were, the want of a complete tonal system,* and the crudeness of musical instruments of the harmonic class.   Before this time vocal music was the almost exclusive product of the art; so much so, that when the first instrumental composers began to write music for instruments, without voices, they used the word Sonata (from *sonare*,

---

* The music of the Troubadours was greatly in advance of the Art, as recognized by the Church and practiced by the leading composers at that period.

to sound).* Hence, a Sonata was originally any kind of an instru
mental piece. The first attempts were naturally without form (and
we might add the remainder of the sentence from Genesis without
prevaricating the truth).

The contrapuntal (polyphonic) style had previously attained a
high degree of scientific perfection in the masses and motets of the
great Belgian, Dutch, French, Italian and English composers, and
this style was afterwards employed as the basis of an instrumental
form, *i. e.*, the development of one or two motives in one movement.
These pieces, being exclusively in thematic style, were lacking in
the primitive outlines of a distinct form. These requisites were most
probably first supplied from the vocal form of the folk-song, which
was necessarily more natural and artless than the ponderous and
scientific ecclesiastical style. The melodies to simple, popular rhymes
naturally resulted in the Ballad Model, and these were adapted to the
prevailing instruments much better than the polyphonic form, which
was necessarily difficult of execution before the appearance of the
Virtuoso.

The first period of an old melody is here quoted, as showing the
natural origin of the ballad form. The song was composed by Witz-
lav, long before the time of Lassus. The music was written in the
ancient hieroglyphical notation, without mensural proportion, except
such as the metre of the poem suggested. The translation and arrangement are by the learned antiquarian and savant, Herr Stade:

LOVE SONG.

Ex. 303.

We have even here a plainly outlined regular period of eight full
measures. This was repeated for the second verse. The metre of
the third verse of the poem changed, and this necessitated a change
in the melody. When a little later the second verse was sung to
another period of music, corresponding to the first, the ballad model
was the result.

---

* G. Gabrieli is supposed to have been the first who applied this word to an instru
mental piece, about 1565.

The music of the old dances, such as the Pavan, Galliard, and Sarabande, became the next, and, perhaps, most important instrumental form. A Dance Tune of the 13th century is here quoted from E. Naumann's excellent History of Music:

Ex. 304.

This is written three times, but each strain is precisely similar to the first, with this distinction: the first phrase of the first and second sections in the second strain commences at (b). Both sections of the third strain commence as at (c), in place of (a) or (b). Otherwise the "three parts," as Dr. Crotch calls them, are identical. In reference to this Dance Tune, Naumann says: "It is worthy of remark that this piece, like *Sumer is icumen in*, is in the key of *F* major, and not in any of the church modes, and is in strict conformity with the rules of modern music in its closes (authentic cadence), which are uniformly composed of a leading-note rising to its proper resolution. This goes a long way towards proving that our modern tonality was natural and spontaneous among our ancestors, although strictly excluded from the music of the Church, and ignored by all the theoretical writers on harmony for three hundred years after that date"—about 1280.†

The various movements and figures of the dances gave to the music of this class a more pronounced rhythmic character, and certain divisions, which constituted the Dance Form. These dances were so characteristic, and so well developed by the middle of the 16th century that composers like O. Gibbons, Couperin, Buxtehude, the elder Scarlatti, and Kuhnau, wrote pieces containing several dance tunes following each other in the same key, and these they termed Suites. In Italy these Suites were called Sonatas, and finally the words Suite, Partita, and Sonata came to be used synonymously. Previous to this time, however, instrumental music had received a

---

* Observe that the first section contains four measures, while the second section has five

† The church modes remained in use until a short while before the birth of J. S. Bach.

great impetus from Monteverde, through his efforts in dramatic music. He first gave prominence to the stringed instruments played with a bow; invented the pizzicato, tremolo, and other styles of playing, and thus stimulated performers to become more proficient, and instrument-makers to improve their wares.

Corelli (born 1653) was a natural sequence of this great improve ment in instruments and instrumental performance, and the Con certos and solo Sonatas of this master are good models even at the present time. But the Sonatas of Corelli were mostly Suites, similar to those we have examined. A few were written in thematic style, with canonic imitations, double counterpoint, etc.

About this time the French composer Lully invented the Over ture, consisting of a fairly developed slow movement, followed by an Allegro, in which the style was changed, and then a repetition of the slow movement. In Italy this order was reversed for the Over ture, and the slow movement came in the middle. This is a more natural arrangement than that of the French. However, both these forms of Overture were incorporated into the Suite during the last of the 17th century. The so-called Sonatas of Frescobaldi, Froh- berger, Couperin, Alessandro Scarlatti, Johann Christopher (the un cle), and J. Sebastian Bach, as well as those of Händel, Purcell, and others, were for the most part a collection of dances arranged gener- ally in the same key, and with considerable taste and variety. The resemblance of the different motives of the dances used by J. S. Bach was more intimate than in the Suites of his predecessors, thereby giving to this cyclical form a unity of design not originally contemplated by its inventors. In the Suites of Händel the differ ent numbers are well connected, and this soon became established as a system, having in this respect considerable resemblance to the classical sonata, which is likewise a cyclical form.

We now come to the germ of the Sonata movement, as described in Chapters XXXIII and XXXIV. In the violin Sonatas of Corelli there occasionally appears an unconscious working towards the Dom inant of the prevailing key, from whence the music naturally returns to the Tonic in the second division, or, after a digression to the dom inant. Domenico Scarlatti, however, was the principal agency in transferring this form to the harpsichord, and enriching it with the more harmonic treatment of the keyed instrument. In the Sonatas of this master we find several instances in which, after concluding the principal subject, there is a second subject in the dominant. The

second subject, however, was not so nearly related to the first as in
the modern Sonata. After the strain in the dominant, the first part
was repeated. No Conclusion appeared in the movement; but it
was a very good piece of clavichord music nevertheless. (We have
here a prophetic suggestion of the main features of all established
classical Forms, namely: A Principal theme in a certain key; a second theme of a different color and in a different key; and then a recurrence of the Principal theme in the original key.)

Benda, Frohberger, Kuhnau, Sarti, and others, also contributed
to the improvement of this germ, so that by the time Philip Emanuel Bach (favorite son of J. S.) began his public career he found
something more than the seed which had been planted, and which
was to bring forth such rich and abundant fruit. The seed had
already taken root, and he had but to train the sprouts and guide
them in their somewhat uncertain course. Emanuel's father seems
not to have made any serious attempts in this form; he was engaged
too thoroughly in his great problems of harmonizing the conflict
between Art and Science, the solution of which he has left us, and
without which the modern Sonata would have been impossible.
Nevertheless, there are numerous instances in his music of the dominant Transition at the end of a first period or part, and the subsequent natural return to the tonality of the key-tone. In his first
French Suite the Allemande begins in *D*-minor, and the first period
ends at the double bar in *A*-major. This is true of the following
Courante, Sarabande, and the first Menuet. The same plan is followed in the Gigue. The other Suites, both major and minor, nearly
all have this peculiarity of tonal construction, and in the fugues also
the episodical part is frequently carried into the dominant.

There is a cause at the bottom of this transitional effect as natural
and as educible as that of polar radiation, or the law of actuation.
The most important accessory sound in acoustics after the octave
(which is here synonymous with *key-tone*) is the fifth or dominating note of the tonic. In transition it is therefore the most important key above the tonic. The cycle of keys also proceeds ton-
ally by fifths, thus returning to the original starting point, *c*. This
dominant transition is, moreover, typical of actuation, of an end
reached, an object accomplished. It is in the direction of onward
progress; not merely of progression, but of *objective progression*.
From the standpoint of the Dominant the composer may show us
other scenes, or return to the key-tone without further transitional

effort. Or by flattening the seventh of the new key he may a te a distant transition, return to any desired key through the modulation by fourths, which corresponds in descending to the fifths ascending.

The student should know that at this time the ear of the ordinary listener was not accustomed to the rich harmonic combinations and distant transitions, such as we find in Mozart's second G-minor Symphony. In fact, the transitions seldom ventured far beyond the circumscribed limits of the Ecclesiastical Modes until after J. S. Bach wrote his "Well tempered Clavichord" (48 Preludes and Fugues in all the major and minor keys). Hence, the composer was obliged to choose such transitions as could be readily appreciated, and in which the relationship to the prevailing key was easily apprehended. The principal key was made more prominent by always keeping it near at hand, and only passing to those related keys in which the connection was readily understood. Tonic major and tonic minor were thus (apparently) closely related, the key-tone and dominant chord being identical:

Ex. 305.

The only difference here is in the third, major (a) and minor (b). After changing from G-major to G-minor, the relative major of the new minor tonic would be readily comprehended, though in reality a distant key from the original. The first period of the second part might begin in G-minor and end in B-flat major (same signature). The next period could begin in B-flat and end in G-minor. The repetition of the first part in G-major could then follow in natural order.*

Before proceeding with the Sonatas of Emanuel Bach, it will be necessary to give some attention to those of his immediate predecessors. Of these, D. Scarlatti, already mentioned, is the most important, at least, in connection with the Harpsichord Sonata. The Sonata movements of this pioneer virtuoso are mostly divided by a double bar into two equal parts. The first part begins in the key of the Tonic, with a plainly outlined Principal Subject. This is followed by a transition to the Dominant, in which the first part ends. So much is very well, with exception of the fact that the second subject is

* See Tonality, in Chapters VII, XV, XVI, XVII, XXII, XXXIII, XXXIV, XXXV, XXXIX, and XLIV.

scarcely recognizable in the midst of so much thematic treatment. The second part is an extended development of one or more of the motives of the first part, and the whole ends with a repetition of the Conclusion of the first part, transposed from dominant to tonic. Neither of the principal themes recur after the development; in fact, the latter is merged into the final conclusion. This is why we accepted the bar divisions, as indicating two divisions, though in the modern Sonata there are three.

(Domenico Scarlatti, Ch. Wagenseil, and a few other composers of this period made a distinction between the Suite and Sonata, and endeavored to give to the latter a more compact form than that of the Suite, and to disassociate it from the dance form. Therefore we shall not hereafter consider the Sonata as synonymous with Suite or Partita, which latter are the same.)

A brief summary of the principal features of a representative Sonata from Wagenseil will be presented here :

Principal subject in the Tonic;

Second subject in the Dominant;

Short Conclusion in the Dominant, all very plainly outlined and easily recognized. The Elaboration is somewhat exhaustive, and deals with the principal themes. The Return is to the Conclusion transposed into the tonic, the first and second subjects being omitted after the Development.

Many similar examples occur in the Sonatas of that period, and in more modern works of this class we frequently meet with instances in which the principal subject is so considerably developed that it is not re-introduced after the development, but in place of that we have the repetition of the Second subject and Conclusion for the Reprise. That this is a material advance towards a more perfect instrumental art-form no one can doubt.

Following in the wake of the younger Scarlatti we come next to Paradisi (1712), sometimes written Paradies. This was an excellent harpsichord composer and performer. His Sonata in *A*-major (which contains the favorite Toccata as Finale) is superior in design to those we have noticed, though the treatment is more free. His Neapolitan Sonata in *D*-major is still more elaborate. But even here the structure is more in Fantasia than in Sonata form.

J. Kuhnau (1667) has been credited with the invention of the Sonata form, but the author cannot agree with this statement. Kuhnau did write some instrumental compositions entitled Sonatas

and not composed of dances; but the form was obscure, and the out
lines rather subjective than objective. The vocal compositions of this
master, especially his sacred works, were valuable contributions to
music of his day, and upon these his fame must rest. And, as a
matter of fact, we cannot ascribe the Sonata form to any particular
composer. It was not an "invention," but a natural growth from
an incipient seed, planted by an invisible hand. In its first appear
ance it was scarcely recognizable; but when it was once placed
under the aerating influences of genius and art it pursued its steady
growth until it had become fully matured.

We now arrive at the period of Philip Emanuel Bach's artistic
productivity. The Sonata came to him as a thematic or fantastic
movement in two parts: the first part ending in the dominant, and
the second part ending in the tonic. He also found in the Sonatas
of his predecessors an embryo design as to first, second and third
subjects, development, and return to the first. But the divisions
were somewhat obscure; no design appeared as to the different
tonalities of a Sonata in the minor mode, and the remaining movements were also undefined and lacked coherency.

The motive of the first subject in Emanuel Bach's *A*-major
Sonata is this:

Ex. 306.

which continues for twelve measures. The second subject is in the
dominant, as follows:

Ex. 307.

This is more extended than the first, and less lyrical. The Conclusion is brief:

Ex. 308.

extending but two measures beyond the quotation.

A glance at these motives will show the intimacy of their rel:
tionship to one another. The style is brilliant, but without bein
in the least trival or incongruous.

The Elaboration commences with the chief subject, and is ski
fully lead through various tonalities, including a Passage which lead
to C-sharp minor. In this key a fragment of the second subject i
introduced. Finally the original key is restored and we come t
the Reprise. This is identical with the first twelve measures, incluc
ing the half cadence. The Second Subject then recurs, slightl
altered, but mostly in the tonic, as is the Conclusion also. This i
to be repeated from the Development. After the repeat, the cadenc
in the second ending is avoided, and a short Coda is introduce
to connect the Allegro with the Adagio. (This seems to be th
first instance of the kind.) The Adagio is in the relative minor
The last movement is an elaborate Allegro Vivace, excellently wel
written.

The Sonata in A-flat major contains some novel features, whicl
we will pass in brief review.

The Second subject and Conclusion are each introduced by ?
measure of Adagio. The Second subject, though somewhat modula
tory, is chiefly in the dominant. The Conclusion begins in toni
minor, but ends in the dominant. The two chief subjects, including
the episodical passage in the first part, are then reviewed and elaborated in the development. The Return of the three subjects is quite
systematic and well defined. The Second movement is an Adagio.
and the Finale is an Allegro, somewhat similar in construction to
the last, being developed almost as much as is the first movement.

The Sonata in F-minor, beginning like this:

Ex. 309.

contains the first instance of the second subject (to a sonata in
minor), being in the Relative Major. It is this:

Ex. 310.

The motive, as well as the change of mode, affords an agreeable and consistent contrast to the first minor subject, and this ever after became the rule for Sonata movements in minor.

The Conclusion, consisting of an equal period, is in the tonic minor, and is in the beginning similar to the first subject.

The Elaboration deals exclusively with the first subject, twelve instead of eight measures, and so the Reprise begins with the second subject, changed from major to minor, as the development was changed from minor to major.

The Conclusion is in the tonic minor, but otherwise the same as at first.

A few concluding remarks will apply to all of the Sonatas of Ph. Em. Bach which we have reviewed, and to his orchestral Symphonies as well. They reveal a musician of the highest type: scholarly, painstaking, of unerring musical instinct, and with a mind capable of receiving and moulding artistic impressions. His most brilliant figures and passages are not mere exhibitions of virtuosity, but component parts of an organic whole; and considering that his piano* compositions are more difficult than those of Haydn, this is all the more remarkable.

The Sonatas of Rolle (1718) were written in the new style, and one in particular in E-flat is very clearly defined and well developed; but as he added nothing materially new to the form, we may pass on to the next great composer after Ph. Em. Bach.

This was no other than Joseph Haydn (1732—1809). Haydn lived such a remarkable length of time, and during such an important epoch in music (which he helped to create), that his music should be indicated chronologically by opus numbers. His piano Sonatas mostly seem to have been written at an early period, and founded upon the plan of Em. Bach. At this time the Austrian labored under some disadvantages, as compared to Ph. Em. Bach. He was not so skilful a performer, nor had he in his youth such thorough musical schooling as Emanuel received from his illustrious father.† We have seen that Haydn adopted the form as established by Bach; but here the resemblance ceases. The works of Haydn

---

* The piano-forte was generally introduced during the life-time of this composer (1714 1788), the first having been submitted for the approval of his father.

† A lad who would voluntarily metamorphose himself from a music student into an uncommissioned *valet-de-chambre* to a pedantic and crusty old singing master, must indeed have had some usance as well as appetite for information.

are much more melodious and playful. In fact, the age of popular melody was just beginning to dawn, and it could have had no better pioneer or champion than the author of "The Creation." This marked difference in style, from thematic to lyric, offers an easy solution of the divergence of Haydn's Sonatas from the character of those by Em. Bach and his predecessors. With Haydn every impression was an unsung melody, and was naturally expressed in the more euphonious lyric style. Hence the music of Haydn abounds in variations and melodic embellishments. A thematic motive may be altered in form, reversed or developed; but it does not lend itself so readily to variation and embellishment as a lyric motive. The lyric motives of the new dispensation also brought the outlines of the Sonata form into stronger light, and in a Haydn Sonata one need not be an experienced listener in order to recognize the different divisions. The other changes introduced into the Sonata as a whole were (besides the more Cantabile slow movement) a Minuet, with "Trio" in a different key as third movement, and a vivacious, sportive Finale in Rondo form.

The Menuet was also lyrical, retaining the accent and rhythm of the old dance, but having infused into it a more sprightly and graceful charm than it had possessed before the advent of Haydn.

The Finales, however, are inferior to those of Paradisi, Bach and Rolle. The Finale to nearly all of Haydn's Sonatas was a species of dance-rondo, divided into short ballad-periods, each of which was repeated with numerous embellishments and variations. This gave to the work as a whole a monotonous, as well as a primitive, trivial character. Indeed, nearly all of Haydn's finales remind us of juvenile merry-making.

In his Symphonies and chamber music we shall see Haydn in his higher element. In the meanwhile we will proceed with our review.

ILLUSTRATIONS.

The Sonatas by Em. Bach, already mentioned; the one by Hässler in *A*-minor (in canonic style); a selection from D. Scarlatti and Paradisi, and the Sonata in *C*-sharp minor (No. 10), by **Haydn**.

Chapter XL.

-

THE DEVELOPMENT OF THE SONATA FORM.
CONTINUED.

WE have seen how the word Sonata came to be first applied to an indefinite, primitive instrumental piece, and how the term was afterwards applied to a collection of popular dance tunes. Then it gradually drew away from the Partita form and became an independent, though imperfect, instrumental composition in two or three movements, and entirely emancipated from the style of song or dance music. Its consequent growth and development into a logical, artistic and homogeneous instrumental form we have also observed. (Even the fully developed Sonata movement, however, presents a striking resemblance to the old Dance form. The three divisions of the former correspond to the First part, Second part in a different key, and Repetition, of the Dance form.)

We have seen how a more euphonious and human (though less artistic) character was infused into the form by Haydn, Boccherini, Nardini, Hässler, and others. We now come to Mozart (1756) He was not alone the most precocious musical genius of any age, but an accomplished theoretical musician and skilful pianist; the father having been a well-informed music teacher and violinist. As Mozart himself has informed us that he had "diligently studied" the works of the great masters, both anterior and contemporaneous, we know that he found the sonata in an advanced state of development.

Emanuel Bach and Haydn became his models. The thorough schooling of his youth, his foreign travels, and, more than these, his genial fancy and wonderful perception soon enabled him to impart to the Sonata a more artistic grace and charm, without lowering its purely instrumental character. His C-minor Sonata (No. 18) and the D-minor piano Concerto are not the only evidences of this fact Haydn now drew as many art-morals from the works of Mozart as the Prodigy had previously extracted from the creations of his senior.

As several Sonatas from Haydn, Clementi, and Mozart have been analyzed as exemplifications of the modern Sonata form, we are already familiar with their outlines and general construction. In the later Sonatas of Mozart there is a manifest enlargement and broadening of the form, and a more natural and spontaneous uniformity existing between all the parts and movements. In respect to Mozart a better estimate of his style can be formed from his piano works than in the case of Haydn. Consideration must be made, however, of the fact that many of Mozart's piano pieces were written from impecunious rather than from inspirational motives, and the author regrets that many worthless effusions by Mozart and Haydn have been so persistently and slavishly included in the great European catalogs, simply because they bore those illustrious names. Indeed, many students have failed to complete their first studies of those masters on account of coming in daily contact with so much of triviality and commonplace giggery. *

Mozart also varied the Sonata form by writing it in Adagio movement, not as an introduction, like the Haydn Symphonies, but as a regular Sonata Movement, with the chief subjects, and Development, and Reprise. It will be sufficient to mention his Sonata in *E-flat* major, No. 9; Adagio, Menuet I and II and Finale. Owing to the Development of the first subject in the sonata part, the Return is to the second subject, with a brief Coda after the repeat. He was also the first to write a theme and variations as first movement to a Sonata, and in all his important works there is a richer harmonic coloring and more distant transitions.

Of the Sonatas of Clementi (nearly ninety in number) we have already written. Being solely a piano virtuoso his sonatas incline more to the bravura style than do those of Haydn and Mozart; and though generally musical, as well as brilliant, they frequently exhibit more constructive ability than poetic fancy.

Our next author is Dussek (1761). He was a finished pianist, a well-informed musician, and a man of great artistic talent. His principal Sonatas are excellent models of poetic fancy and interesting subject-matter clothed in the garb of classical formality. That he improved upon Mozart would be saying too much in his favor, but he was a valuable contributor to sonata literature.

Before mentioning the great exhauster of the Sonata form, we will revert to the piano works of his rival, J. N. Hummel. Hummel was a pupil of Mozart, a great pianist, profoundly versed in all the details of the Art, and a composer of some excellent masses

---

and chamber music. Owing to the enlargement of the piano forte, and to his executive skill, his sonatas are more in the bravura style than those of Mozart and Dussek. Indeed, some are extremely difficult. But this does not, in his case, imply a want of inspiration. His compositions are fresh and spontaneous, generally free from artificiality, and nearly always of serious import. His earlier sonatas, including the one in *E-flat*, with the Hallelujah motive, are as plainly outlined as those of his master. Even this Sonata, Op. 13, is an example of the completely developed form. The chief subjects are formed from elevating motives, the different divisions are of sufficient length to produce a permanent impression, and joined to one another in a most natural manner. Another important feature is the Finale, which is an improvement upon both Haydn and Mozart. Yet almost every young piano virtuoso, newly weaned from his Parnassum and his thorough bass exercises, totally ignores the works of Dussek and Hummel, though he has no hesitation about performing his own abortive effusions.

A short analysis of the Op. 13 of Hummel is here presented.

The first fortissimo phrase is a Preliminary motive, or a condensed epitome of the entire work. Though it stands in a prefatory position, it was not intended as a mere preludatory chord. The Principal Subject commences upon the last of the second measure, thus:

Ex. 311.

[The numbers refer to the measures from the beginning.) The transition commences at 19, with the hallelujah motive (above quoted) in *B-flat*. The Second Subject commences at 35, in the dominant. Observe how naturally the termination of the first subject leads into the second. The Second subject is brought to a close at 81, and the Conclusion begins at once. The intermediate strain, commencing at 62, has at first sight the appearance of being the Conclusion, but this is a reminiscence of the second subject (compare measures 37 and 39 with 62 and 63).

The first eight measures of the Development deals with the Preparatory motive. At 100 the hallelujah motive is introduced in *C*-major. 117 the introductory phrase is again elaborated with an affirmative response in the middle part. After three measures of

Eingang the Principal subject recurs, but without the prefatory measure, as at first.

The Reprise from this point (133) is similar to the first division, but sufficiently diversified to sound spontaneous. The Second subject recurs in the tonic.

The Conclusion is slightly curtailed (but only the regretful part is omitted), and the Coda continues thirteen measures. This is a Recollection (eight measures), and Stretto (six measures). It is significant that the hallelujah motive is here completed (continued to the end of a period) for the first time throughout the piece.

The Adagio contains two principal subjects. The second begins in *F*-major, and the first division closes in this key. After the double bar there is a transitional section, in order to introduce the second subject in *D*-flat. This, and what follows, is in the nature of Elaboration until the return of the Principal theme in *B*-flat, with somewhat different treatment. The first part of the second subjects also recurs (in the tonic) and in the close, portions of both subject are contrasted. The Finale (neither a Rondo nor a Scherzo) is written in Sonata form also, with two Principal subjects, Development, Return and brilliant Coda, or Termination.

BEETHOVEN (1770-1827).

In this chapter we propose to review the first two periods of Beethoven's career, and these merely in respect to his development and perfection of the Sonata form. His last period forms a part of the Romantic epoch, and must be referred to that subject.

The first three piano sonatas of this master, dedicated to Haydn, are a graceful tribute to the genius of Emanuel Bach and Mozart, as well as to Haydn. These are conceived in the strict classical style, the principal peculiarities being these:

In the No. 1 there is a strongly contrasted Middle Theme (or third subject) in the midst of the Prestissimo. Though this is a natural outgrowth from the motive of the first Allegro, it presents an altogether brighter view than anything preceding it.

The No. 2 contains a Second subject in dominant minor, and afterwards in tonic minor, with strokes of alternate light and shade in the continuation of the theme. Here also we first meet the Scherzo.* In this Sonata it is strongly tinctured with the Minuet essence, but more free and sprightly than the regular form.

---

* The Form of the Scherzo is similar to Diagrams B or F, though frequently more extended. See Chapters XVI, XVII, and XXVI.

In the No. 3 there is an Episode introduced between the conclusion of the First subject and the introduction of the Second subject in the Dominant. The Episode is in G-minor, then C minor, A minor, G-minor again; and finally terminates upon D, just before the Second subject. This Episode is composed of adventitious matter, the resemblance between it and the principal theme being very slight. (This diversion has been called by various names, which the author regrets he cannot accept.) The Coda contains some passage work, a Cadenza, Recollection and Stretto.

The Scherzo is a still farther departure from the Minuet form

The fourth movement contains three subjects, and is a decided improvement upon the Haydn Finale.

Passing over ten or fifteen piano and chamber music compositions we will review the Sonata in E-flat, No. 7. This has the dimensions, and, to a certain extent, the style of a grand Sonata. (The first movement contains nine pages, aside from the repetition.) There are several phases of the Principal subject, to which attention should be directed, principally on account of their subsequent use and connection. These are:

Ex. 312.

The motive (1) is plainly constructed out of the E-flat chord. No. 2 is a simple arabesk figure woven around this chord. The same may be said of No. 4, though it is more progressive. No. 3 is the first diatonic motive that appears prominently. No. 5 is composed of the intervals of a major chord ascending. (The original motive both ascends and descends.) No. 6 is a reversion of No. 1

The strain commencing at the 41st measure has been called by the strangely anomalous compound, first Second theme, i.e. "Second theme I." If it is a second subject, let it be called such, for it is better to be logical and consistent than to rigidly follow a nomenclature of outline-analysis which was in vogue during the time of Mozart, but is now disregarded by every first-rate composer.

Let us go back to the beginning. After the positive and somewhat doctrinal motive is announced (1, 2, 3 and 4), the piece speeds
away on its sportive course; one part taking up the thread as another comes to a close, so that the strain is quite continuous until it
is arrested at twenty-five by the sudden and *ff* appearance of the first
motive, here made more positive and momentous by the addition of
the minor seventh. The response to this by the little sportive, let-
us-be-gay figure in the treble parts is the natural, or rather the Beet-
hovenish continuation of the period begun at 25. A similar period
commences at 33, responded to and continued by the sportive element. Another period, perfectly connected with the preceding, begins at 41. This it is which the author believes has been misappre-
hended. It might be called an auxiliary theme, but "first second
theme" is too anomalous and too misguiding. The strain in question is a perfectly natural continuation of the sportive element which
has thus far prevailed. To be sure, there is a warning voice:

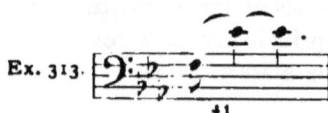

Ex. 313.

in the lower counterpoint, but this is not capable of arresting the
onward flow of the treble part.

Each of the periods commencing at 41 and 51 contain nine
measures, two measures by way of anticipation and change of harmony being included between the two irregular periods. Upon the
last half of 59 the Second theme commences. There can be no doubt
as to this, the contrast being so strong. In the Cotta Edition this is
marked ten metronomical degrees slower than the first subject—a
very just interpretation of the character of this lovely theme. The
first period is repeated in a very graceful variation, which is merged
into a considerably extended period, ending *ff*. We then hear a
rather plaintive and persuasive bit of subsidiary melody in the contralto:

Ex. 314.

After being repeated, this melody passes into the baritone part, accompanied by the sportive figure of the first subject (see 18 and 19).

At 93 this is interrupted by a still more positive motive (an inversion of the chief motive), but without the descending feature.

The Conclusion commences at 111, and is founded on a pedal note throughout (an excellent example of this device). The pedal note, aside from its tenacious and persistent character, adds considerable unity to the upper design. At the conclusion of this there is a short Coda in antiphonal style. Observe the peculiar effect of the syncopation, and the connection between this and the first motive of the Allegro. (Coda seems to the author more appropriate than "Close II," as it is in the nature of an afterthought.)

The Development is rather brief, and merely presents a slightly different phase of the dual character of the first division. The Syncopated motive of the Coda, with its impatient accent, also attracts our attention. The only new feature is the melodic section at 173, and again at 181. Observe how the first is suddenly interrupted at 177 by the positive, chief motive *ff.* The Reprise, with the subsidiary themes, the Second subject and Conclusion, is not materially different from the first division. (The differences should be sought out by the student.)

The original Coda is considerably extended, and contains a Recollection of the second subject, and also of the other subjects. The last eight measures form a Stretto.

The Largo.

This beautiful and soulful lyric exhibits the tender side of a proud and heroic nature. (From this M. Gounod seems to have borrowed the motive of his Ave Maria.) The first period is perfectly regular, and this is followed by a characteristic Intermezzo of six measures, and then the principal theme is led off in a different direction, and somewhat impatiently. Notice the peculiar Avoided Cadence at 201, and the fate-like rappings of the staccato chords, *ff.*

After the cadence on *C* there is a brief transition to *A-flat* major for the Second theme. The first period of this ends in *minor.* Then it is taken up in *D-flat* major, the continuation becoming more yearnful, and ending, all unsatisfied, upon *G.* The distant pourings above serve to recall the principal theme, a part of which soon follows in *B-flat.* Observe the use that is made of this fragment of the first motive in measures 45 and 46:

Ex. 315.

The recurrence of the Principal theme is only slightly different from the first. A notable exception is to be found in measures 65 and 66, where the repeated figure:

Ex. 316.

sung by a higher voice, is very significant. The Coda begins with the motive of the second subject. The curtailed period at the close has been previously mentioned.

The Allegro.

This movement is a quasi Scherzo, full of lithesome grace and happy humor. The manner in which the first period is extended to twenty-four measures is worthy of note. The second period beginning with the canon founded on a diminished seventh chord is more serious; but the first period soon recurs. After the silent measure there is a sportive, intermediate theme constructed upon this figure, from the principal subject:

Ex. 317.

which ends in a similar manner to the first period. The last nine measures form a Coda. In the "Trio" the form is changed, and, in truth, nearly everything is changed—key, mode, rhythm, movement, and melody. The first period of sixteen measures is perfectly regular. The second is curtailed to twelve, and then the first recurs, with a different continuation. At the termination of this period there are a few plaintive measures of Coda leading back to the Allegro.

The Rondo.

The principal theme is sixteen measures. Then there is an intermediate strain in form of an intermezzo.

After a perfect cadence this ends upon the dominant. The Second subject begins in C-minor, and consists of a double motive, or a subject and accompanying counter-subject. This terminates with a short Cadenza leading to the return of the principal theme. After an Eingang of one measure we have a Third subject in two parts (two periods) in C-minor. This is something of a digression, even

though its chief motive is employed in the termination of the Rondo
At the end of the Third subject a few transitional measures are
added to lead to the third appearance of the Principal theme, as
before. The intermediate strain, with the antiphonal answers in the
upper part, is also the same, excepting the transposition. Then we
hear the second subject again, commencing in *F*-minor. After this,
the Principal theme is heard for the fourth time, though now con
siderably altered by means of embellishments, syncopation, and a
descending chromatic progression. The Coda begins rather abruptly
in *E*-major, but soon modulates back to *E*-flat. Here the Termina
tion ("close") commences, with the arpeggio accompaniment in
thirty-seconds, and founded on the melody of the Third subject,
changed from Minor to Major. The entire Termination is calm
and reposeful.

As illustrations to this chapter it would be well to play, by way
of review,
The Sonata in *B*-flat, by Mozart; *
Sonata Op. 75, or 35, No. 2, Dussek;
Sonata Op. 13 in *E*-flat, Hummel;
Beethoven Op. 2, No. 1, first, second and fourth movements, and
the Op. 7 entire.

QUESTIONS.
(*For each Movement.*)

1. Measure and Modes.
2. Rhythm of the different motives.
3. Number of subjects.
4. What motives developed.
5. Forms (how many).
6. Cadences.
7. Eingang, Episode.
8. Pedal-note, Passage, Cadenza.
9. Styles (Lyric, Thematic, Harmonic, etc.).
10. Conclusion, Coda, Termination.
11. Echo, Counter-Subject.
12. Middle Theme (or third subject).
13. Recollection, Stretto.

* There is so much confusion in the numbering of these Sonatas in the foreign Catalogs
that a thematic indication will be given in the Compendium.

The Sonata movement as a Form; the Scherzo, or Minuet, Rondo, or Finale, should be recognized and specified. This might be a general question.

Chapter XLI.

THE ENLARGEMENT AND PERFECTION OF THE SONATA FORM—Concluded.

IN passing chronologically over the piano Sonatas of Beethoven we meet with only slight deviations from the recognized form and arrangement, until we come to the Op. 27, Nos. 1 and 2. As regards the natural and psychological impressions, and his mode of conveying them to us, these are ever new, progressive, and truly remarkable. These considerations are necessarily far more important than the external ones as to form, outline and tonal construction, and may be compared to the relationship between casket and jewel, body and soul.

In the Op. 10, No. 2, we notice a principal theme recurring after the Development in *D*-major, in place of the key-tone, *F*. In the Op. 26 the first movement is a theme of two periods (one form), followed by five variations, and a final Coda of fifteen measures. The remaining movements are: a Scherzo, Funeral March (in place of the usual song), and a Finale, partly in Rondo and partly in Sonata form. The theme and variations had previously been used as a first movement by Haydn and Mozart, but not such variations as these. The introduction of the Funeral March was Beethoven's invention, which he afterwards applied in the Heroic Symphony. (It is curious to observe that the *marche funèbre* was written while Beethoven's sometime hero was not only yet alive, but the shining light of the first French Empire. But when he caused himself to be crowned, Beethoven's Republican enthusiasm vanished, and the dirge became a lament over insatiate ambition. In later years, when our composer was told of the death of Napoleon, he simply answered: "I have already written his funeral march.")

We now come to a new epoch in the sonata form. Heretofore (especially with Haydn and Mozart) the first movement was the most important. Nay, the finale was very often of no consequence whatever. Both of the Sonatas, Op. 27, are entitled "Sonata quasi una Fantasia," *i. e.*, a Fantastic, or Free Sonata.

In the first movement of No. 1 we have a Principal subject, Intermezzo, and return of the principal subject, all in the tonic E flat, excepting a few abrupt transitions in the intermezzo. The Second subject is in C-major, with a change of key, metre and movement (though the beats remain about the same). After a transition, this leads to the third appearance of the principal theme in E-flat. The Intermezzo is here omitted, and the movement ends with a rather mystic Coda. A Scherzo of peculiar construction then follows. The third movement is an Adagio in single form (one subject), ending with a Cadenza, or transition, to the dominant, which becomes the key-tone of the Finale. This is a Rondo in Sonata Form, with three subjects, Development, Return and Coda. This stops upon the dominant seventh chord, and then the first part of the Adagio is re-introduced, and the whole ends with a Stretto, *Presto.*

Op. 27, No. 2. The plan of this (if it is allowable to apply such a term to this wonderful improvisation) bears some resemblance in its fantastic form to the No. 1. After five measures of prelude we have a song without words, Adagio. This is a single form, with but one Principal subject of two periods, regular and extended, and a Coda, in which the upper bass repeats the rhythm of the subject as a pedal-note.

The Second movement is an Allegretto* (*a la* Menuet), with two repeated periods and a "Trio." Observe the extension of the second period, and the peculiar significance of this. The Finale, *Presto,* is in Sonata form, and, like all the movements to both numbers this opus, it is joined to the others without interruption.

The Principal subject (thematic) is joined to the second subject (lyric), which first occurs in the relative minor of the dominant. The Conclusion, in the same key, is somewhat extended, containing a Coda and return to the first.

The Development deals with the two chief subjects and a fragment of the third. After this we hear the Reprise, with the second and third subjects and Coda transposed to the tonic, and in exten

* Von Bülow appropriately terms this an "Intermezzo between two tragical night pieces."

sive Coda, or Termination, in which the different subjects are again
passed in review. These are interspersed with some Passages and
a Cadenza. This is, as we have seen, a considerable deviation from
the regular sonata plan.

Amateurs, who have read the romantic account of how Beethoven composed this piece in the lampless music-room of the blind
girl, with the streaming moonlight as a guide and a text, know very
little of the deep sorrow and disappointment, the hopeless fervor,
and the almost dreadful despair which this sonata expresses. The
moonlight fancy has served its purpose, and hereafter the Sonata
should not be associated with its former fictitious title.

The principal peculiarities of Op. 28 are, au enlargement of the
Second subject, an extended Elaboration, principally of a small fragment of the first subject, and a Coda taken from the first theme.

Op. 31, *No*. 1. From the beginning of the first subject to the
introduction of the second there are no subsidiary themes or digressions. The Second theme appears in *B*-major (the original key-tone
is *G*). The Conclusion is short. The Development deals exclusively
with the principal theme, and contains considerable Passage work.
The re-appearance of the first theme is curtailed. After the Conclusion there is an extended Coda, with a few new features. The
middle movement, *Adagio grazioso*, is a very material enlargement
of, and deviation from, all previous middle song movements. The
Rondo, also, is of peculiar and original design, with several subsidiary themes, some development of the chief motive, and a capricious
Coda. This latter seems to be incorrectly or, rather, prematurely
indicated in the standard editions. No cadence is effected until just
before the Adagio. Here, with the alternate Adagio and Allegro,
is where the afterthought occurs, and accordingly this is the Coda.

Op. 31, *No*. 2. This is written upon a Dual Theme. The first
is this *Largo:*

The effect of the long-drawn chord is emphasized in the original by
the suspension of the *A-major* chord below.

Here is the other and more animating part of the subject which
follows the first:

Eg. 319.

The motive of the second subject is taken from this latter, while the development deals principally with the *largo* phrase. This subject (a) and response (b) alternate again in the relative major, the second part of the subject being continued through twelve measures. The original motive then appears in minor, allegro, as a bass subject, responded to by this soft but plaintive phrase:

Ex. 320.

This is continued throughout the page, the bass all the time growing in importance until the response above consists of merely a mono tone. The Second subject is more extended and continuous. It is in *A*-minor, and consists for the most part of vanishing and re-ap pearing figures. This movement has no Conclusion, strictly speak ing—and why should it? The composer was in Fairy-land (fairies also have their woes), and not obliged to be philosophical.

The Development begins with three long-drawn major chords. *D*, *B*, and *F*-sharp, *Largo*. The Allegro is then resumed, and the Elaboration continues somewhat after the fashion of what has been mentioned as to the bass solo and treble response. This wanders through various regions, and at the end there are ten measures of Coda as a return to the first theme. After giving out the first *largo* phrase, as before, there is a remarkably human Recitative in *D* minor. Then a Section of the Allegro motive, and the Recitative is repeated in *F*-minor. Now, in place of the natural Allegro se quence, as at first, there appears an Episode of twelve measures, leading to the return of the Second subject, as at first, except the transition. The last eleven measures may be considered Coda. The middle movement is an Adagio, and the Finale a remarkable con clusion to the whole.*

This analysis of the first half of Beethoven's piano Sonatas has already led us to a very decided anticipation of the Romantic style in music. This path, which his genius conceived, and his strength accomplished, has gradually led to the Anti-classical, the Romantic.

___

* The student's attention is here directed to the Development in Op. 31, No. 3. It is easily analyzed, and will prove instructive.

and the Realistic styles of the 19th century. With the thematic and necessarily pedantic style of the forerunners of Haydn, Beethoven had little affinity; the almost exclusively lyric style of the Italians and, to a great extent, of Haydn and Mozart, attracted him only for a while, as he soon found that his sermons upon Art and Immortality could not be preached in such a consonant language. As for the bravura displays of Steibelt and Kalkbrenner, he never accepted their doctrine, and so had not the trouble of putting it aside. He was to this extent an eclectic: that he used all styles when they served a purpose, besides creating a style of his own.

The Sonatas of Onslow, Von Weber, Schubert, and others, were mostly influenced by the grand sonatas of Hummel, and especially those of Beethoven from his opus 7 to the still greater concluding ones. The romantic tendency of Von Weber was more the result of the romantic librettos which he selected for his operas than a natural impulse in that direction. Moreover, the romantic style was created by Beethoven, and this is the other clue to Von Weber's romanticism, despite the fact he considered the composer of the Romantic Seventh Symphony "fit for a mad-house."

As for Schubert, he was an original creative artist, to whom melody and harmony came without the asking. But he was a silent worshiper of the Titanic Beethoven, whose personality was to poor little Schubert so colossal that for many years he never ventured into Beethoven's actual presence! Like Haydn, Schubert had no money to pay for lessons in Counterpoint, but who shall say that he learned less from the mute pages of his idol than he would have learned from Herr Professor? Schubert has been classed among the originators of the Romantic School, and in a sense this is true, as many of his works, especially for Orchestra, have a romantic vein. But the natural bent of his thoughts was lyrical, combined with a rich harmonic structure and a ceaseless flow of melody, which, as in the case of Mozart, gives to his subsidiary themes a connection which unites them into a continuous chain. In this respect Schubert has scarcely been equaled by any other composer. The purists have scolded about his "erratical forms" and his "want of contrapuntal knowledge," but as a matter of fact Schubert was a severe student, and, after his twenty-first year, a well-informed musician, not alone in theory, but in orchestration. If not, then he must have been a greater genius than even Dr. Grove believed him to be, for his last three Symphonies, as well as some of his Sonatas, are master creations, full of the most charming melodies ever conceived, rich and varied harmonies, originality of conception and form, and skilful contrapuntal treatment. * After studying and hearing Schubert's great Symphony in *C*, Schumann, the most prophetic of critics, wrote as follows :

"In listening to symphonies like this, we are transported to a region where we never remember to have been before. Here we have, besides masterly power over the musical technicality of composition, life in all its phases, color in exquisite gradations, the minutest accuracy and fitness of expression, and permeating the whole work a spirit of romance such as we recognize in other works of Franz Schubert. This heavenly, long-drawn-out symphony is like some romance of Jean Paul's, which ought never to end."

Schubert composed not for gold, nor even for fame; but simply as the birds sing, and as the flowers exhale their perfume. He used no chart, no square and compass, but he conceived such music as prompted Beethoven in his last hours to remark, "There is indeed a divine spark in Schubert."

Certainly it ought to be the privilege of such a man to create a model, or to vary the accepted models of his day. What became of the classical form when Beethoven composed his *D*-minor Symphony? It became a thing of the past, as we shall see in the last chapter. In the meantime let us be glad that the tardy verdict of his native city has at last placed the coffin of Schubert beside that of his illustrious ideal.

With respect to Mendelssohn (most of whose music rests upon the classical foundation) we will say but little until we come to the end of the classical period.

ILLUSTRATIONS.

Beethoven, Op. 27, Nos. 1 and 2; Op. 31, Nos. 1, 2 or 3.
Hummel, Op. 20, 81 or 106.
Schubert, *A*-minor, Op. 42 or 143.
Onslow, Ops. 7 and 22 (four hands).
Von Weber, Op. 24 or 49.

---

* His song, The Erl King, ought to be sufficient to establish his reputation among the immortals.

Chapter XLII.

THE SYMPHONIC FORM.

STRINGED QUARTETTE.   CLASSICAL OVERTURE.   CONCERTO.

THESE are based upon the Sonata form: in fact, they are frequently identical as to formula.

The Symphony is usually more extended than the Sonata. This is principally owing to the fact that the various principal and secondary themes admit of repetition in the symphony more readily than they do in the sonata. For example, a theme given out by the stringed orchestra may be repeated by the wood-wind * or the brass instruments with such different effect that the repeated melody' sounds almost like a new subject. In adapting the same theme to different kinds of instruments the composer is naturally led into a different arrangement, which also adds variety to the repetition. This is illustrated by the following example:

Ex. 321.

At (a) and (b) we hear the difference in tone-quality between the blow and the stringed instruments, and also the difference in execution. The reiterated notes are perfectly easy on the violins, and these

---

* The composition of a full Orchestra is as follows: 2 Flutes, 2 Hautbois (*Oboi*), 2 Clarinets, 2 Bassoons (*Fagotti*), 4 French Horns (*Corni*), 2 Trumpets (usually Cornets), 3 Slide Trombones, 1 Tuba, 1 pair Kettle Drums (*Timpani*), and stringed instruments in proportion —about thirty-five. Other instruments employed for special effects are: English Horn (*Corno Inglese*), Bass Clarinet, Double-bass Bassoon, Saxophone, Piccolo and Small Clarinets, Triangle, Cymbals. Tenor and Bass Drum, Gong 'Tam-Tam', Tambourine, Castanets, Bells, Great Organ, and Harp. The Violins, Violas, Violoncellos, and Double-Basses are spoken of as the *Strings*; *Wood-wind* applies to the wooden blow-instruments—Flute, Oboe, Clarinet, English Horn (when employed), and Bassoon; *the Brass* includes Horns, Trumpets. Trombones, and Tuba; the *Percussion* instruments (pulsatalic) are those which mark the rhythm and the salvos—Drums, Triangle, Cymbals, Bells, and Tam-tam.

give to the repetition of the phrase a more animated character
Another difference in the Symphonic Form is, that the principal
subjects are more extended, or certain secondary themes, which grow
out of the principal ones, are more frequently employed. What is
called Conclusion in the Sonata seldom appears in the Symphony
but in its place there is a Return, or brief Coda, either for the repetition or the Reprise. After the Reprise there is a final Coda more
extended. Sometimes this consists of a brief citation of the last
themes, and sometimes it is in the nature of a Conclusion or Termination. In Mozart's first Symphony in G-minor there are three
subjects in the First division, which is repeated. The Second division contains but a few measures of development, and then comes
the Reprise. In this the Second subject is given in tonic minor in
place of relative major. The second division is also repeated, and
finally there is a Coda of fourteen measures. In such cases there is
no third division. In the Symphonies of Haydn the first division is
invariably repeated, as in the Sonata. In the Mozart Symphonies
the first division is seldom repeated, and frequently the themes are
so numerous, or of such nature, that no development appears.
These are the main points of distinction between the Sonata and
Symphonic forms, and though the observing student will find exceptions in numerous standard works, the Symphonic form may be
generally understood as we have stated it.

Herewith is a brief analysis of one of Haydn's most popular
Symphonies, and one that was written in his full maturity, that
It is known as the "Oxford." Preceding the *Allegro Spiritoso* there
is a short Introduction, Adagio. The Allegro commences with these
four measures:

as a Preliminary Motive, and as a preface to the more important
Principal Subject, which is this:

This continues for fifteen measures, when the Preparatory motive is
again introduced in the capacity of an intermezzo. This time it is

extended to five measures, and then the main subject recurs and modulates to *A*. The first motive is then introduced in *D* (four measures), to lead to the Episode or Transition in *D*-minor. Simultaneously with the ending of this, the Second subject appears in the Dominant, thus:

Ex. 324.

At the end of this (which is but eight measures in length) we have a briefly extended period, or Coda of three measures! The Development begins first with the Second subject, and then the First, and afterwards fragments of both are employed simultaneously, and in canonic style. The Episode is also employed, as well as the principal part of the first subject. The Reprise is the same as at first, with exception of a subsidiary theme as solo for the basses, and some transitional matter. The Second subject recurs in the tonic. The Coda begins with this:

Ex. 325.

After this is a brief Recollection (of the second subject) and a Stretto founded upon a fragment of the first subject.

The second movement is a very graceful and lovely Adagio in *D*-major, followed by an episodical second subject in *D*-minor. The return of the first subject is the same as at first, with an interesting and rather plaintive Coda.

The third movement is a bright and characteristic Minuet. Part II to this contains the three-measure phrases previously mentioned.

The fourth movement, a Presto, is thoroughly characteristic of the genial old composer. The First subject is repeated, with slight changes in the orchestration, and then a second strain (not a second subject) follows. After a subsidiary theme we hear a series of harmonic sequences leading to the dominant, in which key the Second Subject appears. There is a short Conclusion and Coda in form of a transitional return to the first division, D. C. After the double bar we have the Development, principally of the first subject, then, after the transition, the Second subject in *C*, modulating through *D*, and to *E*-minor. Then an anticipatory Return from the Elaboration to the Reprise. This latter takes place where the first two periods (Principal subject) recur, exactly as in the beginning of the Presto, excepting the repeat. After a short transition out of the key and back, the Second Subject recurs, as in the first division, transposed to the tonic, G. The Coda begins in the basses, just as the violins and flutes are making the cadence of the second subject:

Ex. 326.

The fragment of principal theme used as the motive of the Conclusion in the basses forms an United Period here (third measure of our quotation). After twelve measures of this, the Recollection commences.

From this it will appear that the outlines and construction are not materially different from the classical sonata form. The internal arrangement and the incidental details are necessarily more varied and polyphonic, owing to the large number of instruments. (This Symphony was scored for one flute, two hautbois, two bassoons, two horns, two trumpets, two kettle drums, and the string quintette— about twenty-five or perhaps thirty performers).

A sketch of one of Mozart's Symphonies composed in 1773 will now be given as a contrast to the one from Haydn. This Symphony in D is No. 14 in Litolff's Catalog; No. 23 in that of Breitkopf and Härtel. It opens with an introductory section (M. P.) *tutti*, and the Principal subject commences in the string orchestra, with the motive in the bass. This first subject, with its subsidiary passages, is of unusual length (for this symphony), but the different periods are closely connected, and contain some clever bits of counterpoint. (Observe the 39th, 40th, 41st, 42d and 43d measures.) The Second subject, composed of antiphonal phrases (the hautbois responding to the violins), is in the dominant. The Conclusion begins at the end of the Second theme, and as it illustrates one of the essential differences of internal construction between piano and orchestral music, the first few measures of the Conclusion will be quoted:

Ex.327.

None of these parts except the horns can properly be termed complemental, for each is important and characteristic, yet they are all conceived so clearly that they can be comprehended even upon first hearing. As this design is clearly impracticable upon the piano as a solo, and yet, as the parts are all essential, it is plainly a symphonic one. At the end of this there is a short Coda, as a return to the Principal theme (in the bass). No Development appears anywhere in the Symphony, except that the entire work is in one sense a development of these notes of the principal subject:

Ex. 328.

(Mozart's motives require but little illustration.)

After the Coda the entire first division is repeated literally, with the prescribed transpositions back to the tonic. The Coda leads directly into the Andante, without any pause or rest. This Andante contains two distinct themes, with an Eingang of five measures after the Second, as a return to the first. This Eingang is again used as a means of connecting the Andante with the Finale, * Presto assai.

* This is the first instance of the kind which the author has noticed (P. E. Bach's plan being different). This continuity and connection of movements has recently been revived, as in the favorite E-flat Concerto by Liszt, and many recent Symphonies.

This is a peculiar species of Rondo, the Principal subject of sixteen measures occurring five times without alteration! As a relief to this there are three short periods in the dominant, then the repetition of the first theme. Following this is a Middle Theme in *D*-minor, with a short appendix as a Return. The three-period part is then transposed to the tonic as a Second subject. After repeating the first theme for the last time there is a short Coda constructed out of the chief motive of the first movement :

Ex. 329.  etc.

and the movement is at an end. The second and third movements are decidedly inferior to the first. There is, however, a remarkable affinity and unity between the various motives of the different movements, and it would be difficult to imagine a more naïve and sunny piece of music than this little symphony with its bright and confident Allegro, its amiable Andante, and its frolicsome, hurrah-for-a-good-time Finale.

It would be manifestly unjust to this great musician to close even this brief review of his works without mentioning some of his more important Symphonies. Attention is therefore called to the second *G*-minor Symphony (No. 550, Köchel), beginning like this:

Ex. 330.

which, with the " Jupiter," was composed in 1788. It is not only a mature work, but, in the author's opinion, the greatest piece of symphonic writing up to that date. It represents Mozart in his most artistic and serious mood. The themes are purely instrumental, and of a loftier type than most of the music of that period. The formal construction is unrestricted by arbitrary rules, yet the theoretical details are as correct as if they had been arranged by the erudite Albrectsberger. The first movement is an enlargement of the Symphonic form of that day. Each of the principal subjects is extended, and that, too, without tacking on a Coda here and there; but by means of native growth and a finely conceived thematic development.

The Elaboration is most effective, and truly remarkable. The two principal themes are first reviewed, and then made to battle

against each other.   During this and what follows, much is made of
the first three notes quoted in Ex. 330. The last eight measures
before the Stretto are particularly touching and beautiful.   There
are four movements to the work, three in *G*-minor and one in *E*-flat
major.   The Finale is also in Sonata form.   A characteristic of the
melodic structure of this symphony is the frequent use of the harmonic form of the minor scale, with the augmented second both ascending and descending.   The full score of this Symphony should
be examined; but if that is not practicable, the author would recommend Kirchner's very clever arrangement for two pianos, eight
hands.   By making a detailed analysis of the work it can then be
played as Kirchner has arranged it, without difficulty, and with instructive as well as pleasurable results.   But without the analysis
the Symphony had better be left in its mute paper cover.

THE CLASSICAL OVERTURE.

Mention has been made in Chapter XXX of the popular Operatic
Overture being, so far as form and contents are concerned, a Potpourri; but the Classical Overture is written as a musical exposition
of some scene, or poem, or historical character.   When Mendelssohn
was asked to describe the wonders of Fingal's Cave, he replied:
"It cannot be told—only played."   Accordingly his overture upon
that scene is the musical record of his impressions and recollections
of that marvelous subterranean cavern.

Schubert's Overture, Op. 26, to the story of "Rosamunde" is a
good example.   The plan is this: Introduction in *C*-minor, somewhat dramatic, and with a lovely, short theme, heard in various
unrelated keys.   The principal movement then commences in *C*-
major, *Allegro vivace*, with a First subject of considerable length,
and a subsidiary theme to lead to the Second subject in the dominant.   This is succeeded by an elaborate Conclusion and Coda, and
then a transition back to the first theme.   There is no Elaboration.
The repetition of the principal themes is the same as at first, with
transitions to and from the tonic, and the overture finally ends (this
was the hardest part for Schubert) with a rather brilliant Termination, in which he changes the metre from ¢ to ⁶⁄₈.   The themes are
very fascinating and the workmanship good.

From what has been written about the Potpourri-Overture the
student must not conclude that all operatic overtures are in this
formless style.   Those of Mozart, Cherubini, Von Weber, and the

still greater ones of Beethoven, are pure classics, being inferior to the Symphony only in length.

THE CONCERTO.

The great Concertos are written almost exclusively for Piano, Violin, or Violoncello, with orchestral accompaniment. The former are the most numerous, owing to the advantages which the piano possesses in power, compass, and *timbre*—the latter being so different from that of the orchestral instruments that its softest tones are easily distinguished.

Though the Concerto is ostensibly an elaborate solo with orchestral accompaniment, the construction is something of a compromise between the solo Sonata and the Symphonic form. Since Beethoven composed his Choral Symphony the lines of demarkation between these two forms have become wider, as will be seen in the last chapter.

The orchestra usually sounds the principal motives in their unembellished state, by way of Introduction. In Hummel's *A*-minor Concerto, Op 85, the orchestral introduction is considerably extended, introducing to our notice all the principal motives, even the transposition of the Second subject from the relative major (where it first appears) to the tonic major, as in the last of the Allegro. After a transition in the horns back to the original key-tone, the Solo enters. The formal construction usually begins here, as the Solo takes up the different subjects in their natural order, surrounding them with fioriture, arabesks, embellishments, variations, passages, cadenzas, etc. This plan is similar to that of Mozart, who was the creator of the modern piano concerto. This natural expansion and amplification, together with the more or less antiphonal style which results from the frequent responses between Solo and Orchestra, constitute the distinguishing features of the Concerto. We should also mention the orchestral intermezzos which come in simultaneously with the closing of the different periods or climaxes by the solo instrument. These Intermezzos are termed "*tutti* passages," [*] and are naturally extraneous to the Sonata form, as we have seen it, though the tutti frequently does more than mark the climax and sustain the interest created by the development of a Solo passage. It frequently acts as a continuation of the musical representation, and prep...

---

[*] Tutti refers to the employment of all the instruments simultaneously but in sense it applies to the orchestral passages, without the solo instrument

the way for other views which are to be unfolded. There are usually
three movements to the Concerto—the Dance form seldom being
included.

The Concerto is the highest exemplification of the Bravura Style
and possesses some advantages over the solo piece. The orchestra
coloring not only affords great variety, but in cases of complex am
plification or variations of a motive by the solo instrument, the
melodic outlines may be given to the orchestra, thus elucidating
what might otherwise be difficult of comprehension. Nearly all
composers have written concertos, from Bach and Mozart, down to
our own Whiting, Nicholl, and MacDowell. The tutti parts may be
played upon a second piano, or organ, which is still better, as it does
not require so great a strain upon the imagination as a two-piano
arrangement. A partial list will be found in the Compendium.

CHAMBER MUSIC.

Chamber music includes all classical music intended for a small
and select audience, written for a few instruments, from a duet to a
decet—a flute, oboe, clarinet, horn or piano being added to the string
quartette or quintette, which is the standard of chamber music.

If we select as an example the String Quartette (first violin, second
violin, viola and violoncello), it may be briefly described as a miniature Symphony. The contents and form are nearly the same as those
of the Sonata. The String Quartette is, however, a characteristic
class of music, which, if it lacks the variety and grandeur of the Symphony, yet has these advantages: The parts are more intimately related to each other, and there are comparatively few extraneous or
superfluous parts. Each instrument has its own individual melody
or sub-melody, and tells its own story, or joins in chorus with the
others. At the same time the voice-parts are not so numerous as to
prevent their thorough and complete comprehension and enjoyment.
And this four-voiced polyphony is a great advantage which the Quartette possesses over the solo Sonata, without mentioning the dreamy,
delicious and ethereal quality of the sustained passages in a quartette
—an effect which the greatest pianist can never hope to equal. Indeed, it would not be saying too much if we class the String Quartette
and Quintette as the purest and most exclusively musical of all styles
of instrumental music. The human voice can alone outrival the
tone of the violin; but the violin can, with perfect ease, execute
so many passages and transitions that would be impossible to sing-

ers, and with a continuity and variety of tone-color, also impossible in vocal music, that the advantages are greatly in favor of the Violin Quartette The Chamber Music of Bocherini, Haydn, Mozart, Hummel, Beethoven, Onslow, Schubert, Mendelssohn, and Schumann must be heard to be appreciated. A piano arrangement of chamber music is so unsatisfactory that the author does not recommend it as an illustration of this style.

ILLUSTRATIONS.

Symphonies: Haydn, "Oxford" in *G*.

Mozart, No. 23, *D*, and the one in *G*-minor arranged by Kirchner (Edition Peters, No. 2273, b).

Beethoven, Larghetto to Second Symphony, Op. 36, or Allegretto to the Eighth Symphony, Op. 93.

Overtures: Mozart, Don Juan or Magic Flute.

Beethoven, Fidelio (in *E*).

Schubert, Rosamunde, Op. 26.

Mendelssohn, Fingal's Cave, or Ruy Blas.

These and the Symphonies should be played as duets or duos, or with eight hands, two pianos. Selections, including Concertos, will be mentioned in the Compendium to this book.

PART XI.

Chapter XLIII.

PROGRAM MUSIC.

REALISTIC, CHARACTERISTIC AND DESCRIPTIVE.

SINCE the production of Don Giovanni, The Creation, Oberon, and especially the Op. 67 of Beethoven, there has been a gradually increasing tendency among creative artists towards a more definable and tangible musical expression. Previous to the birth of Haydn, instrumental music was not sufficiently known and developed to assume the functions of a Language, except in the hands of those giants, Bach, Handel, and Gluck. Those masters wrote not alone intellectual and ideal music, but considerable tone-painting also. But the imperfection of many of their instruments, the undeveloped state of instrumental music, and the restraining canons of musical theorists, were serious obstacles in the way of characteristic or descriptive music. Haydn was sixty years acquiring the skill which enabled him to compose The Creation. In addition to his musical inspiration and spontaneous flow of melody, he had here not only a connected narrative, but a detailed, guiding text from beginning to end. Haydn's previous life of servitude, even with the vexations and entanglements included, never could have inspired such music as his great oratorio contains. A higher motive and a more definite plan than could be gathered among courtiers, lackeys and *intrigante* was necessary to the production of his greatest work. Mozart, who had quicker perception, and the benefit of a cosmopolitan life, learned the lesson before he was thirty; and whoever has listened to his Figaro, Don Giovanni or Magic Flute (not to mention his great symphonies), must realize that instrumental music, even one hundred and four years ago, could portray other sentiments than those of vague fancy and psychological phenomena. The operas of Von Weber are still more realistic, and confirm the impressions left upon our minds by Mozart. (The Opera is here mentioned on account of its pronounced character, which does not require a skilled analyst to point out the significance of this passage or that. If the operatic scene represents the iniquitous Don being engulfed in the infernal abyss, every one may judge for himself whether the accompanying music is appropriate and descriptive, or whether it is a mere blatant fanfare.)

In the Pastoral Symphony Beethoven has drawn the veil from instrumental music, and with no other text than scenes remembered and impressions formed he proceeds to tell us in his own inimitable way of the freshness and simplicity of rural life; of the " scene by the brook," with its smooth musical flow; the carols and twitterings of the quail, cuckoo, nightingale, and yellowhammer; of " the merry gathering of the country people," the characteristic dance the gathering storm, its full raging fury; the lull, and the final Allegretto, marked by Beethoven " Pleasurable feelings, interwoven with thanks to the Deity, after the tempest." Fearing that certain musicians might ascribe more to the music than he had in mind, Beethoven appended to the score these words: " More an expression of feeling, than a painting." As for the critics, Beethoven cared little for them. \ They called him mad, neglected Mozart, starved Schubert and condemned to musical perdition Berlioz, Wagner, Schumann, and every creative artist who did not continue to plant their seeds in the sterile soil of Bach and the classical formalists. / When these same critics review a new work they seldom fail to draw on their imaginations for interpretive details and translated meanings, many of which would greatly surprise the composer of the music. But, *au contraire*, let an humble author (in his desire to correct the common belief that music is a mere mechanical conveyance of agreeable sounds) endeavor to point out the more significant passages in a tone-painting, and, lo! a numerous tribe of these excellent gentlemen will unsheath their swords and proceed in the most systematic manner to decapitate and mutilate him. Woe to the unwary wight who dares to brave their ancient canons! (This inconsistency has been pointed to before.) But it has evidently become a part of the unwritten creed of these reviewers to pshaw every attempt, whether literary or musical, that is not in their catalog of " purely instrumental music."

But the student is herein advised to accept the teachings of the great creative artists whose genius has raised music high above its former terpsichorean and dry, ecclesiastical character. Our rules and our theories must conform to the productions of the men who have created the art of music, not to the dictum of those whose duty is merely to point out the results which have been accomplished by the productive artists. When theorists informed Mozart that his music was " wrong," he had the courage to reply: " Heretofore it was wrong—henceforth it shall be right."

Every year since the production of the Pastoral Symphony has added to the list of Program Music; and a considerable quantity of the best music of the present time is either Realistic, Characteristic, or Descriptive. One has but to examine a first-rate catalog to be convinced of the multitude of high-class compositions of the Program order. And even the most obstinate of critics, in reviewing a work like Rubinstein's " Tower of Babel," cannot resist the temptation to enter this new realm of music. The following quotation from J. S. Dwight will prove this: * * * " Next the Hamites chant a monotonous and *arid* tune in *C*-sharp minor, with ceaseless tramp in empty fifths and fourths in the accompaniment. A gray picture of Sahara, worthy of Félicien David." And Dr. Grove, in his excellent esthetic analysis of Beethoven's Pastoral Symphony, ventures upon hypothetical ground in several instances, as thus, writing of the very droll episode in the Scherzo: * * * " but, it, perhaps, may picture some burly rustic in hob nails taking the dancing ground to himself for manifestation of his special clumsiness, after it had been occupied by the prettiest lass of the village, whose lithesome grace made everybody envious of her happy partner." This refers to the short movement in ¾ metre in the midst of the " merry-making." The description is most excellent, and shows keen analytical perception, as well as a considerable confession from a critic who is ever placing a finger to the lips, and disclaiming all intention of telling what the music means.

Much stronger and more explanatory is the foot-note which Von Bülow wrote to the joining of the last two movements in Beethoven's Sonata on the Departure, Absence and Return. He says: " The mourner's grief at the absence of the beloved friend has found expression in plaintive monologue, and then follows a moment of unconsciousness, softly mingled with a suspicion of his speedy return. We can almost see the solitary one, wandering with downcast look,

which suddenly brightens; a lifting of the eyes, a cry of rapture and
then a hastening to meet the newly found friend!" Von Bulow
makes no apology for this revelation. He is something more than
a theoretical scholar and a critical annotator. He is a disciple of
Liszt and Wagner, an interpretive artist, and a man of immense
information and profound knowledge.

The author had occasion, in another work, to refer to the enlarged
sphere of music as it now exists, and the innumerable means of ex
pression which the art now embraces. Indeed, the material avail
able for tone-painting to a man like Rubinstein or Saint-Saens is
(aside from their inspirational power) so immense as to be almost
incomprehensible!

But even with these vast resources they have never attempted to
represent, by means of instrumental music, a detailed narrative.
Nor has any reputable author endeavored to deduct abstract ideas
from a tone-poem, or to name the color of a musical heroine's hair.

There are certain freaks who attempt to describe in music " the
entrance of General Taylor into the city of Mexico," the " advance "
of a particular regiment at Waterloo, etc. There have, also, been
certain quasi musical scribblers who have tried to pull away, not
alone the veil, but the very draperies from Music's Goddess. But
certainly the sins of these misguided transgressors should not be
charged against composers who select a motto, or a poetic text, as a
basis for their inspirations, nor against the author who endeavors to
point out the particular connection between certain of the poetic
contents and the analogous passages in the music.

"Am Genfer See," by Bendel, is an excellent book of music,
without the accompanying poem of Leo. But with the addition
of this we are taken into the confidence of the poet-musician and
permitted to accompany him on his delightful journey. In place
of detracting from the music, the poem rather enhances and eluci
dates it. Not every composer would attempt a musical exposition
of this romantic poem, and certainly none but a gifted musician
would have succeeded, as Bendel has, in producing a highly artistic
series of tone-pictures, appropriate, suggestive, and beautiful.

Indeed, if so many music-teachers and reviewers were not either
too obtuse or too biased to give their pupils and their readers
more information with regard to the descriptive and realistic char
acter of certain compositions, our people would find more enjoy
ment in listening to music, and we would have fewer cases of

bankrupted orchestral and choral societies. And until this infor
mation is more fully given, a large majority of people will continue to withhold their patronage from what *they* consider a
merely agreeable auricular sensation. Far from being repelled by
a piece of Program music, we should rather be attracted to it,
for a poor composer will show his incapacity much sooner on
account of the betraying text which he adopts than if he had
confined himself to the "pure instrumental style," in which the
form and structure may be as correct as the "Consecration of
Tones," and yet have no relevant meaning.

Compositions of a realistic or descriptive character, in short,
all high-class Program music, is herein recommended, not altogether
on account of the peculiar interest (born, perhaps, of curiosity)
which attaches to them, but as matter of instruction and general
benefit to the earnest student of music. With a *morceau* like
Schumann's Warum it will be sufficient for the class to know that
a question is asked and a regret expressed. The imagination, of
course, is not to be robbed of its vocation.

There is considerable analogy between the painter's and composer's art; not only in results attained, but in the *modus operandi*.
Form, rhythm, tonality, etc., have their corresponding processes in
painting. A colorless picture, such as "The Crossing-place," by
Halfnight, may be taken by way of comparison: First, there is a
Draught as to the bounding lines, and enough of the general character of the picture to indicate whether it is a marine view, a land-
scape, or a portrait; next comes the Sketch, in which the details are
sufficiently indicated to show a foreground of the opposite banks of
a small stream, with trees on either side, and something of linear
perspective; finally we come to the Delineation. Here the details
are perfected by means of light and shade, and the natural distribution of the illuminating rays. The result may be briefly stated: In
the foreground a small, shallow stream, winding from left to right,
and away in the distance; on the left a female figure merging from
the path through a river forest to the open; a boat moored to the
nearest bank; water-lilies and swans floating upon the water in the
foreground; stone steps leading to the landing on the left, with a
corresponding pier on the opposite shore. In the distance a cottage
and a church, half hidden by the oak and elm trees, with a broad
streak of light in the center, outside of the shadow lines and extending in perspective to the limit of optical vision—altogether a faith-

ful and pleasing pastoral, and one that might inspire a composer
with very musical sentiments, for there is a peculiar similitude
between painting and music. Both appeal to the imagination, and
depend largely for their effect upon the connection existing between
outline and seemingly adventitious details. Thus we may ascertain
from the picture the location of the scene, the life of the people, and
that the housewife is returning from the field beyond to her home
on the opposite bank of the stream. We may also determine whence
the light proceeds, and the time of year which the scene represents
In like manner a bit of Spanish rhythm, a fragment of Scotch, Hun
garian, or Chinese melody might be the means of elucidating a
musical composition; for it is such peculiarities as these infused into
the music which gives it what Mr. Edgar Kelley calls *atmosphere*
Thus a smack of bell melody, or some well-known chime; a boat
like motion; a bugle call, or a hunting-horn signal; a rapid spin
ning accompaniment and innumerable other adventitious details,
become important indices in descriptive music; and are as proper
as the devices in painting which enable us to say, the hour is noon,
because we see no outlying shadows, or the season is autumn, on
account of the color of the foliage. These are extraneous circum
stances, but they add to the completeness of the picture, and assist
the imagination in its endeavors at divination.

ILLUSTRATIONS.

F. Bendel, Op. 135, "Six Stories in Tones," Little Red Riding Hood,
    Cinderella, etc.
"Fairy Tales," by Gurlitt, Max Vogrich, Merkel, and Reinecke.
Van der Stücken, Op. 8, "Gnomes, Nymphs and Reapers." Dances,
    after Shakespeare's "Tempest."
Jos. Löw, Op. 485, "Paul and Virginia" (Piano Duet).
Saint-Saëns, Op. 40, Danse Macabre (Dance of Death), after the poem
    by Cazalis.
Von Weber, Op. 65, "Invitation a la Danse."
Templeton Strong; Sounds from the Hartz Mountains. Seven
    Characteristic pieces (four hands).
A. Jensen, "Erotikon," Op. 44. Seven tone pieces. 1, Cassandra. 2.
    The Enchantress; 3, Galatea; 4, Elektra; 5, Lament of Adonis
    6, Eros; 7, Kypris.
Bendel, Op. 139. "Am Genfer See." Six tone paintings, following
    the poetic text of Leo.

The author has seen no translation of this strange poem, but it furnishes so many keys to the beauties and significant parts of the music that the teacher is advised to procure at least a rough transcript for the benefit of the class. The illustrations should be performed somewhat in the order of their enumeration, as the first is especially characteristic, and every one who remembers their childish lore will appreciate the significance of the music.

Another beautiful selection is the Op. 485 of Löw. A brief poetic text in German and French is placed as an explanatory motto at the commencement of each of the musical numbers. The composer has caught the poetic spirit of the poem and transferred it to sounds in a remarkably artistic humor, and it is one of the most characteristic and beautiful of all the small Program pieces. In the Fairy Tales the interpretation may be mostly left to the imagination. The Selections from Conductor Van der Stücken are excellently written and happily conceived; but these should be preceded by a short study of Shakespeare's Tempest which has inspired so many composers.

The Op. 65 of Von Weber has been so thoroughly analyzed that the author will merely call attention to the delicate suggestiveness and characteristic nature of the piece. (Notwithstanding the beauty and significance of the music, it is usually strummed out after the two-pints-to-a-quart measure of ball-room waltzes.)

The Symphonic Poem by Saint-Saëns is probably the most realistic piece of descriptive music ever written, and it is important that the class should hear a performance of this opus, but they must be forewarned to expect nothing euphonious or beautiful. The subject, though once looked upon as a portentous and credited phenomenon, is, of course, too antinomious a matter to be considered otherwise than as a phantasm. It is, moreover, the very antithesis of whatever might be properly called beautiful. In short, it is a very ugly theme. But it inspired M. St. Saëns to produce a remarkably weird, ghoulish, and spectral composition, and one that would have done honor alike to the scientific skill and the abnormal imagination of Berlioz. This opus was scored for orchestra, but the most effective arrangement for our present purpose is that of E. Giraud, two pianos, eight hands.*

---

*A complete explanatory analysis of the Danse Macabre will be given in " The Language of Music."

The Op. 44, of Jensen, will require some explanation from the teacher if it is to be understood by the pupils.

In a review of this lesson it would be well to read a brief description of some tone-picture like the "Paul and Virginia," and then play selections from the work in miscellaneous order, to prove the ability of the class to specify any of the eight numbers.

Chapter XLIV.

THE ANTI-CLASSICAL EPOCH, AND THE MODERN ROMANTIC SCHOOL.

INTELLECTUALISM, REALISM, MODERN-CLASSICAL, AND ROMANTIC-CLASSICAL.

THE causes which led to the modern Romantic styles in music are too multifarious and conflicting to admit of detailed enumeration in this volume. And, independently of these agencies, the author has for a number of years past been satisfied that for enlargement of design and novelty of expression we owe as much to the natural spirit of progress as to the extraneous influences of poetry, legend, politics, and social revolution.

Human interests and motives are so prone to cupidity and lead in such sordid paths, that artists are instinctively impelled towards some self-existent or ideal state, the antithesis of what goes to make up our daily life.

The influences of nature, on the contrary, offer consolation, delight and elevating precept. The flowery aroma of the garden; the graceful winding stream midst blooming valleys or towering mountains; the gorgeous, thousand-hued sunset—all these fill the ear with a sense of perfection and satisfaction. Even the smallest flo of forest or glade is a type of perfection! And so there is a const strife between the carnate flesh and the ethereal spirit: one, already in the abyss, endeavoring to drag us down; the other, dwelling among the flowers and the stars, striving to elevate us.

Though it will be in consonance with our previous course and progress to look upon the new styles and forms as the natural process of art-evolution, yet every new path must have some objective direction, and so we must inquire, what expression is sought, and what goal is to be reached. We must first separate the real from the unreal, the natural from the supernatural. With the entity of the former we are supposed to be familiar. The latter includes Dragons, Griffins, Giants, Gnomes, Ghouls, Goblins, Witches, Spectres, Dryads, Tritons, Naiads, Nymphs, Elves, Fays, Genii, Sprites, etc. The Elves, Fays, Sprites, Nymphs, Sylphs, and Naiads come within our conception of the beautiful; the others are either repulsive, terrible, or awe-inspiring. Among these creatures and spirits are those which inhabit the interior of the earth, water, air, and fire.

Empiricism, transcendentalism, spiritualism: the doctrines of Schelling, Hegel, Mesmer; in short, whatever is strange or incomprehensible has had its effect upon Romanticism. The legends of Lorelei, of the Erl King, Frithjof, and the race of giants also had their share, as we have seen. Add to these the numerous vital and chemical phenomena, some of which were analyzed in Chapter XXVII, and it will be apparent that practical life and Baconian philosophy possess but little attraction for the poet, the artist, or the composer. As for the romantic poets, the following quotation from Novalis will serve as a criterion: "We dream of journeys through the universe— is not the universe in *us?* The mysterious road leads but to our innermost soul; we are Eternity. The outer world throws but shadows upon this realm of light." Yet this is not stranger than the miracles which form part of the three principal religious creeds: Buddhism, Mohammedism, and Christianity. And yet the very mainspring of animal life is a mystery, not less remarkable than the seemingly unsupported planets of the universe.

Music, not being a definite language, must be preceded by poetry, painting, or sculpture, wherever the expression goes beyond physical or psychological emotion, or vague fancy. No Art can give complete expression to an ideal; but what one lacks, another may supply. And thus the peculiar power and province of each has at last become known and recognized. As a rule, what is most vague and mysterious is best adapted to music; hence the Romantic finds its most natural expression through the medium of melody, harmony, and rhythm.   The Music-Dramas of Wagner all founded upon mythical subjects, are proof of this.

Though the romantic style in music is a product of the present century, yet the elements and subjects of romanticism are coeval with vital existence.   It was not, however, until the latter part of the 18th and beginning of the 19th century that the many legends doctrines, phenomena, and supernaturalisms which have been men tioned, began to coalesce and center around the new temple of thought, wherein the unreal becomes real—fiction and legend be come truth and philosophy.

Inventors, innovators, and discoverers have ever been discredited and jeered by the world, who, like the flock of sheep, will continue to scramble over the fence, even though the bars be down   Galileo, Columbus, Fulton, Monteverde, Beethoven, Berlioz, Schumann, Wag ner, have all been persecuted and maligned.   Happily these clouds of prejudice have been dispelled, and all will be clear again until some other genius of innovation appears, when history will repeat itself in conventional fog and tirade.   This will surely come to pass; for time and the elements are constantly adding new conditions to the old.   And we may expect ere long to see a piano-forte whose imperfect mechanism will not require from fifteen to twenty years to overcome, and perhaps a violin which will not remind us of *felinus intestinus* when out of the hands of a Joachim, a Sarasate, or a Wilhelmj.

BEETHOVEN.

By the time the music critics had become accustomed to Beet hoven's Romantic Seventh Symphony the giant was ready to hurl his Choral Symphony at them, 1824*.   This puzzled them still more and they were not long in concluding that the choral part was "heterogeneous," and that the entire work should be cut down and trimmed into a "producible form."   But the master was sure of his doctrine, and fortunately there were those like Schumann who real ized that the evolution of art is as inevitable as the evolution of nature.   The purists and the conservatives beheld with dismay the gradual disintegration of their favorite forms and models, and at once sounded the war-cry—*the preservation of the Classical*.   What ever went beyond, or fell short of their abstract idea of form, became known as Anti-Classical.

* Grove's historical and critical Analysis of this greatest of all Symphonies is published in pamphlet form, and ought to be read by every student of music.

The last and greatest compositions of Beethoven, the Program
Music of Berlioz and Liszt, and even the piano works of Schumann
and Chopin, all fell within the pale of their displeasure, and were
accordingly condemned.   Schumann, at an early age, buckled on the
editorial armor, not so much in his own defense as that of Beethoven,
Schubert, Berlioz, and Chopin, and in favor of progress and art-
development.   In this he was greatly aided by Mendelssohn, who,
though now considered a classicist, was shortly after the death of
Beethoven enrolled under the revolutionary banner of the anti-
classics.   In addition to the newspaper panegyrics and frequent per-
formances of Beethoven's and Schubert's greatest works, which
were brought about by the Schumann coterie, they devoted themselves to the general advancement of Art, to the encouragement and
defense of Chopin and Berlioz, and afterwards of Gade, Brahms, and
other rising geniuses.   Schumann and his party, realizing that human
joys and woes had already formed the burden of too many songs and
symphonies, brought forward the doctrines and tenets of Romanticism in all its different phases of beauty, mysticism, grandeur, terror,
and diabolism.   Berlioz and Liszt were soon attracted to the new
school; then came Wagner, Raff, Von Bülow, Rubinstein, and the
other illustrious ones.   Though not all sharing in the weird fancies
and radical mysticisms of Jean Paul, Novalis, and Schumann, yet
there was this common bond between them: They were all enthu-
siastic advocates of the continued advancement of Art-principles
(which included the last sonatas and string quartettes of Beethoven
and his Choral Symphony), and were opposed to the non-progressive
purists, whom they called Philistines and fossils.*

An examination of the music composed immediately after the
death of Beethoven reveals the principal styles of the present day.
The Romantic world, already introduced by Beethoven, Schubert,
and Von Weber, was more fully explored and illustrated by Berlioz,
Schumann, Mendelssohn, Gade, Raff, Heinrich Hofmann, Rubinstein, and others.   The only features of Romanticism which attracted Mendelssohn and his followers were those naïve and sunny
elves of the fairy world of Oberon and Titania.   Berlioz and his
followers seized upon the transcendental ; demons, ghouls, spirits
of evil, satanic power, and even the horrible din and uproar of
Pandemonium—these were the themes in which they delighted, and

* Among these were Steibelt, Kalkbrenner, Von Weber, Field, and Moscheles.

which they expressed so powerfully that their style may be called the Realistic.

BERLIOZ.

Hector Berlioz, the greatest of all French composers, was almost exclusively an orchestral writer. He discarded the arbitrary out lines of form and the prescribed rules of construction, trusting to the consistency of the subject he chose to illustrate. Berlioz never undertook the composition of a work until he had formulated a plan embracing the incidents to be illustrated by means of music. Being a literary scholar he wrote his poetic program first, and then set himself to the task of expressing through the agency of instrumental music the scenes, emotions and incidents indicated in the program. If a scene is devoted to Marguerite, the motive remains the same; but when Mephisto enters, we have diabolical music to indi cate the fact in no uncertain manner. That he should write a sec ond subject in a certain key, at a certain point in the movement, because there was a rule to that effect, these things he never seri ously contemplated. Had he been obliged to do so, he would have preferred to remain a medical student. In addition to his literary and musical gifts, Berlioz was the inventor of " Program Music," and, in his prime, the greatest of all masters of the Orchestra.*

CHOPIN.

Chopin, though he has had as many imitators as Schumann or Mendelssohn, and more than Berlioz, never aimed at the establish ment of a school. Caring but little for Chorus or Orchestra, he de voted his genius exclusively to the Piano. Though he discarded the abstract form of the Classicists, and composed in a manner both original and beautiful, yet his music is classical in this sense that the conception and execution are in the highest degree artistic. Many of the dances of Chopin are perfectly common in form, like other dances; but the peculiar turn of the melody, the rich and varying harmonies, and the exquisite grace of the ornamentation stamp them with the seal of genius.

Chopin's natural tendency was, however, towards more compact and coherent single forms. In place of a preconceived and formal plan, as to number of subjects, elaboration, tonality, etc., he followed

---

* At the beginning of his musical career, Wagner wrote a letter from Paris to Liszt in reference to Berlioz, and concluded with these words: "There are to-day only three musi cians alive in this world—you and I and he."

fancy on its natural course, keeping the same motive, but ever changing and beautifying it to the end. The Berceuse is one of the best types of these remarkable single forms.

Another peculiarity of the Polander's music is, the numerous chromatic progressions, both melodic and harmonic, wherein the tonality, like a phantom, becomes vague and indefinite. From a technically analytical standpoint the works of Schumann are anal ogous; but here the resemblance ceases. (*So many discriminating articles have been written about the music of these two masters that the author has designed to include merely a few critical paragraphs upon the relationship of the different composers to the prevailing styles of the present day.*)*

LISZT.

Another style, the Rhapsodical form, as we have previously termed it, owes its origin principally to the King of Pianists, Franz Liszt. The idea of appending to the music a descriptive Program of the scenes and emotions to be portrayed was borrowed from Berlioz, but the form and the manner of conveying these impressions are different. The Symphonic Poems, "Les Preludes" (after Lamertine), "Tasso," "Mazeppa," the music to Dante's "Inferno," etc., are in the Rhapsodical form. Here we have the first instances of the continuous, uninterrupted melody, the constantly changing tonality, and the characteristic motives of Berlioz, all united with the most brilliant and *bizarre* effects of orchestral coloring. However much these works may be decried, it is well to remember that Art is boundless, and that the *Inferno* serves a purpose.

INTELLECTUALISM.

There is still another school, and an important one, headed by Johannes Brahms. As this is something of a compromise between the two opposing styles, it might properly be termed the Romantic-Classical.

Certain natures are at all times conservative, as opposed to radicalism. This is true in art as in politics. Herr Brahms and his colleagues belong to this class, and it must be admitted by whoever looks on from a neutral standpoint that the conservatives have preserved society from annihilation, though frequently driven by Radicalism into a more liberal and progressive policy; and so one becomes a complement to the other, like storm and sunshine.

---

* See Frederic Chopin—His life, work, and letters. By Moritz Karasowski. 2 Vols. The John Church Co.

The Romantic-Classical style preserves as much as possible of the outlines of classical form, while enriching it with all the advantages of the most recent orchestral and harmonic possibilities. In other words, whether Herr Brahms undertakes to express his own emotions and psychological aspirations, or chooses the motto of a Romantic subject, the classical ideal is ever before him, with its conservative edict, "thus far shalt thou go"; and the powerful impressions which his music leaves upon us are mainly the result of his strong individuality and consummate mastery of the laws and details of the art. Hence it has been termed (and not without reason) musical Intellectualism. (Those who find Brahm's music "dry" and "non-melodious" will do well to remember that purely euphonious melody has been nearly exhausted, and that a single melody is not calculated to express more than a passing fancy or a transient emotion.)

WAGNER.

With regard to the music of Richard Wagner but little can be said in the present work. His Music-Dramas are conceived upon so broad a plan, and require the co-operation of so many arts and sciences, that an adequate idea cannot be formed from the music alone. However, it is too important a matter to be thus passed over, and we will include a brief review of the main features of the music.

An important feature of Wagner's Music-Drama consists, as is well known, of the characteristic and symbolical phrases and sections, called Leading Motives. These motives are used from time to time as the action of the Drama may require, and serve to connect the incidents and elucidate the text. They are also employed as the basis of the musical development—whole scenes frequently being elaborated out of one or two of these small themes. Another feature of these music-dramas is the uninterrupted and seemingly interminable melodies, which keep expectancy at its highest pitch, until relieved by subsequent action or interest. The harmonies are immensely various and highly colored; the conception bold and poetic; and the orchestration may be classed among the wonders of human accomplishment. The composer was also a poet, a scientist, and a connoisseur of painting, sculpture, scenic-effect, stage mechanism, and even of terpsichorean figures and evolutions; for all these accessories are constituent parts of his scheme. That a radical of his class should create unjust enemies and over-zealous friends is but a natural consequence; but the student is earnestly advised not to be unfair in

influenced by the former, who look upon Wagner as a methodical
lunatic, who wrote merely jargon and cacophony; nor by the latter,
who confidently assert that the Prophet of Bayreuth was the only
truly great musician, and who do not scruple to throw literary dirt
even at the statue of Beethoven! This is bad policy and worse
ethics.

MENDELSSOHN.[*]

The history of art affords few exceptions to the rule that misery
is the mother of genius; and when an exception does occur we are
wont to say that it lacks heroism, or is too plastic and effeminate—
forgetful of the fact that not alone grace and charm and gentle spirit
belong to woman, but that fortitude is also stronger in the feminine
than in the masculine character. Heroism is mostly the product of
circumstance. But we cannot always recite the chronicles of Homer.
Hood and Burns, Drake and Bryant also have their niches to fill. In
fact, the world is as deeply indebted to Reinecke for his beautiful
little Sonatinas and Cantatas as to Rubinstein for his colossal Ocean
Symphony. Years ago some crotchety critic affirmed that Mendelssohn's music was "only fit for school-girls," and we have heard the
remark quoted by village professors who, if they should live centuries, would never become as thorough musicians as was Mendelssohn
at the age of fifteen. If every composer is to be compared with
Beethoven, few will survive; but the detractors of Mendelssohn
never think of comparing Haydn to Beethoven, for that would
destroy a popular idol; and yet, if a considerable quantity of
Haydn's music were published under an American name it would
be pronounced unmitigated trash.

Few musicians have exercised such a powerful and beneficial
influence upon the art as Mendelssohn. It was he who resuscitated
the Cantatas and Masses of Bach; who first conducted worthy per-
formances of Schubert's then unheard Symphonies, and who helped
to popularize the greatest works of Beethoven. It was he who first
recognized Gade and Joachim, and extended a helping hand to the
neglected Berlioz; and to him the world is indebted for the Leipzig
Conservatorium. Small minds do not conceive or execute such
designs as these; nor do inferior composers create a style of their
own, with such imitators and followers as Jadassohn, Hiller, Reinecke, Taubert, Gade, Sterndale Bennett, Heinrich Hofmann, and

---

* See "Mendelssohn, a Memoir," by F. Hiller, or the life of Mendelssohn in Grove's
Dictionary.

Brahms. If we are to judge (as some have done) by the "Lieder ohne Worte," or his unsuccessful attempts at dramatic music his position in art would not be a very high one; but we might as ill, judge Schubert by his volume of dances, or Beethoven by his Baga telles. Let us rather acknowledge that it was Mendelssohn who conceived the most characteristic musical representations of the fairy world, and that his "Elijah," "St. Paul," 42d Psalm, Scotch Symphony, and most of the concert overtures are masterpieces of the most refined grace, deep learning, and ingenious fancy. Aside from this he was an accomplished and courtly gentleman, with a lofty sense of justice and honor, and whoever passes animadversions upon him should do so with a respectful salutation. Mendelssohn was by nature and education a classicist, and many of his composi tions betray rather too much of the lyrical tendency, a fault com mon to both Mozart and Schubert. Yet his best works contain but little of the conventional form and outline. The Scotch Symphony is a wider departure from the abstract form, and quite as original as the "Im Walde" of Raff.

ANALYSIS OF THE SCOTCH SYMPHONY, OP. 56.*

The first movement, *Andante con Moto*, is in the form of an Introduction, though it opens with the leading motive, which is this:

Ex. 331.

The entire Andante is confined to this motive, which appears in various forms; but the tonality is principally that of *A*-minor, as the introduction is in the nature of a meditation.

The *Allegro*, also in *A*-minor, commences very softly, thus

Ex. 332.

This section is repeated in *C*-major. The theme then returns to *A*-minor, and is led in a different direction from the first quotation. As this Allegro movement savors somewhat of Intellectualism

* For interesting particulars concerning the scenes and memories which in pi 1 th opus, the reader is referred to the "Standard Symphonies" by Upton These details are necessary to a perfect understanding and enjoyment of such works

(being mostly a development of one motive), it will be instructive
to observe the thematic treatment:

The last of this is a descending, rather than an ascending melody.
    The germ of the whole movement is this:

The rhythm of this plays an important part.
    The next phase of the subject is this:

This becomes continuous by means of the duet. Just before the
lower part makes its cadence upon the tonic, the upper part re-com-
mences the first theme as before—measure 22. The melody is then
led in a still different direction (see 26, 27 and 28), and the cadence
postponed till the *Assai animato*, which occupies the place usually
assigned to the Second Subject; though, to be precise, there is no
second subject to this movement. Here again the continuity is
maintained by means of the duet, each part making its cadence as
the other begins.
    At the end of this stretto passage (*ff*) the first theme returns in
this form, accompanied above by a plaintive melody—a natural and
graceful outgrowth of the leading theme:

Ex. 336.

After a brief transition there is a strain of peculiar construction and
effect beginning at 99. The harmonic accompaniment is almost
dramatic in its coloring, while the melody is typical of bouyancy
and freedom—especially these intervals:

Ex. 337.

Attention is also called to the transition commencing at 111 and
the charming effect of the chromatic progression founded upon the
pedal-note *B :*

Ex. 338.

This leads to a climax upon *E*-minor, in which key the Refrain is
heard. This strain forms what would be, technically, the Coda but
it expresses so well the burden of one's thoughts in connection with
Holyrood and its hallowed memories, that a more suggestive title
than Coda seems necessary. Besides, it corresponds perfectly to our
definition of Refrain.

At the end of the Refrain, after a beautiful *perdendosi* the first
part is repeated.

The Elaboration commences with a vague reminiscence of the
chief motive, very skilfully interwoven with a characteristic hint of
Scotch music:

Ex. 339.

The harmonic outer parts (*c*-sharp and *g*-sharp) are plainly suggest
ive of the drones of the bagpipe.

The interior melodic design is continued until the 175th measure,
where the regular Development commences:

Ex. 340.

Observe the difference between the principal theme in the bass and
the same theme at the beginning of the Allegro. (The student will
learn more about thematic development from such comparisons than
from whole volumes of dissertations upon the subject.)

The counter-subject above is also to be noticed—firstly in regard
to its contrapuntal construction, (Mendelssohn was a complete mas
ter of Counterpoint,) and then in reference to the esthetic effect of
this counter-theme against the more animating melody below.

From 185 a new and brighter element is introduced into the
upper part:

Ex. 341.

The bright little flute figure, the principal theme in the violins, the
harmonic accompaniment in the middle, and the interrupted imita
tions between the 'Cellos, Faggots, and Basses, as they respond to
one another, all these are to be observed. Attention is also called
to the transitions, and the mode of development from 206 to the fol
lowing stretto, 214, which is an abridgment of the Stretto in the first
part. Following this is a fragment of the Refrain in *E*-major (origi
nally *E*-minor), though the minor sixth (*C*-natural) is still retained
as a local coloring.

The Elaboration is continued through the Return, with a lovely
theme in the 'cello part from 250 to 270. The harmonious construc
tion of this Return, and the manner in which the cadences are post

poned, are worthy of careful examination. The Reprise takes place just before the 'cellos make their cadence, thus forming an united period, and preserving the continuity of the design

Ex. 342.

The Reprise, mostly in *A*-minor, is similar to the first division, with slight differences in the treatment and the tonality. The Refrain is in *A*-minor, and at the end of this the Coda commences. This is mostly a Recapitulation, with the addition of a somewhat stormy passage in chromatics.

The Stretto then follows, and the movement closes tranquilly with a recollection of the Andante.

The entire movement is an elaboration of one principal motive, and it is well to remember that this is one of the earliest examples of this style, which has since become very common among living composers.

The Second movement, *Vivace non troppo*, in *F*-major, is a rustic scene, very different from the melancholy and mystery of Holyrood. This movement is known as the Scherzo (owing to the position it occupies between the first Allegro and the Adagio), but it is not a Scherzo either in form or character; it is rather an Idyllic Caprice, the construction of which is peculiar and worthy of study. The principal theme is so characteristic and full of good humor that we quote the first eight measures:

Ex. 343.

This forms the basis of the entire movement, being developed in the most capricious but artistic manner. The auxiliary theme commences upon the last of the 71st measure, and this is also elaborated

---

* This melody is composed exclusively of the old Scotch (Pentatonic) Scale

But the auxiliary theme is a mere relief and passing fancy, whh
serves as an episode to the song and dance and contentment of ·e
peasantry.   Altogether it is a very wholesome antidote for mel.·
cholia or ill-humor.

This is the movement to which Schumann referred in the follc·
ing eulogistic words: " I doubt whether a Scherzo more full of gen's
has been written in modern times."

The third movement is the song, *Adagio*.   The leading melo/
is mild and plaintive, with occasional touches of the heroic, ming'l
with the song of regret for past glories.   The movement is free fru
conventionalism, save that a few strains remind one of the sai:
composer's "Lobgesang."   Another gem of the Symphony is t:
fourth movement, *Vivacissimo*, ₵, a species of Scherzo of remarkal:
animation and continuity.

There is nothing remarkable in the construction, though it;
perfectly free and spontaneous.   The principal charm lies in t:
conception and the total effect, which are altogether delightful.   T:
Scherzo is joined to a short Finale in $\frac{6}{8}$ metre, *Allegro maesto*,
which is much more reposeful and sedate than the other par,
reflecting the serious and religious character of the people.

All the movements are to be performed continuously from beg·
ning to end.

SCHUMANN.

Robert Schumann made the same discoveries as did Berlioz ¡
reference to the necessity of a new style.   But each labored in a d
ferent country, uninfluenced by the other.   Schumann also wrc·
from a definite plan, and though he used fewer connected narrativ
than the Frenchman, yet nearly all Schumann's music was the resı
of thought, as well as feeling, and seems to have been inspired I
some definable idea, emotion, or incident.   The Scenes of Chil·
hood, Papillons, and Carnival, with their suggestive titles and me
tos, are faithful miniature tone-poems, of which the Manfred mus
Op. 115, with its continuous text, is the climax and culmination.   '

Though Schumann never wrote a page of common music, y
his compositions are not so uniformly excellent as those of Chopi
The last works of Mozart and Beethoven were their greatest: b
the later opuses of Schumann are overclouded and sometimes di
torted by the mental and physical sufferings of his declining year.
Very little apology, however, is necessary ; his works are firmly co
ceived, artistically executed, original, earnest, and significant.

ANALYSIS OF THE ANDANTE AND VARIATIONS FOR TWO PIANOS
OP. 46 (COMPOSED IN 1843).

This Opus has been selected for review, partly because it repre
sents an important style of composition, and also on account of the
peculiar charm and originality of these variations.

The Principal Theme consists of two regular periods. We quote
the last section (which is similar to the first) in order to illustrate
the transformations which follow:

Ex. 344.

The notes of anticipation and the harmonic appoggiaturas are the
principal features of the theme. The first variation consists in
diminishing the value of the melodic notes, and echoing the different
groups, first by one piano and then by the other :

Ex. 345.

The second period is similar in treatment, though in the last sec
tion the direction of the melody is slightly altered, and a chromatic
bass progression introduced, which has an important bearing upon
what follows.

The next period, marked *un poco piu animato*, is something of a
relief to the preceding; but by preserving the same rhythm, and in
troducing the chromatic bass progression, previously mentioned, the
effect of unity is maintained :

Ex. 346.

'From this quotation it is apparent that neither the original theme
nor the original harmony are visible ; and it is doubtful if any one
except Schumann could conceive a period like this, so seemingly
different from the original, yet so intimately connected with it in
effect.   It is, therefore, to be considered a variation.

From the second period of our last quotation the composer con-
structs a subsidiary theme (reference-letter C) of which this is the
first section :

Ex. 347.

To show the origin of this, we will copy a few measures of the previous strain :

Ex. 348.

The intervals are almost identical, the rhythm, phrasing, and sequence being different.   (The slurs in Ex. 348 merely show the
similarity of the intervals in the two strains.)

The period commencing at C is continued without a second period, by means of material changes in the tonality and the antiphonal treatment incident to a Duo.   The period beginning at D is
a variation of a variation, thus :

Animato.

Ex. 349.

There are two periods in this style, which have someth g ɩ a catch-me-if-you-can character peculiar to Schumann. (Compare the strains B and D.)   At E the first Piano has the first period of a Refrain, the motive of which is founded upon the theme of the .b ʋa ʋ in contrary motion.   The rhythm is similar to the original a:

Ex. 350.

Lento.

The second period is given to Piano II. beginning in *D flat* and with the melody in reverse order, but accompanied by the trumpet calls as before:

Ex. 351.

The original *Andante* then recurs, slightly altered in harmonic structure, but unembellished.   At F the original *Andante* theme appears, thus varied and transformed:

Ex. 352.

Animato.

f

The melody is not easily traced through this labyrinth of syncopation and appoggiaturas, but the notes with stems turned upwards will assist in showing the design.   The better way, however, is to sing the original theme while the variations are playing, which can easily be done, as the *harmonization is identical.*   But this only applies to the repeated first period—sixteen measures—as singularly enough the second period is taken, not from that of the original theme, but from the second period of the *Animato.* (Compare G with B f. st harmonically, and then with regard to the melodic outline, which also similar.)   It is neither possible nor desirable with such variations to indicate by means of accentuation the melodic theme. b t it is necessary that the performer should trace the design th ʋ ʋ and know every note of the *original theme* in order to imagine

a foreground and basis for the variations. Some prominence is als
to be given to the harmonic parts, which, being identical with th
original (especially at G), will assist the auditor in appreciating th
composer's thought and design. The original accents upon the dif
ferent phrases,

(Melodic outline of the Var. at G.)

Ex. 353.

remembering that every section and period begins upon 3 and end:
upon 2, are also necessary in the performance.

The Episode in *E-flat*, beginning at H, is intended as a contrast
to the preceding. The rhythm is borrowed from the variation D
though the sounds suggest a bolder sentiment :

Ex. 354.

The second period is something of a variation of the theme of
the Refrain, E. The last variation (I. Piano 1) is like this :

Ex. 355.

This is upon the original theme, slightly altered in its harmonic
substance. The original second period is worked out in the same
style, K. After a repetition there is a recollection of the umem-
bellished melody, L.

The Coda commences in the second piano part :

Ex. 356.

with the response by piano 1:

Ex. 357.

And so the vanishing melody is merged into a ritardando Passage M, in two parts, and ends tranquilly.

One objection to the ordinary variation form is the monotonous rise and fall of the cadences, owing to the frequent repetition of two regular periods. Our composer has obviated this difficulty to a considerable extent by commencing a period by one piano simultaneously with the ending of the other.

One quotation will illustrate this method:

Ex. 358.

Unity and continuity are thus preserved, and these add materially to the interest and the artistic effect. Of this style of variation our composer was both master and originator; and though it is in a comparative sense fragmentary, yet it possesses the advantage of being less labored and more of an artistic unfolding of a musical germ.

Schumann wrote a few sonatas and chamber pieces in the strict classical form, but these are inferior to his incomparable songs, and to his single and rhapsodical forms.

The Piano Quintette, Op. 44, is in Sonata form only so far as the first movement goes. But even this contains fewer motives and more continuity of design than the regular classical models.

Critics are generally agreed in placing Schumann's orchestra
works and cantatas below the piano pieces; though the *A*-minor
Concerto and the *B-flat* Symphony will always occupy high ground
But in the author's opinion his greatest opus is the Melo-Drama
"Manfred." Byron's weird and forcible poem seems to have pro
duced a powerful effect upon the composer, and inspired him to his
greatest effort. It is a masterpiece which will never grow old, for it
is possessed of the living spark of immortality.

CHOPIN. BRIEF ANALYSIS OF HIS RONDO, OP. 73, FOR TWO PIANO-FORTES.

It is not necessary to give a detailed analysis of this opus, for it is
so characteristic of the composer that nearly everything previously
stated in reference to the peculiar style of Chopin will apply to the
Op. 73.

There is a short introduction in antiphonal style, an ascending
Passage being responded to by a fragment of lyric melody in the
other piano part. The theme of the Rondo would be recognized by
any one familiar with his style, as the work of Chopin. It is this

Ex. 359.

This occurs three times in the course of the Rondo, besides the
variations and elaborations of the theme, and the recollection at the
close.

The main features are: An Intermezzo, digression, Second Sub
ject (lyric), occurring first in *A*-minor, and afterwards in *E*-minor
elaboration of the leading motive, and numerous abrupt and brilliant
transitions, of which the following is a specimen:

Ex. 360.

Several modulations and chromatic passages occur, in which, as was previously observed, no prevailing key is discoverable, but in place of that the scene constantly changes.

The principal transformation of the theme may be seen by comparing the extracts below with the original motive:

Ex. 361.

At (a) we have but the first two measures of the theme; after which a mere outline appears in place of the original second phrase, and this is accompanied in the *Secondo* by the principal motive in reverse order. The theme then passes into the second piano part in a still different form:

Ex. 362.

Ex. 363.

At (c) the peculiar turn of the melody is to be noticed; also the constantly changing tonality. Following this is a Cadenza, *a tempo*, and a perfect cadence.

After the pause the Coda commences with an exquisite recollection of the principal theme, founded on a tonic pedal-note. The last thirty-two measures form a Stretto.

The music of Chopin is more equal and uniform in point of excellence than that of any other composer. Mozart, Haydn, Schubert, and Raff composed too voluminously, and, per consequence, a considerable portion of their music is not only unequal, but unworthy of such names. But Chopin wrote just enough; and from the Op. 1, to his posthumous works, we are always sure of polite, as well as brilliant company. It may be that the green-house, the ball-room, and the art gallery are less satisfying than the meadows, the woodland songsters, and the pictures of nature; but these are mere opposite phases of life, and of the former, Chopin was the poet laureate.

This chapter will be concluded with a brief technical analysis of a work composed after the death of Chopin, Mendelssohn, and Schumann, and one which is remarkable even among the productions of the present time. This is the Piano Concerto in *A*-minor, Op. 16, by the representative Norwegian composer, Edvard Grieg. Thirty-five years ago this Concerto would have been considered angular in form, and lacking in euphonious character. At the present time there are few who would dispute that it is a faithful and artistic characterization of the genius of the North. The Concerto is written upon a Dual subject. After a prelude of one measure, by the horns and drums, the piano begins with the Preliminary Motive in unison, *ff*:

Ex. 364.

Attention is called to these intervals:

Ex. 365.

as they form the basis of the second subject, and also the motive for the subsidiary theme of the Orchestral Intermezzo. After five measures by the solo instrument the orchestra gives out the principal theme, and at the end of this (twelve measures) the piano commences its regular work:

Ex. 366.

The lyric phase of the principal subject follows this. Observe the peculiar effect of the augmented fourths in the melody, and the same melody in reverse order, in the bass:

Ex. 367.

also the harmonization of the first two melody notes by means of the sixth resolution of the Dominant seventh. In the 13th measure this is joined to the *animato*, forming an united period :

Ex. 368.

The accompaniment to this is the principal motive in the bass as counter-subject. An idea of the harmonic structure may be formed from this quotation :

Ex. 369.   Orchestra.   etc.

This consists principally of a series of secondary discords followed by an imperfect or a perfect triad. The harshest of the discords is introduced without preparation. After a return of the Scherzo figure, as per Ex. 368, the sequence of discords and triads is repeated in *G*-minor.

The next quotation illustrates a Continued Thesis :

Ex. 370.

Molto cresc.

This is accompanied by the orchestra in canonic imitation. The effect is as mazy as a half-remembered dream. The thesis contain four measures besides those quoted. Upon the final resolution the Second Subject appears, *più lento :*

Ex. 371.

The peculiar grace and tenderness of this theme afford a strong contrast to the prevailing sentiment of the music, and yet it is founded upon a fragment of the Preliminary Motive, as may be seen by comparing (a) with (b) :

Ex. 372.

The difference consists in omitting or including the passing tone between *b* and *g*.

Attention is also called to the effect of the echo by the flute and clarinet in the second measure (Ex. 371), and to the unexpected charm of the transition to *A-flat* and back to *C*. The same theme is then given to the piano, and embellished and enlarged. The last section of this theme is repeated, *più animato,* and this leads, without cadence, to a transitional Passage finally terminating upon the major key-tone (*ff*), *D*. Simultaneously with this cadence the full orchestra begins its first regular Intermezzo :

Ex. 373.

Here we have the dual subject more nearly combined; the flutes
and clarinets sound the Preliminary motive, and then the basses
give out a paraphrase upon the first part of the Principal theme.
This is continued for sixteen measures, when the principal theme is
thus developed:

Ex. 374.

While the melody and two violin parts remain the same during this
section, the scale progression in the bass supplies variety and change
of tone-color. This is accompanied by arabesque figures in the solo
part, and repeated a minor second higher. Just before the Reprise
the dual subject is again introduced, the orchestra having the principal motive, while the piano responds with the preliminary motive
slightly altered:

Ex. 375.

and afterwards to this:

Ex. 376.

Four measures of *tutti* lead from this to the Reprise, which is similar
to the first division. The Thesis previously mentioned now occurs
on the dominant, and the second subject is re-introduced in *A*-
major.

The Cadenza is fully indicated by the composer (a wise proceeding), the last part being in recitative form. The Coda then commences by the Solo, with a paraphrase of the principal theme, mostly
unaccompanied. This commences pianissimo, and works up to a

stormy climax, with portentous rumblings in the bass. The second phase of the leading subject here occurs in augmentation After eight measures of tutti the termination begins, and brings the movement to a close, with the preliminary motive descending and ascending.

The second movement is a dreamy *Adagio* in *D flat* major The Orchestra announces the subject, which is then embellished by the solo instrument. It is a finely conceived elaboration of one motive

The Finale returns to *A*-minor, *Allegro Moderato*, ¾ metre This is mostly an elaboration of the principal subject, which is thoroughly illustrated. The second theme is in *F*-major, beginning

Ex. 377.

p **Poco più lento.**

and continuing in the vague manner of an endless melody, through various tonal regions. After a brief exposition of this, the principal theme recurs, and the second theme is heard no more until it appears in a heroic form in the Termination. We have a few brief subsidiary themes as reminiscences of the first *Allegro*, but the prevailing sentiment is that of the principal theme of the Finale, which has the character of a Scherzo. Toward the close the metre is changed to ¾, with the same motive as a basis. The termination is in *A*-major, ¾ metre, with the second subject as theme, given out by the brass instruments *ff*, with the solo and orchestra combined. From our notice of the work it is evident that the outline and arrangement, though not formal or restricted, are not materially different from the improved model of Beethoven. The charm of Grieg's Concerto, however, lies in the peculiar nature and mold of the themes, the harmonization and the dignified treatment of the solo part Variations are not included as mere displays of bravura style, but as the natural embellishments of Fancy's weaving. The weird and rugged nature of the sounds are more an expression of Norwegian life and character than of any particular program: but, as the composer's native land was originally the favorite haunt of Romance, it is possible that legend has supplied some of the peculiar nuances.

It is of the highest importance that music students shall a just and accurate understanding of the merits of the great m

*The advantages, in point of unity and connection, in favor of the development single motive, have already been pointed out, and need not be dwelt upon here

posers and their different styles. The basis of this information must
necessarily be acquired through reading—after which the student
may continue his onward progress, and form his own opinions. But
a somewhat serious obstacle presents itself at the very outset, in the
prejudice, not to say ignorance, with which a considerable portion
of musical criticism is tinctured. Most of our critical opinions
come from Germany and Austria, and, per consequence, we see
through German spectacles, instead of viewing the different styles
through the lenses of an International field glass. The result is,
that after reading the current musical literature of the day (most of
which is a mere copy), one would conclude that there are only a few
great names in music, and these exclusively German : Bach and
Händel, Gluck, Haydn, Mozart, Beethoven, Von Weber, and Spohr.
And even then our Teuton friends quarrel among themselves as to
who comes after Beethoven : One party will exclude all except Berlioz,
Liszt, Wagner, and Brahms ; while the great Vienna critic, Hanslick,
will tell you that Wagner and Liszt represent noise, not music, and
that the successors of Beethoven are, Schubert Mendelssohn, Schumann, Chopin, Gade, Rubinstein, Hiller, Reinecke, Jadassohn, etc.
It is not difficult for a neutral with sober sense to discern the errors
and fallacies of these two extreme parties. In respect to Bach and
Händel, their position is secure, and no one now disputes their title
to fame. But this title was not bestowed by the music critics, but
by the great composers, such as Mozart and Beethoven. The position of Gluck, as an intelligent and gifted opera composer, is also
secure. The fame of Haydn owes much to a propitious star.
Placed at an early age in a financially independent position, with
one of the few fine orchestras in Europe at his complete disposal, he
enjoyed the rare privilege of trying his experiments with the orchestra in private, and thus correcting whatever was illy conceived.
Being industrious and talented, and with a permanent position, he
contributed not a little to instrumental music, and his " Seasons "
and " Creation " will always be heard with pleasure. A few of his
chamber compositions are also beautiful ; but his piano works could
very well be spared from the catalogs, and of the one hundred and
eighteen symphonies there is not a single one which, as a whole,
would interest an audience of musicians or connoisseurs. In our
review of the sonata form we gave due consideration to the works
of this composer, especially on account of the form, of which he
was a master; but a sense of justice compels the remark that he is

overrated, and that if Mozart or Schubert could have occupied such a position the result would have been much more gratifying. Boccherini, born two years before Haydn, was as much the "father of the Modern Quartette" as Haydn; and if the great Italian did not compose a Creation, it must be said in his favor that he wrote a much smaller quantity of trash. Meanwhile we hear very little of the Italians, Monteverde, Alessandro Scarlatti, Durante, Cherubini and Clementi. The Masses and Operas of Cherubini are in every respect great works, yet how seldom are they performed! The Sonatas of Dussek, Hummel and Clementi, though not equal to the great ones of Beethoven, are yet worthy of reproduction, and certainly far superior to the ear-tingling euphonism of Haydn's sonatas which have been drummed into our ears from infancy.

Mozart was a more universal genius, whose tomb no musician would think of visiting with covered head. Yet circumstances of penury betrayed him into the perpetration of many trivial effusions which, out of respect to his memory, ought to be destroyed, with the plates from which they are printed. His fame, however, will rest secure upon the last Symphonies and Chamber music, the Masses and Operas, and some of the Sonatas and Concertos.

Another hero, who owes his position to national pride and prejudice, is Spohr. An excellent teacher and a great violinist he surely was. A master of musical laws and mechanics, and a prodigious composer he was also. But that he ever had the slightest symptoms of inspiration, the author has been unable to discover Franz Schubert, though "to the manner born," remained during his life-time unacknowledged, save by a solitary friend. The critics saw only a small man, indifferently clothed, whose exterior was unromantic. But thanks to Beethoven's discovery, and to the exertions of Schumann and Mendelssohn and Grove, we now hear considerable about the Viennese composer. His fame is not yet fully acknowledged, but it will be. And what of the French composers? From current opinion, one would conclude that Berlioz was a lunatic; that Gounod, Bizet, Thomas and Massé wrote some "pretty, sensuous melodies," and that Saint-Saëns and Delibes and Godard are "promising young composers"!

Fortunately art is as broad and boundless as prejudice is narrow and restricted, and the genius of French character and invention forms an integral part of all that is artistic. That Berlioz was erratic and mad does not detract from his music, which deals with erratic

subjects. Beethoven also was mad when, in the fever of compos
tion, he poured a bucket of water on his hands—and into the apart
ments below. *Erratic* is such an excellent definition of genius tha
we will not take issue upon that ground, but merely record ou
opinion that a personality such as Berlioz's is one that cannot b
spared from the records of musical art. The operas of Gounod
Bizet and Massé are such an immense improvement upon the pot
pourris of Rossini, Donizetti, Lortzing, and Bellini that they ough
to be welcomed by every lover of music. That some of the melodie
in Faust are "sensuous" is merely a compliment to the composer
for what other kind of music would you write for Marguerite an
her devil-beguiled lover!

As for Saint-Saëns, he is one of the greatest composers of th
present day—serious, learned, and gifted. Even Delibes and Godar
are something more than promising—they are excellent composer
of the French school.

And the English composers also suffer the effects of nationa
prejudice—though at home they receive fair treatment, owing to th
commendable pride of the English people. But the names of Pur
cell, Bennett, Macfarren, Mackenzie, Cowen, Stanford, Gorin
Thomas, McCunn, ought to be known in every country when
music is cultivated.

Chopin also has been given a lower position on the roll of fam
than others of inferior genius—probably because he was of the Sla
vonic race. Contemporary criticism has always been imperfect an
contradictory, but with regard to the names like Monteverde, A
Scarlatti, Cherubini, Berlioz, we certainly should have accurate
information.

But some learned critic of the old world, with the film of preju
dice covering his eyes, gave a place among the illustrious to Spoh
and Haydn, to the exclusion of Cherubini, Schubert, and Berlioz
and directly it is translated into English, repeated as original by the
penny-a-liners, and eventually becomes standard opinion. Such i
the force of prejudice.

ILLUSTRATIONS.

Italian Symphony, Op. 56, Mendelssohn. (Four hands. Editior
 Peters.)
Andante and Variations for Two Pianos, Op. 46, Schumann.
Rondo for Two Pianos, Op. 73, Chopin.

Concerto in *A*-minor, Op. 16, Greig. (Orchestral parts arranged for a Second Piano appear in score with the Solo.)

For other selections, see Compendium, p. 331.

Chapter XLV.

AMERICAN ORCHESTRAL AND CHORAL WORKS.

AMERICAN musical compositions have for so many years been pshawed and elbowed into a corner, that the author is gratified to present a number of works which are entitled to the highest consideration. Yet there is still prevalent a belief that outside of the mechanical arts and sciences everything must bear an import stamp or a foreign label in order to give it value or credence, forgetful of the fact that a people who could conceive and establish the most powerful and beneficent government in the world's history are also capable of creating art-works. Thanks to a few patriotic music journals, and especially to that exalted master of Pianism, Wm. H. Sherwood, American compositions are now receiving general attention; and it is from a sense of justice, as much as from patriotic motives, that this chapter is undertaken.

SPRING SYMPHONY.

J. K. PAINE, *Op.* 34.

The poetic program for each of the different movements of this Symphony is as follows:

"Departure of Winter,
Awakening of Nature.
May-night Fantasy.
Romance of Springtime.
The Glory of Nature."

Ia. The Introductory Movement, Adagio, ⁴⁄, represents the dis
appearance of the wintry elements.   The 'Cellos give out the Winter
theme in *A*-minor, as follows:

Ex. 378.

This is succeeded by a secondary theme, and the Adagio is buil'
upon these two subjects:

Ex. 379.

At the close of the Adagio the Winter theme re-appears in Canonic
form, leading gradually to the Allegro, in *A*-major, ⁶⁄ metre.   Afte
sixteen measures prelude by the first violins the Awakening Motive
is announced by the 'Cello and Viola, and afterwards distributed
among the wood-wind in antiphonal style, like the songs and re
sponses of birds:

Ex. 380.

The principal theme then passes into the upper parts, and an effect,
ive anti-climax is attained by the introduction of this gay and
'sprightly rhythm:

Ex. 381.

Following this is a Transition to *F*-major, in which key the second
subject is announced by wood-wind:

Ex 382.

After one measure of triple metre (with a chromatic progr... ...)
the bass), the Conclusion begins like this:

Ex. 383.   Con.

At the end of the Conclusion, and before the Reprise, there is a tran-
quil Middle Part in place of the customary Elaboration. During this
part the Winter theme appears, somewhat altered, in both ... ...
tion and augmentation, interspersed with fragments of the Awakening Motive.   The Reprise is similar to the first in A-minor.

The Second Subject is introduced in a novel manner, after ... few
measures of Anticipation:

Ex. 384.   An   oboe   B.
Strings.   p

As the Violins end, the Oboe takes up the Second theme. The ...
is both bright and unexpected.

The repetition of the Conclusion is somewhat altered and
tailed, and merged into a Coda of considerable dimensions, ...
upon fragments of the two principal themes.

Throughout the entire Allegro there are frequent reminiscences of the Winter theme, in various guises, as may be seen from the quotation:

Ex. 385.

Numbers 2, 3, 4 and 5 are derived from the original, No. 1.

II. MAY-NIGHT FANTASY.

Scherzo, Allegro. The first part is in *D*-minor, ½ metre; Part II is in *D*-major, ⅔ metre; after which, Part I is repeated, with the addition of a Coda and Stretto.

Two noticeable features of this movement are, its unity of design and continuity of execution—there being but few terminal cadences in proportion to the length of the movement.

III. A ROMANCE OF SPRINGTIME.

Adagio, *F*-major, ¼ metre. This slow movement is a Rondo, with principal and secondary themes, episodes, etc. The treatment of the first theme is varied at each recurrence, and the movement closes with a beautiful Recollection.

IV. THE GLORY OF NATURE.

Allegro giojoso. *A*-major, ₵ and ⅜ metre. The final movement, in Sonata form, is constructed upon the same outlines as the first Allegro; *i. e.*, First Subject, Second Subject, and Conclusion; Middle Part, Reprise with transitions back to the principal tonality, and a Coda in form of Termination.

The Symphony is constructed upon the classical model, but the treatment is sufficiently free for the demands of the text.

As for the orchestration, it is characteristic, scholarly and effective.

NOTE.—For further particulars see "Standard Symphonies."

"THE PRODIGAL SON." SYMPHONY IN A, No. 2.

By S. G. Pratt. *Op.* 33.

The story of the improvident youth wandering from home breaking the commandments, reduced to penury and remorse and finally returning, amidst paternal joy and forgiveness, has been so frequently enacted that there can be no doubt as to its human interest, and adaptability to musical treatment.

Mr. Pratt has made three parts to his Symphony, corresponding to the natural divisions of the text from St. Luke.

I. *Allegro Moderato Maestoso.*

"And the younger son gathered all together and took his journey into a far country, and there wasted his substance with riotous living."

II. *Adagio. Andante.*

"And when he had spent all, there arose a mighty famine, and he began to be in want, and he went and joined himself to a citizen, who sent him into the field to feed swine."

III. *Allegro.*

"And he arose and came to his father. But when he was a great way off, his father saw him, and had compassion, and ran and fell upon his neck and kissed him."

From this it is clear that the music belongs to the Program order.

I. ALLEGRO MODERATO MAESTOSO.

The composer's program motto is "Pride, Pleasure, Carousal."

The first movement is constructed upon three principal themes, as follows:

Ex. 386.

A represents youthful confidence and bright anticipations.

B suggests something of the tempter's voice, and is antiphonal in its
    construction.

C typifies the dance, and the whirl of bacchanalian revelry. In the
    midst of these unlicensed orgies the warning voice of a good
    spirit is heard, but not heeded, for the Carousal theme proceeds
    on its wayward career.

These are the main outlines and significant features. Let us observe some of the details.

After the first theme has been continued in various forms, and,
by various instruments, it passes into the basses, accompanied by
two counter-themes:

Ex. 387.

The violin part represents a pleading voice, which is frequently
heard throughout the movement. It also forms good counterpoint
with the flutes and hautbois above, and the principal theme below.
The continuation of the first subject in the 25th measure:

Ex. 388.

becomes the counter-subject to the second theme, accompanied by
flutes and harp. The parts are then inverted and continued in transition and variation with good effect. An intermezzo in antiphonal
style intervenes between the second and third themes, founded on a
pedal-note by drums and basses. The first subject is then repeated
followed by a paraphrase upon the second subject, and a transition,
terminating upon a diminished seventh chord on ƒ-sharp. This pre-
pares the way for the Carousal theme, which immediately begins in
C-sharp minor, accompanied by castanets, tambourine and drum.
In the midst of this lascivious carnival, but after a diminuendo, the
clarinet and first horn sound the voice of warning, but without
entirely interrupting the carousal. This is in the nature of an Episode, as may be seen from the quotation:

Ex. 389.

It is somewhat remarkable as being the only instance we have observed of an episode introduced adventitiously without interrupting the prevailing theme. Observe that the violins have the continuation of the carousal theme, while the rhythm of this theme is kept up by the violas and 'cellos. The harmonic structure is also peculiar. The Elaboration deals principally with the first and third themes in the key of *F*. During this part there is an ingenious development of the chief motive in canonic imitation :

Ex. 390.

The second violins and viola each imitate the first measure of the first violin, the minor thirds of the diminished chord being favorable for this treatment. 'Cellos and wood-wind also join in this design. The first of the Reprise is similar to the initial part, but only the motive of the second theme is employed, and this passes from one instrument to another canonically, accompanied by fragments of the first theme. Farther on the three principal themes are employed in simultaneous juxtaposition. The design may be seen in the following compressed score :

Ex. 391.

The basses and fagots have theme I, horns, cornet and tromboues have theme II, the violins take the repeated figure of the motive to theme III, while the flutes, hautbois and clarinets sustain the upper harmony. This is continued for some time, until the strings scamper down the scale with the Carousal motive. Here the angel voice is several times heard, with its brief admonition; but the spirit of evil prevails. The movement ends with an exciting stretto.

II. ADAGIO. ANDANTE.

The motto in the score is: "Remorse, Repentance. Vision." The *Adagio* is an introduction to the *Andante*, and expresses the natural feelings of the spendthrift after his resources were exhausted, and he came to realize that he was bankrupt, not alone in money, but in morals.

The Adagio motive is this:

Ex. 392.

which is echoed by hautbois and fagot. The same motive is then repeated a fifth above, and continued as per example below:

Ex. 393.

By recalling the second verse of the text the student will not fail to perceive the significance of these tones. Note the peculiar effect of the rests in the second measure, the *b*-flat of the violins against the suspended *a* below, and finally the despairing wail of the 'cello, echoed by the second violins and viola. This is continued in transition, with an occasional impatient phrase of Allegro interspersed, and leads to the Andante. Here the motive is the same, but by means of a slight increase in the movement, different harmonic coloring, and especially the more definite course of the theme, a somewhat hopeful expression is attained:

Ex. 394.

This may be termed the Penitential theme: at least it is a very clever attempt at expressing through music the feelings of repentance. Still more of contrition is portrayed in the following section, of which we quote the first phrase:

An expression of grief pervades each of the voice parts he the counterpoint is also good. This is continued in an exte period and repeated with the theme in the first violin part Follow ing this is theme II, somewhat in episodical form.   It represents in retrospect the haunting remembrance of Prodigality :

Though this Prodigality theme (viola) stands in the place of the second subject, it is not included in the program of this movement (*i. e.*, Remorse, Repentance, Vision); yet what more natural than to suppose that in the midst of his poverty, dejection, and repentance the cause of this condition should force itself upon his mind?   The suggestive resemblance of this middle subject to the carousal theme of the first Allegro is to be noticed, also the effect of the pizzicato accompaniment by the rest of the stringed orchestra.   This is somewhat developed, and interspersed with a subsidiary theme resembling the more serious phrase of the second subject from Part I :

The Penitential theme then recurs, as in the first of the Andante, and gradually dies away in this dreamy maze of canonic harmony :

Something of the oblivion of sleep is here expressed, wherein the outlines are yet vague and indistinct.   The mind is thus prepared for the ensuing prelude of the Vision of Home.   The violins tremolando, with the remaining strings sustaining the *E*-flat harmony, all pianissimo, represent the peaceful state of slumber, while the harp, in gentlest touches, completes the fancied perspective

Ex. 399.

This dual state of present actuality and distant fancy of the dreamer seeing through hypnotic lenses his distant home, is thus expressed the violins, *here;* the harp, *there.* These four measures lead, by means of a perfect cadence, to the brighter key of *G*-major. The conception is not only original but beautiful.

Immediately following our last quotation is what may be considered, euphoniously, the handsomest strain in the Symphony. This is the third theme; or, in strict designation, the Episode:

Ex. 400.

The horns sing the familiar melody of days agone, accompanied by the aerial quivering of the violins, and the affirmative response by the basses, altogether a lovely and satisfying picture. After an equal period in this style, the duet theme passes from the horns to the clarinets, with this alteration in the accompanying parts:

Ex. 401.

With these themes the movement is continued and developed to considerable length, and finally ends in merest whisper.

III. THE RETURN. JOY AND RECONCILIATION.

The Finale is preceded by a brief Introduction. The first phrase portrays the rapture of father and son upon their reunion, followed by a plaintive monologue by 'cello and fagot in unison—a fragment of the Penitential theme. The themes of the *Allegro* are as follows:

Ex. 402.

The joy caused by the return of the Prodigal, and the feeling of thankfulness for his deliverance, are the principal sentiments of the last movement. Interspersed with these is the Penitential theme, somewhat altered, symbolizing the chagrin and repentance of our crest-fallen hero. The various principal and subsidiary motives are ingeniously combined and elaborated into an effective climax. Towards the close the organ is introduced for the hymn of thanksgiving, and the themes are broadened out by means of augmentation and fuller instrumentation.

SCENES FROM LONGFELLOW'S GOLDEN LEGEND.

SYMPHONIC CANTATA.

FOR SOLOS, CHORUS AND ORCHESTRA

By DUDLEY BUCK.

[Prize Composition, Cincinnati Festival, 1880]

There are so few leading characters and controlling principles in this work that we will give a brief epitome of the main incidents of the legend.

Prince Henry of Hoheneck is afflicted with an incurable malady, and having written to the famous physicians at Salerno, they inform him that he can be cured only by the blood of a maiden who will freely consent to die for his sake. Regarding the remedy as impossible, the Prince gives way to despair, when he is visited by Lucifer, disguised as an itinerant physician. The Fiend tempts him with an intoxicating nostrum, to the fascination of which the Prince becomes a victim. He wanders from home, and finds refuge in the cottage of one of his tenants, whose daughter Elsie, moved by a religious compassion for his fate, determines to sacrifice her life that he may be restored. Prayers and entreaties being of no avail to alter her determination, Prince Henry, Elsie, and their attendants depart for Salerno. On their journey they encounter a band of Pilgrims with whom is Lucifer disguised as a Friar. Upon reaching Salerno our friends are received by Friar Angelo, a Professor of the Medical School. Elsie persists in her resolution, despite the opposition of her attendants and the Prince, who now declares that he only intended to test her constancy. " I come not here to argue, but to die." Lucifer draws Elsie into an inner chamber and she bids farewell to her friends. But the Prince and attendants break open the door and rescue her at the last moment. Prince Henry is miraculously healed, restored to his possessions, and marries the devoted Elsie. The Prolog and Epilog will be noticed elsewhere.

SCENE I. PROLOG.

The spire of Strasburg Cathedral. Night and Storm. Lucifer with the powers of the air, trying to pull down the Cross.

The orchestra commences at once with the delineation of the scene. This descriptive part is mostly thematic, and founded upon what we may call the Storm motive, and the Lucifer motive. The principal features of these are quoted herewith.

Ex. 403.

(STORM MOTIVES.)

Ex. 404.

(EVIL MOTIVE.)

Ex. 405.

The Lucifer motive is given out by the Trombones and Tuba after the ascending climax of the storm music. What we call the Lucifer motive is a theme which suggests and typifies the Spirit of Evil. and it is frequently employed by the composer in this sense, as we shall see. (The continuation of this orchestral prolog affords a good illustration of Chapter XXXV.)

At the end of the cadence Lucifer calls upon the evil spirits to de-demolish the tower. The Lucifer motive here forms the principal orchestral accompaniment. The chorus of Spirits (Sopranos and Contraltos divided), sing their reply: "Oh we cannot! For around it all the saints and guardian angels throng in legions to protect it," etc.

Following this, the Cathedral Bells (represented by tenors and basses) are heard intoning the Latin Hymn, *Laudo Deum Verum.* The storm music, Lucifer's imperious commands, the chorus of spirits proclaiming their abortive attempts at destruction, and the solemn song of the Bells are again heard in alternate succession, until Lucifer admits his defeat and calls away his "Inefficient Craven

Spirits." As they disappear, the storm-music diminishes through a
descending passage of six measures, and the Cathedral Choir is heard
singing the Gregorian Chant with organ accompaniment. As this
chant is afterward used symbolically we will quote the motive

Ex. 406.

Attention is also called to the rococo style of this chant, which is
especially appropriate here. The Prolog terminates with the chorus.

SCENE II.

*Castle of Vautsberg on the Rhine. Prince Henry alone, ill and restless. Mid
night.*

The Orchestra plays an appropriate introduction, founded upon
Prince Henry's motive, the first phrase of which is as follows:

Ex. 407.

A sombre Recitative and Aria by the Prince then follows.
A few of the more instructive passages will be quoted. First is
the setting of the words, " My fervid brain calls up the vanished Past
again, and throws its misty splendors deep into the pallid realms of
sleep."

Ex. 408.

pal - lid realms,   the   pal - lid realms   of

Observe the peculiar effect of melody and harmony
" misty," " splendors " and " pallid sleep."

Another passage, illustrating the meaning of the w
p. 25 of the vocal score :

> " The thought of life that ne'er shall cease
> Has something in it like despair."

Ex. 409.

like   des - pair.

Cl. Fag. Horn.

the diminished seventh chord (forming a species (
dence), the distance of the intervals between the tw
the choice of instruments all contribute to the sign
effect.

SCENE III.

A flash of lightning, out of which Lucifer appears in the ga
Physician.

Following the first salvo we hear the Lucifer mo
as before.   After the Prince inquires the name of his
the motive of Evil appears in a contracted form, thus

Ex. 410.

After some words of apology the Fiend explains
that against your casement drives, in the village belo

etc. Here we have a suggestive reminiscence by the orchestra of the storm music from the Prolog, but mostly *piano*. At the suggestion of Lucifer the victim then proceeds to describe his ailments in a measured recitative, accompanied by the Prince Henry motive, until after the Fiend has read the mysterious prescription from Salerno, when the Lucifer motive re-appears. We pass over to where the Prince imbibes the infernal decoction and begins his song

> " 'Tis like a draught of Fire! through every vein
> I feel again the fever of youth," etc.

Here the voices of a chorus of Angels are heard in their soft admonitions, against the ecstatic song of the Prince and the infernal glee of the Tempter.

The student of part-writing may derive an instructive lesson from this Septette by observing the manner in which each of the parts is made distinct and comprehensible to the listener.

SCENE IV.

Elsie's Home. "Evening Song" on the lighting of the lamps.

This beautiful unaccompanied Quartette is so well known that we will not stop to comment upon it.

SCENE V.

Elsie's chamber. Night. Elsie praying.

This solo is also favorably known. We merely call attention to the religious fervor of the melody and the charming accompaniment.

SCENE VI.

The Pilgrimage to Salerno.

(FOR ORCHESTRA ONLY.)

Onward and onward the highway runs to the distant city impatiently bearing
Tidings of human joy and disaster, of love and of hate, of doing and daring

PRINCE HENRY.

Hark! what sounds are those whose accents holy
Fill the warm noon with music sad and sweet?

ELSIE.

It is a band of pilgrims, moving slowly,
On their long journey, with uncovered feet.

PILGRIMS.

Urbs cœlestis, urbs beata
Supra petram collocata,
Urbs in porto satis tuto,
De longinquo te saluto!

The above quotation from the poem is included as a **Program** to
this orchestral number, and not as a vocal text.   The music to th
hymn to St. Hildebert forms the basis of the movement, being hear
frequently and in different forms in this number.   The motive o
Prince Henry, somewhat altered, is heard in connection with th
Hymn, and the Lucifer motive appears as an episode (his Satani
Majesty being among the Pilgrims, disguised as a Friar).   The Pi
grims' chorus, however, predominates, and forms the refrain of th
Coda.

SCENE VII.

*Convent of Hirschau in the Black Forest.   Gaudiolum of Monks at midnigh.
Lucifer disguised as a friar.   Friar Paul sings.*

At the end of each verse of the Bacchanalian song the Monk
join in Chorus, forming altogether a spirited and characteristi
number.

SCENE VIII.

The Revel and appearance of the Abbot.

(FOR ORCHESTRA ONLY.)

"What means this revel and carouse?
Is this a tavern and drinking house?
Are you Christian monks, or heathen devils,
To pollute this convent with your revels?"

The quotation gives the clue to the music, which is one of th
most descriptive numbers in the book.   The Revel motive form
the burden of this number.   We quote a section:

Ex. 411.

After an extended period of this, the revelers sing a hymn (probably through force of habit), while the carousal theme continues. The theme of the Drinking Song is next introduced, as a component part of the carouse; and then we again hear a fragment of the Gregorian Chant. The themes of the Revel and the Drinking Song continue for some space, crescendo, until the climax of the carousal is reached, when a crash is heard from the full orchestra, representing bustle and confusion. It is the appearance of the Abbot. A brief quotation here will tell the story in tones:

Ex. 412.

Following this are a few fragments of the revel motive, piano, as a reminder, and then we hear the Gregorian chant above.

Ex. 413.

The movement terminates with this theme, Adagio.

SCENE IX.

A terrace overlooking the sea. Elsie Solus. Night.

A beautiful and suggestive idea is expressed here by poet and composer. As our heroine looks out upon the cloudless night

and the ocean beyond, her imagination weaves the **murmuring** ⟨
the sea into a sacred litany, and she fancies that "the stars com
forth to listen." Here an invisible chorus sings, *pianissimo*, "*Chris,*
eleison." The solo and responsive choruses continue until El⟨si
joins in the refrain *Kyrie eleison.* The effect is quite charming, an
serves to illustrate the deeply religious character of this heroin⟨
who would voluntarily immolate herself that another might live.

SCENE X.

Barcarolle.

(FOR ORCHESTRA ONLY.)

SCENE XI.

Chorus of Sailors at Sea.

We pass over these two episodical numbers, as they do no
demand special analysis.

SCENE XII.

The Medical College of Salerno. Lucifer disguised as a Friar. Enter Princ
Henry, Elsie, and their attendants.

The orchestra sounds an Intrada founded upon the Prince's mo
tive in minor. He inquires for Friar Angelo. The response, "H
stands before you," is followed at once by the Lucifer motive in th⟨
orchestra, giving us a symbolical representation of the ever-presen
Spirit of Evil. The dialog continues until the Friar inquires o⟨
Elsie, "Have you thought well of it?" The strings and wood-win⟨
then give forth this motive:

Ex. 414.

answered by the horns in antiphony:

(Noc - - te - sur - gen - tes.)

Ex. 415.

This will be recognized as the motive of the Gregorian Chant (*see* p. 18), *Nocte surgentes*, being best calculated to typify the purpose and character of Elsie. Her reply is characteristic "I come not here to argue, but to die." The chorus is here introduced *pp*, with the words:

> "Against all prayers and protestations
> She will not be persuaded."

After the words "I must fulfil my purpose" the Trombones and Tuba sound the Cathedral motive again:

Ex. 416.

The bright progression into the *B*-major chord is in anticipation of Elsie's sentiment, "Weep not for me, rather rejoice," etc., which immediately follows.

Finally the mock doctor draws her away (we hear the Lucifer motive from the orchestra). The apostrophe of Prince Henry, "Gone! and the light of all my life gone with her," is accompanied by his motive in minor.

The remainder of the scene is highly dramatic. Elsie's farewell is heard from the inner chamber, interspersed with Prince Henry's cries of "Murder! Unbar the door!" etc., repeated by the full chorus *ff*, and the ghoulish reply of Lucifer, "It is too late!" altogether forming an exciting and interesting *ensemble*.

SCENE XIII.

The return. Castle of Vautsberg. Prince Henry and Elsie on the terrace. Evening.

This number is a duet of charming effect between the Prince and Elsie, in which they pledge their love and faith.

SCENE XIV.

Epilog and Finale.

The full chorus here unite in a praise song commemorative of Elsie's self-abnegation:

> "In characters of gold,
> That never shall grow old,
> The deed divine
> Shall burn and shine
> Through all the ages!"

The orchestra commences with the Cathedral motive, and this is heard throughout the finale, as being both suggestive and expressive of the religious nature of the heroine and the sacred character of the chorus. The handling of the voice-parts, the harmonic coloring the numerous lights and shades, the accompaniment, and all the minor details are of such character as must place this chorus among the best examples of choral writing. As a Middle Part the composer introduces the evil spirits disappearing in a storm-cloud in the distance.

> " Lo ! over the mountain steeps,
> A dark, gigantic shadow sweeps.
> ＊　＊　＊　＊　＊　＊　＊
> It is Lucifer, the son of mystery."

The Lucifer motive here passes into the orchestral and choral parts with truly realistic effect. This episode has the double advantage of strong contrast and connective suggestiveness, and serves to elucidate the object of the Prolog. The Finale is brought to a close with the hymn of praise by the full choral and orchestral forces.

THE 46TH PSALM.

("*God is our refuge and strength.*")

FOR SOPRANO SOLO, CHORUS AND ORCHESTRA.

By W. W. GILCHRIST.

This is a short Sacred Cantata, written throughout in the serious ecclesiastic style, with no attempt whatever at mere euphonious effect. The Orchestral Introduction claims our first attention, especially as the form and structure are uncommon. First and second subjects, in respect to their location and relation, have no existence here; but there are two motives which alternately succeed each other as such, and without being thematicised into regular subject or strains:

Ex. 417.

This five-measure section being repeated a fourth above, the signa ture and movement are altered, and we hear the second motive

Ex. 418.

Un poco piu mosso.

There is another section of this brief four-part canon, and then the first motive is repeated in F-sharp and in G-major. So much is a meditation upon the first two sentences of the text. "God is our refuge and strength," A, and " An ever present help in trouble," B An expressive thematic development of the second motive, piu mosso, begins at the reference mark 1, and continues to 5. Commencing with the motive B in free canon as before, the composer introduces as a counter-theme this figure :

Ex. 419.

which is a contrary imitation of the last four notes of the second motive. This may be more readily observed by comparing b) with a) in Ex. 420:

Ex. 420.

As the development proceeds, motive and counter-motive naturally exchange places and appear inversely. Though the sounds are altogether serious, they still express considerable of confidence and determination, as is evidenced by the numerous naturally resolving discords throughout the introduction. There is, however, an occasional sound of penitent sadness, as in the antiphonal passage quoted

Ex. 421.   *p*

The three upper parts, each resolving a minor second, the pedal-note below, and the plaintive bit of melody above, all contribute to this effect.   Farther on there is a forcible and violent expression by the full orchestra, of which this excerpt will convey an idea:

Ex. 422.   *ff*

In listening to these sounds one's thoughts involuntarily revert to the second and third verses of the text: "Tho' the waters roar and are troubled, and the mountains shake," etc.

Another characteristic effect is produced at *Più Mosso*:

Ex. 423.   (a)   (b) etc.

The two upper intervals of the diminished seventh chord at (a) disappear without their proper resolution—observe the quarter rests at (a) and (b)—a very subtle expression of the words which afterward appear in the text: "He uttered his voice—the earth melted." This is twice repeated, showing an unmistakable design in the omission of the resolving cadence which, according to theory, should have been this:

Ex. 424.

These voice effects are more noticeable in the original score where each tone is uttered by a separate instrument, than on the piano, where it is not always possible to trace the progression of the different parts. At 5 the original motive is resumed for eight measures, and at 6 the movement is changed to *Allegro moderato e maestoso*, with a more animated treatment of the first motive:

Ex. 425.

This is increased to a *ff* climax, and then repeated in iterated notes.

The Introduction finally leads, without interruption, to the opening chorus, tutti, *ff*:

Ex. 426.

God is our refuge and strength,

God is our refuge and strength.

This is the principal motive, and is the same as the first of the Introduction (A 1). Observe the strength and dignity of the chorus part and how the three-measure phrases are united into a regular period.

The Cantata is founded upon this leading motive and the other-subjects which grow out of and accompany it; for the second

motive of the Introduction is but a slight extension of the second
half of the chief motive:

Ex. 427.

The last sentence of the first verse now occurs:

Ex. 428.

A ver - y pres-ent help in trou - ble.

The second measure will be recognized as supplying the phrase
which followed the meditation in the Introduction; the descending
tones from *d* to *a* are identical with the descending phase of the
chief motive (Ex. 426), thus showing the unity of design. The tenor
phrase is responded to by the sopranos a fourth above in fugal style,
accompanied in the tenors by a counter-subject, which, in its turn,
becomes a subject:

Ex. 429.

A   ver - y   pres - ent   help   in   trou - - ble,

C. S.

A   ver - y   pres - ent   help.

The sopranos and, afterwards, the other voices, take up this counter-
subject as a regular motive:

Ex. 430.

A ver - y pres-ent help,

A ver - y pres-ent help.

These two phrases alternate until the end of the cadence, when the
basses come in simultaneously with the leading motive:

Ex. 431.

trou - - ble.   God is our

- - - ble.

God is our ref - uge.

Passing over many interesting details, we come to the *Allegro con fuoco* in *D*-minor (11):

Ex. 432.

Allegro.

There - fore will we not fear,   Tho' the earth

ff

All the voices in unison sing this phrase, the boldness and daring of which will not escape notice. Yet even these seemingly strange tones are analogous to the main motive, as we shall see. An imposing effect is here produced by giving the leap of a seventh alter nately to the basses and sopranos, while the contraltos and tenors intersperse with the ascending and descending phrases previously quoted. Upon the return of the words of the first sentence, the original motive again appears, though changed in rhythm and tonal ity (12). Characteristic effects are also produced upon the words " Tho' the earth be removed, and the mountains be carried into the sea "—13 and 14, and the following *furioso* in *F*-minor, " Tho' the waves thereof roar." After a considerable elaboration of this idea the first motive returns (17), accompanied by the second motive as counter-subject. Upon the termination of this first chorus there is an orchestral Intermezzo containing some odd touches of harmony and this is joined without interruption to the soprano solo, *Andante*

The principal features of this are the alternating metre, ⅜ and ⅘, and the pastoral nature of the melody and accompaniment. The theme is also closely related to the original motive. The solo part then passes to the chorus, while the soprano continues with obligato responses. This division reposes on the major chord of *E*, at 34, followed by an *Allegro molto* upon the words of the sixth verse, " The nations raged." The last of this verse, previously mentioned in connection with the Introduction, is treated differently in the chorus parts :

All the voices in unison.

Ex. 433.

He ut-tered his voice, the earth melt-ed.

The downward leap of a sixth, the unexpected tone *g*-natural, and the discontinuance of the chorus parts after the word " melted," all contribute to the good effect.

A curious fragment of Canon in the second, between the sopranos and tenors, here follows, which is especially suggestive, and even descriptive :

f

The hea - then raged,   the na-tions were

Ex. 434. *f*

The hea - then raged,   the   na-

The choral divisions following each other in such close canon order, as in a stretto, give a turbulent, contentious, and somewhat exciting impetus to the music, which is a most vivid illustration of the words " the heathen raged," etc.   A better effect could not be conceived. Observe the first note of each part as it proceeds with the canon :

Ex. 435.

The upper melodic outline proceeds in the same diatonic order. The basses and contraltos then take up the same design in *F*-sharp minor ; and afterwards the motive of the canon is developed into a fughetta.   At the end of this chorus a soprano solo is again introduced for the ninth verse.   Afterwards the male voices have this peculiar scale-phrase:

Ex. 436.

He mak-eth wars to cease

a compound of the minor scales of *B* and *F sharp*. Attention is
called to this entire solo and chorus, which is replete with beauties
and instructive details, and to the *Andante con espress* (p. 5 of
the vocal score). The significance of the orchestral intermezzo
(previously explained by the text) while the voices in unison *pp*,
utter the words " Be still then," as the orchestral coloring proceeds—
all this is finely conceived and deserves special study. The *Allegro
maestoso* (57) is a canonic fugue, founded upon the original motive
extended to a section. The Finale is a massive and spirited *Gloria*
for all the voices and instruments *alla breve*, the same *Gloria* motive
being used in the postlude of the orchestra.

There is an effect peculiar to vocal music to which the student's
attention should be drawn. Several instances occur in the present
work, and we will quote a few :

Ex. 437.

The God of Ja-cob is our ref - uge

The God of Ja-cob is our ref - uge

The Lord is with us

The Lord of

Reference is here made to the crossing of the voice-parts at. In
the second measure the natural course of subject (soprano) and
counter-subject (contralto) causes them to cross each other, but without interfering with the two themes, each of which may be followed
by the attentive listener. In like manner the basses pass above the

tenors in the fourth measure (the tenor sounding an octave lower than written). On the piano these voice progressions lose their effect, and the example in the second measure for instance would merely sound like this:

Ex. 438.

Similar instances occur on pp. 65 and 67 of the vocal score.

As this Cantata is a remarkable development of a single musical motive, we will close our review by presenting, in a condensed form, the numerous transformations and elaborations of the original motive, No. 1:

Ex. 439.

Here is a lesson in thematic development worth remembering and in the orchestral parts may be found other arrangements and trans migrations of the leading motive.

In artistic construction, coherency of design, and total effect, this is one of the finest short cantatas with which the author is familiar, and would do honor to any composer, or any nation.

PIANO CONCERTO IN A-MINOR.

By E. A. MacDowell, Op. 15.

This Concerto contains the usual three movements, and is scored for full orchestra, except the trombones. It opens with the piano solo in form of an Introduction, thirteen measures, being somewhat of a paraphrase upon the leading motive.

The principal subject begins in the orchestra, at the end of the piano cadence, *Allegro con fuoco*. We quote the first orchestral period, as showing the nature of the theme, and the method by which it is continued and connected:

The free canonic imitations between the clarinet, oboe and flute are in antiphonal style; but by means of the simultaneous endings and beginnings the entire fifteen measures are connected into one thematic period. The last ten measures rest upon a dominant pedal note by the contra-basso and timpani, resulting in some odd combi nations of harmony, especially where the chords (G-sharp major and

F-sharp major are suspended above the *e* in bass. At the end of this (A) the regular piano work begins. Violins take the theme in a more melodically developed form, surrounded by passages and figures from the solo instrument. A few measures of this reveal the composer's method of treating the theme: first, thematically by means of canonic imitations of the motive only; second, melodic development, *i. e.*, continuing the motive into a regular subject or melody. Thematic treatment, however, is the predominating element throughout; the intervals of the first half of the motive being inverted, contracted and extended. The rhythm also is imitated as here:

Ex. 441.

and here:

Ex. 442.

Another feature is the dual rhythm which is employed freely throughout the first movement, and illustrated in the extract from p. 15 of the full score:

Ex. 443.

The effect of this is disputatious—as of contention and strife. Immediately after, the Piano begins a Passage founded on the 7th major chord, accompanied by a roll of the kettle-drum on *B*, and during the last two measures, by this fragment of the motive in Repetition beginning *pp* and increasing to an *ff* climax.

Ex. 444.

The succeeding tutti marks the second exposition, and is a still different paraphrase of the first subject, beginning in *E*-minor. Here the horns have another brief variation of the opening phrase

Ex. 445.

The tutti is continued thematically through a diminuendo of twelve measures, with constantly changing tone-color. The theme then passes from flutes and hautbois to the 'cellos, after which the violins have this contraction of the motive, seeming to recall some bygone memory :

Ex. 446.

Two measures after this the Piano announces the second subject in *C*-major, principally unaccompanied :

Ex. 447.

A very simple theme, with something of a retrospective character, and peculiar periodic construction. The solo continues upon the second theme for a considerable space, but on the thirteenth measure, as the piano makes its cadence upon *F*-sharp major, the clarinet sounds the more animated part of the first theme. The harmonization here is novel and interesting, especially where the stringed orchestra accompanies:

Ex. 448.

This part is a thematic development of the two motives of the second subject, with anticipations and imitations by the orchestra. The alterations of the motive may be seen in this quotation:

Ex. 449.

Thematically, this is the same as the first of the second subject.

The nature of the themes, their connection with one another, and the general treatment, all reveal to us a composer with superior talents, and what is yet more rare, with a definite artistic aim.

Upon the final cadence of the second subject (E) the orchestra gives out the first phrase of the principal theme thus altered:

This antiphonal design is continued for sixteen measures, reminding somewhat of a passage in the Coda of the first movement to Beethoven's *C*-minor Concerto, Op. 37. But in the latter work the timpani motive:

is continued without alteration, and the responses (also different) come upon *every other* measure.

The Elaboration commences from our last quotation, with a paraphrase of the first subject, as we have seen. At F the second subject is developed, the ornamentation being in the solo part. The two subjects are then combined. The Reprise takes place at G, in the orchestra. This is in *E*-minor, and considerably varied in treatment. Both themes again appear simultaneously at I. The second subject recurs (in *A*-major) at J, accompanied by the strings with a variation of the first subject and the general treatment differing from that of the first division. From the measure before K an extended thesis is developed out of a fragment of the second theme, which is continued until the pause at L. From this point the Solo part has a cadenza in tempo of three pages' duration, ending with a brief recollection of the Introduction. This is joined in the cadence to the Coda—last ten measures.

Second movement, *Andante Tranquillo*. The orchestra gives the opening period, of which this is the first phrase :

At F the metre is changed to 6/8, and the two pairs of horns are given, in alternate phrases, an Episode beginning thus:

The principal theme then recurs in *E*-major. This is more lyrical than the principal theme of the Allegro, and conveys a genial expression of peace, if not of contentment.

Third movement, *Presto*. *A*-minor, 6/8 metre. The first is an Introduction of twenty-two measures, between the dominant kettledrum and the Piano in *ad libitum* cadenza passages, the latter being emphasized at the commencement of each section by an *sf* chord of the full orchestra. The principal theme is as follows :

Ex. 454.

The Piano in unison delivers the melody, while the strings furnish the tripping accompaniment. Attention is directed to the analogy between this and the first theme of the Allegro. Without further elaboration the second theme follows in *A*-major. This affords a pleasurable glimpse of the fairy world, all gay and sunny. At C the principal theme recurs. The violins and hautbois have an outline of the melody, while the piano gives the theme in variations. This is one of the few instances in the Concerto where variations occur. At F the staccato melody of the second subject is developed into a very graceful cantilena by the violins

Ex. 455.

Following this we hear some reminiscences of the second theme of the first movement, and then the cantilena passes into the solo part, with a murmuring accompaniment by the violins. At M the composer introduces a middle part in *F*, Maestoso, the horns and trumpets having as theme a fragment of the original Allegro motive the Piano accompanying with a repeated chord figure. From O the movement changes to *molto più lento*, and the motive of the first *Allegro* is given by the first horn very nearly in its original form This is continued till the return of the *Presto*, when the same motive is treated canonically. Here the two motives from the first *Allegro* are combined into one phrase; a curious and interesting example

Ex. 456.

The stretto begins with the Prestissimo.

Besides the middle part already mentioned there is a subsidiary theme, and the principal themes of the Finale recur as in a Scherzo But the introduction of the two motives from the first movement together with the various elements of the Finale, which have been indicated, would seem to point to some more definite plan than the expression of undefined fancy or feeling. But as this is a mere technical analysis we merely call attention to the somewhat moorish style of musical architecture in this Finale.

Though differing in details, the Concerto is founded upon the classical model—a wise course for every young composer to pursue It reveals thorough harmonic and contrapuntal skill, a correct under standing of orchestral resources, and, what is better still, a lively fancy controlled by good judgment.

The score of the Concerto is not overladen, and would give satis faction even with a small orchestra. In this respect it is especially recommended to piano virtuosi.

THE CULPRIT FAY.

A FAIRY CANTATA FOR SOLOS, CHORUS AND ORCHESTRA.

BY FREDERICK GRANT GLEASON, *Op.* 14 (*MS.*).

This Cantata is exclusively a native creation, poet, composer and scene all being American. The poem by Drake is the most ro mantically sylvan and gossamer-like piece of imagery in American literature, and well calculated to inspire a composer. Mr. Gleason has not set the entire text, but the quaintness and completeness of the story are preserved. There are eighteen musical numbers, in three parts. Each of the more influential incidents and sentiments of the story is typified by a characteristic motive, and the various numbers are developed from these motives in a highly artistic man ner. Supposing the student to be familiar with the substance of the story, we will quote the leading motives first, especially as they have peculiar significance whenever they are introduced:

(A)   Summer Night Motive.

Ex. 457.

(B) Mystery Motive.

(C) Gathering of the Fays.

(D) Fairy Life.

(E) The Fay's Love.

(Observe the analogy between the Fairy motives, B, C, and D, and between the motives relating to the Culprit Fay, E, F, and I.)

A short orchestral Introduction, suggestive of a midsummer night on the Hudson, leads to the opening chorus, " 'Tis the middle watch of a summer's night." (Play the first motive and imagine the sounds issuing from three French horns, *pianissimo*.)

No. 2 is an accompanied Recitation for contralto, in form of narrative:

> " 'Tis the hour of fairy ban and spell,
>   The woodtick has kept the minutes well."

The "sentry elf from the haunted tree announce: the midnight hour, the triangle strikes twelve, and all is astir in fairy land. The scene is founded upon the mystery motive (B), which is frequently heard as being suggestive of the spell of fairy influence. After the triangle solo we hear a brief summons from the horns, and then the fairy revel begins (C). The gathering of the Fays is well expr d by the motive (C), passing very lightly in tripping staccato from instrument to another, interspersed with an occasional summon from the horns in more animating rhythm. This leads to the chorus in *A*-major:

> "They come from beds of lichen green.
> They creep from the mullen's velvet screen."

The vocal parts are principally harmonic, while the fairy revel motive is continued by the orchestra as local coloring. And here we should observe that the characteristic motives are, for the most part, orchestral, or at least their special significance, as they are introduced and reintroduced throughout the cantata, nearly always proceeds from the orchestra, the vocal parts being mostly narrative. The motive representing Fairy Life (D) is also heard in this number from the orchestra; in fact, it is all-important here, the gathering motive being but an incident of the Fairy Life. (D) is also used for Intermezzo between the verses of the chorus.

The second half of the Fairy Life motive:

Ex. 458.

is ominous, and gives a premonition of the transgression which forms the mainspring of the action; it is therefore omitted when the motive first appears, and is not heard until just before the words in the chorus:

> "An Ouphe has broken his vestal vow."

The ominous part of the motive is then frequently voiced by the orchestra, and it is also combined with the Task motive The unity and connection of motives is more frequently an intuitive process, rather than a studied design on the part of the compo His mind being engrossed, and, as we may say, saturated with composition and its connecting details, he unconsciously conceives many designs apparently unrelated, but which, upon close exam

tion, are found to be perfectly coherent and indicative. An explanation of this vague inner power would lead us beyond the jurisdiction
of the five known senses and into the realm of phenomena. It will
be sufficient for present purposes to trace the results of this mysterious agency as they are manifested in the composition.

No. 4, a Tenor solo, is a narrative of the Fay's transgression:

> " He has loved an earthly maid."

The orchestra commences with the mystery motive by the string
quartette in unison, and in a darker tone than No. 2. The Fay's
Love motive follows in delicately conceived instrumentation. After
the words:

> " To the elfin court they haste away
> To hear the doom of the Culprit Fay,"

the 'cellos and basses have this premonitory theme:

Ex. 459.

interspersed with fragments of the motives of Night and the Fay's
love.

No. 5 is a descriptive recitative by the King of the Fairies, passing sentence upon the culprit. In view of the fact that the maiden

> " Is pure as angel forms above,
> Such as a spirit well might love,"

the doom of the Fay is modified to the accomplishment of two difficult and dangerous tasks. Let these be told by the poet:

> "Thou shalt seek the beach of sand,
> Where the water bounds the elfin land;
> Thou shalt watch the oozy brine
> Till the sturgeon leaps in the bright moonshine.
> Then dart the glistening arch below,
> And catch a drop from his silver bow.
> If the spray-bead gem be won,
> The stain of thy wing is washed away;
> But another errand must be done
> Ere thy crime be lost for aye:
> Thy flame-wood lamp is quenched and dark,
> Thou must re-illume its spark;
> Mount thy steed and spur him high,
> To heaven's blue canopy;
> And when thou seest a shooting star,
> Follow it fast and follow it far;

The last faint spark of its burning train
Shall light the elfin lamp again.
Thou hast heard our sentence, Fay:
Hence! to the waterside, away!"

The **Penalty** motive (b) is now heard, together with phrases of
the Fay's love melody (e), as being the cause of his transgression
At the last of the words:

"Shall light the elfin lamp again."

the orchestra gives forth the motive of Fairy life (d), with the omi
nous part prominently accented, a highly suggestive and appropriate
effect. Part I ends here with an Amen cadence

PART II.

No. 6 commences in deep monotones by the *B* kettle-drum and
basses pizzicato, followed by the Night on the Hudson motive issuing
from the four horns. This leads to the chorus, which describes the
adventure of the Fay upon the river. Motives E, F, G and I are
heard during these numbers. The encounter with the water imps is
preceded by the River theme from the horns as before, and then commences a Barcarolle founded upon the water sprite's motive (H)
The accomplishment of the first task is hailed by the chorus with

Ex. 460. Joy to the Fay!

The **Intermezzo** is founded upon the Fay's Love and the Task
motives, with a snack of the River theme at the close.

PART III.

An **Orchestral Prelude** and Chorus describe the ascent of our
tiny hero into the starry regions:

"But the elfin made no stop nor stay
Till he reached the bank of the milky way."

Here, among the ethereal spirits, a delightful episode transpires

"With warblings wild they lead him on
To where, through clouds of amber, resplendent rose
The palace of th_ .ylphid Queen."

Here the violins sound her Love motive, somewhat altered and developed into a period.

Then follows a description of the Airy Queen, her love for the earthly fay, and the entreaty to

"Remain in the everlasting realms of light."

But he has resolved to cherish in memory his earthly love, his "virgin bride"; hence, at the end of the Queen's melodious exhortation, the love motive of the Fay resounds from the orchestra. (If it were our custom to dwell upon the sensuous charm of melody, we would linger long upon the fascinating strains of this soprano solo.) The motive itself (j) appears but once in the voice-part, which is an independent melody, while the regular love motive of the Queen is frequently heard in the orchestra above the voice.

In No. 15 the two love motives form the basis while the Fay is fluctuating between his earthly associations and duties in one scale, while in the other he weighs the incandescent splendors and coruscating charms of his present surroundings, and the not less tempting plaint of their ethereal mistress. But the predominance of the earthly love motive in the music is a sure precursor of what is narrated in the recitative, No. 16:

"Lady," he cried, "I have sworn to-night
To do my sentence task aright."

The Penalty motive is heard in the orchestra. He continues:

"My honor scarce is free from stain."

Here the Task motive is heard. After his words:

"Betide me weal, betide me woe,
Its mandate must be answered now,"

the orchestra sings a touching farewell upon the burden of the Queen's unrequited love motive.

No. 17 is a characteristic chorus, *Allegro con fuoco*, descriptive of the course of the Fay,

"Borne afar on the wings of the blast,"

in quest of the shooting star. His encounter with the storm fiends and the flaming rockets, and his final capture of the "glimmering spark," are here related. A realistic and original effect is produced in this number by the peculiar manner in which the Tam-tam is introduced as the "flash and flame" of the bursting star is described by the chorus.

The rhythm of the accompaniment and the unceasing modulations in this chorus and tenor solo also deserve particular mention. The last number begins with a summons by the trumpets, and a phrase of the task motive in brighter colors:

Ex. 461.

This is repeated in *A*, and then we hear the Fairy Life motive *Allegro*. The following chorus,

> "Ouphe and Goblin, Imp and Sprite, hither wend your way," et

tells of the joy and welcome to the wanderer. The Fairy Life motive forms the burden of the interludes to both the final choruses and also the Postlude after the words:

> "The day-glimpse glimmers on the lawn,
> The cock has crowed and the fays are gone."

Our review has been sufficient to show the significance of the characteristic motives, and the skill and judgment with which these are variously employed and combined to elucidate the text. To observe that the harmonization, counterpoint, instrumentation and forms are well conceived and correctly set down, would be but a trite compliment to one of the most accomplished and gifted of the young composers of the present day. Students of orchestration and even some well-known composers, will find a valuable lesson upon the treatment of brass instruments in Mr. Gleason's scores. Those who have heard his "Otho Visconti," or "Montezuma," will not be surprised at this statement.

The author had anticipated making some critical mention of a representative opus from Messrs. Bristow, Chadwick, Kelley, Foote, Nicholl, Whiting, Templeton Strong, Huss, Hille, Nevin, Parker, Converse and Fairlamb; but the limits of this chapter have already been exceeded, and we must conclude with the illustrations. Unfortunately several of the works last analyzed are either still in MS or published only in full score. A piano arrangement of the 46th Psalm, or the Culprit Fay, would be so unsatisfactory that it is not recommended.   Therefore, as a general illustration of American works, the following list is appended:

Buck, Revel, and appearance of the Abbot, from "Golden Legend." (Arranged by the composer for four hands.)

MacDowell, Concerto, Op. 15. (Published for two pianos.)

Paine, Serenade, Op. 12, or Prelude and Fugue, Op. 41.

Gilchrist, Une Petit Suite.

Gleason, Vorspiel to "Otho Visconti," arranged by **Clarence Eddy**.

H. W. Nicholl, Concerto in *D*-minor.

G. E. Whiting, Concerto in *D*-minor.

Kelley, Royal Gaelic March, from "Macbeth" music. **(Two or** four hands.)

Wm. H. Sherwood, Medea, Op. 13.*

S. G. Pratt, Grand Polonaise in *A*-flat.

A. M. Foerster, Romance for Violin and Piano.

Burmeister, Concerto in *F*-minor.

Maas, Concerto in *C*-minor, Op. 12.

G. W. Chadwick, String Quartette.

* Special analytical edition just issued (1890) by the publishers of this work

COMPENDIUM.

THE plan of the Compendium is arranged to correspond to the different topics, styles, forms, etc., as they are explained in the body of the book. Preference is given to works either new or little known, for the reason that standard compositions need no recommendation.

ILLUSTRATIONS FOR PART I, CHAPTERS I AND II

AURICULAR EXERCISES.

Bargiel, Three Clavierstücke. (Nos. 1 and 2. Major ; 3, Harmonic Minor
Henselt, Love Song in *A*-flat. (Harmonic and Melodic Minor.)
Chadwick, Scherzino, Op. 7, No. 3. (Harmonic and Melodic Minor.
Hyllested, Album Leaf in *G*. (Alternate Major and Minor.)
Behr, Polonaise, Op. 55, No. 1. (Chromatic.)
Godard, Waltz in *A*-flat, Op. 26. (Chromatic.
Chopin, Etude, Op. 10, No. 2. (Chromatic.
Gade, Aquarellen, Op. 19. (Ten short pieces, Enoch Edition, 469.)

CHAPTERS III, IV AND V.

Hans Huber, Thoughts of Home in the Desert, Op. 41, arranged by R. Hoffman. (Syncopated accompaniment and change of Movement
Marston, Bagatelle in *F*. (Change of Mode, Metre, Movement and Rhythm
Hyllested, Melody in *G*. (Compound Rhythm.)
H. Hofmann, Elegie. (Change of Metre, Movement and Mode ; also different Rhythm in accompaniment of each period.)
De Prosse, "Little Classics," Nos. 3 and 10.

PART II. CHAPTERS VI AND VII.

Hiller, Choral in *E*-minor from Suite.
Heller, Cradle Song in *G*.
Saran, March, Op. 6, No. 2.
Gleason, Allegro, Op. 8, No. 4.
Seymour Smith, Dorothy.

(Major and Minor Chords and Natural Transitions.)

CHAPTERS VIII AND IX.

X. Scharwenka, Op. 62, No. 6.   (Cadence No. 1—end of First Section.)
Taubert, Etude, Op. 4, No. 2.   (Cadences Nos. 2 and 3.)
Joseffy, Mill, Op. 23.   Nos. 2 and 5.)
X. Scharwenka, Op. 62, No. 1.   No. 3, last measure.)
Reynaud, Lily of the Valley.   (No. 4.)
Chopin, Prelude, No. 4.   (No. 4.)
Heller, Cradle Song in *G*.   (No. 5.)
Seymour Smith, Dorothy.   Nos. 4 and 3, last period.)
Czibulka, Sarabande, Op. 316.   (Secondary Seventh Chords.)
Chopin, Prelude, No. 4.   (Dominant, Diminished, and Secondary Seventh Chords.)
Sidney Smith, Tarantelle, Op. 8.   Dominant, Diminished, and Secondary Seventh Chords.)

PART III. CHAPTERS X TO XV.

X. Scharwenka, Op. 62, No. 5.   (First measure contains Motive or Semi-phrase.)
X. Scharwenka, Op. 62, No. 11.   (First measure contains Motive or Semi-phrase.)
X. Scharwenka, Op. 62, Nos. 1 and 2.   (Semi-phrases.)
Gade, Canzonetta, Op. 19, No. 3.   (Semi-phrases.)
Behr, Pearls of Dew, Op. 575, No. 10.   (Single Types.)
Chopin, Mazurka, Op. 7, No. 5.   (Single Type. The period in *G* is identical with that in *C*. This is a Round.)
C. Cui, Canzonetta in *A*-flat.   (Ballad Model.)
H. Hofmann, Op. 34, No. 3.   (Ballad Model.)
Hensell, Love Song in *B*-flat.   (Ballad Model.)
X. Scharwenka, March, Op. 62, No. 1.   Primary Form.)
Jno. Orth, Mazurka in *G*.   (Primary Form.)
Chadwick, Congratulations, Op. 7, No. 1.   (Commencing on Second Eighth.)

PART IV. CHAPTER XVI.

DANCE FORM—COMMON SPECIES.

MARCHES.

Gounod, Marche Pontificate.
E. Mollenhauer, Palisades March.
S. B. Whitney, Processional March, Op. 25.
Dulcken, Canon in form of a March, Op. 127.
L. Damrosch, Arion March.
Lavallée, Marche de Concert.
Gleason, Egyptian Priest's March from "Montezuma."
Schubert-Tausig, Marche Caracteristique.
Schubert-Tausig, Marche Militaire.
Bargiel-Joseffy, Marche Fantastica.   (The original is simpler.)

SCHOTTISCHE.

Durége, Sailor's Return.
Mattoon, Woodnymph Schottische, op. 16.
A. J. Davis, Alma Schottische.

POLKA.

S. B. Mills, Polka Caprice.
Van Laer, Polka Brillante, Op. 10.
Henselt, Polka Brillante, Op. 13.
Bendel, Invitation to the Polka.
Kroeger, Polka Gracieuse, Op 8 No. 6.
Sherwood, Polaria, Grand Polka.

GALOP.

Rubinstein, Galop, from "Le Bal."
Bachmann, Rendezvous Galop.
Elson, Dash along Galop.
Tours, Plus Vite Galop de Concert.
Brandeis, Irresistible Galop.
Gregh, Scherzo Galop.

MAZURKA.

Saint-Saëns, Two Mazurkas, Ops. 21 and 24.
Sherwood, Two Mazurkas, Op. 9.
F. Dewey, Mazurka in *G*-minor.
Fairlamb, Mazurka de Salon.
Robyn, Mazurka, Op. 38, No. 4.
Dayas, Mazurka.
Rivé-King, Mazurka des Graces.
Hyllested, Second Mazurka in *G*.
S. G. Pratt, Joyous Breeze, Mazurka.
A. E. Warren, La Gazelle, a la Mazurka.
Foote, Mazurka in *G*-minor.
Lavallée, Souvenir de Toledo.
Wieniawski, Mazurka de Concert, Op. 41.
Leschetizky, Mazurka, Op. 24, No. 2.
Chopin, Fifty-one Mazurkas.

WALTZ.

Von Bülow, Waltz in *B*-flat, Op. 21, No. 7.
Dvořák, Two Books of Waltzes, Op. 54.
Moszkowski, Five Waltzes, Op. 8.
Löschhorn, Valse, Op. 37, No. 1.
Jadassohn, Valse, Op. 62.
Schulhoff, Second Valse Brillante.
Keler-Bela, On the Beautiful Rhine. (Ball-room Waltzes.)
Warren, Autograph Waltz.   (Ball-room Waltzes.)
Lambert, Valse Impromptu.
Neupert, Valse Caprice, Op. 57, No. 2.
Hyllested, Valse Sentimentale.
Seeboeck, Valse Caprice.
Maas, Valse Allemande, Op. 21.
Carreño, Springtime, Valse Brillante.
Flörsheim, Valse Gracieuse.

Mills, Valse Caprice.

Baermann, Clavierstuck in Waltz Form.

Raff, Nine Favorite Pieces.   (Waltz, Minuet, Gavotte, Bolero, etc.   Enoch Edition, 455.)

Schubert, Dances, complete for Piano Solo.   (Edition Peters, No. 150.   Four hands,
    Edition Peters. No. 719.)

DANCE FORM—ROCCOCO SPECIES.

(Minuets, Sarabandes, Etc., may be found among the Suites hereinafter mentioned.)

Bach-Mason, Gavotte in *G*, from Sixth 'Cello Suite.

Bach-Joseffy, Gavotte for left hand alone.

Gluck-Brahms, Gavotte in *A*, from "Iphigenia."

Gluck-Mason, Gavotte.

Morley, Musette.

MODERN GAVOTTES.

Pabst, Gavotte and Musette, Op. 1?

Popper-Kirchner, Gavotte in *D*, Op. 23, No. 2.

Saint-Saëns-Dayas, Gavotte from Septuor.

Saint-Saëns, Gavotte in *C*-minor, Op. 23.

Strelezki, Gavotte Moderne in *A*.

M. Vogrich, Gavotte Hougroise in *A*-minor.

Von Wilm, Gavotte in *G*, Op. 33, No. 3.

Flörsheim, Morceau a la Gavotte.

Seeboeck, Florence Gavotte.

W. G. Smith, Gavotte Antique.

H. N. Bartlett, Grand Gavotte in *D*, Op. 45.

Durand, Gavotte, Op. 84.

Sgambati, Gavotte, Op. 14.

Liebling, Gavotte Moderne.

M'me Helen Hopekirk, Gavotte in *B*-minor.

Carl Venth, Gavotte, Op. 16.

C. L. Capen, Gavotte in *F*-minor.

M. Roeder, Two Gavottes.

Foote, Gavotte in *C*, Op. 8, No. 1.

A. Cortada, Gavotte.

Sternberg, Gavotte, Op. 32, No. 1.

H. W. Parker, Gavotte in *E*-minor

W. R. Johnston, Gavotte, Op. 40.

Gounod, Musette.

E. Nevin, Gavotte and Musette in *G*-minor and **G-major.**

SARABANDE.

Mattheson, Sarabande and Variations.

Zipoli, Sarabande in *G*- minor.

Corelli, Sarabande in *E*-minor or *D*-minor.

Von Procházka, Sarabande.

Emery, Sarabande (and Scherzo), Op. 6.

CHACONNE.

Händel-Liszt, Chaconne.
Neustedt, Chaconne Favorite.
Reinecke, Chaconne in *B*-minor, Op. 123, No. 3.
Durand, Chaconne in *A*-minor, Op. 62.
Seeboeck, Chaconne in *B*-minor.

TAMBOURIN.

H. Huber, Tambourin.
Raff, Tambourin from Suite, Op. 204.

BOURRÉE.

Bach-Joseffy, Bourrée in *F*
Moszkowski, Bourrée, Op. 38, No. 1.
Reinecke, Bourrée in *A*-minor, Op. 175, No. 2.
Tours, Bourrée Moderne, Op. 32.
Dupont, Bourrée in *B*-minor.
E. Silas, Second Bourrée.
Thayer, Bourrée in *D*.
Seeboeck, Bourrée Antique, No. 1.

COURANTE.

Dom. Zipoli, Courante from *G*-minor Suite.
Muffat, Courante in *D*-minor.
Von Wilm, Courante, Op. 33, No. 2.
Thayer, Courante in *D*.

GIGUE.

Händel, Gigue in *G*-minor.
Rameau, Deux Gigues en Rondeaux.
Mattheson, Four Gigues.
Zipoli, Gigue from *G*-minor Suite.
Corelli, Gigue in *A*.
Leschetizky, Gigue, Op. 36, No. 3.
Sternberg, Gigue, Op. 32.

DANCE FORM—MODERN CLASSICAL SPECIES.

POLONAISE.

Rivé-King, Polonaise Heroïque.
Foote, Polonaise in *D*, Op. 6, No. 5.
M. I. Espstein, Polonaise.
Jno. Orth, Polonaise in *A*.
S. A. Emery, Polonaise.
Henschel, Polonaise in *G*.
Nicodé, Polonaise Caracteristique. Op. 5.

BOLERO.

Jadassohn, Bolero, Op. 75, No. 1.
Raff, Bolero in *E*-flat, Op. 111, No. 1.

Reinecke, Bolero, Op. 86, No. 2.
Devrient, Bolero Seguedille, Op. 20.
Löschhorn, Bolero, Op. 108, No. 4.
C. Johns, Bolero and Minuet.

TARANTELLA.

Nicodé, Tarantelle, Op. 13, No. 1.
Raff, Tarantelle in *A*-minor, Op. 99.
Rheinberger, Tarantelle, Op. 53, No. 1.
Ph. Scharwenka, Tarantelle, Op. 45.
Rossini, La Danza. (Vocal Tarantelle arranged by Liszt.)
Gottschalk, Tarantelle Brillante.
Mills, Tarantelles, Nos. 2 and 3.
Maas, Tarantelle, Op. 10.
Van Laer, Tarantelle, Op. 3.
Sternberg, Tarantelles, Op. 35, No. 3 and 40, No. 2.
Baetens, Tarantelle in *C*.
Woolf, Tarantelle, Op. 111, No. 1.
Poznanski, Tarantelle.

SALTARELLO.

Nicodé, Saltarello, Op. 13, No. 2.
St. Heller, Saltarello, Op. 77. (Theme from Mendelssohn's Fourth Symphony.)
Löschhorn, Saltarello, Op. 108, No. 2.
Raff, Saltarello, Op. 108.
Satter, Saltarello, Op. 147.
Mills, Saltarello.

CZÁRDÁS.

Liszt, Two Czárdás, *A*-minor and *B*-minor.
R. Willmers, Makoi, Czárdás.
Behr, Hungarian Dances. (Czárdás Album.)
Brahms, No. 17, from Hungarian Dances. (Published for two or four hands.)

MINUET.

Jensen, Minuet, Op. 33.
Bargiel, Tempo di Minuet in *E*-flat.
Bizet, Minuet de l' Arlesienne.
Sherwood, Ethelinda, Tempo di Minuet.
Levett, Minuet.
W. G. Smith, Minuet in Canon Form.
Sternberg, Minuet, Op. 32.
B. O. Klein, Minuet from Suite, Op. 25.

HABANERA.

Neustedt, Habaneras, Op. 174.
Northrup, Habaneras, Ops. 49 and 52.
G. D. Wilson, Cuban Dance.

PART V. CHAPTERS XIX TO XXI

Hiller, Gavotte in *G*, from Piano Suite. (Uneven phrases and sections The Mensural proportion is not good.)

Von Wilm, Playfulness, Op. 12, No. 5. (Intermezzo and Coda, simple example

Bachmann, Dance Bretonne. (Intermezzo and Cadenza, Passage in Coda

Bachmann, Sur la Brêche. (Extended Periods and Coda

Bachmann, Village Festival. (Introduction and Intermezzo

Bohm, La Fontaine, Op. 22. (Second period extended, Principal period of Trio extended, last six measures Coda.)

Seymour Smith, Dorothy. (Prelude. All Periods regular except last

E. Liebling, Feu Follet, Op. 17. (United period before middle part in *G* and again before Coda.)

CHAPTER XXII.

Chopin, Etude, Op. 10, No. 1; also Op. 10, No. 11. (Dispersed Harmony

N. B.—The best examples of uneven mensural proportion may be found among the Piano Duets.

Lassen, Andante Amoroso. From "Love above all Magic." Arranged by Liszt (Abrupt transitions, especially Coda.)

Wagner, Prelude to "Lohengrin." (Abrupt transitions.

PART VI. CHAPTER XXIII.

B. Woolf, Allegretto Scherzando, Op. 67. (Lyric and Thematic

Spindler, Buntes Leben, Op. 300, No. 3. (Antiphonal.

Manzotti, Tempo di Marcia. (Unison passages, Harmonic and Antiphonal.)

C. Cui, Canzonetta. (Lyric.)

Kullak, Scherzo in *F*. (Partial Canon. Thematic style in middle part

X. Scharwenka, March, Op. 62, No. 1. (Harmonic.)

Hiller, Choral from Suite. (Harmonic.)

Geo. Henschel, Canons for Piano. (An improvement on the old style.)

Dulcken, Canon en forme de Marche, Op. 27.

Goldbeck, Melody and Canon.

Ales. Scarlatti, Fuga:

Händel, Six Grand Fugues.

Raff, Fugue from Suite, Op. 75, No. 5.

Rheinberger, Fugue in *G*-minor, Op. 5, No. 3.

Saint-Saëns, Preludes and Fugues, Op. 52, Nos. 3 and 5.

Schumann, Four Fugues, Op. 72.

Jadassohn, Six Preludes and Fugues, Op. 56.

Clara Schumann, Three Preludes and Fugues, Op. 16.

J. K. Paine, Fugue, Op. 41, No. 3.

Foote, Prelude and Fugue, Op. 15.

MacDowell, Prelude and Fugue in *D*-minor, Op. 13.

338

COMPLETE MUSICAL ANALYSIS.

BRAVURA STYLE.

Mozart-Liszt, "Don Juan," Fantaisie.
Liszt, Tarantella.
Paganini-Brahms, Theme with Variations.
Schubert-Tausig, Marche Militaire.
Chopin, Scherzo, No. 1, "Infernal Banquet."
Chopin, Polonaise, Op. 61.
Henselt, Concerto in *F*-minor.
Beethoven, Emperor Concerto in *E*-flat.
Brahms, Concerto in *F,* or *B*-flat.

CHAPTERS XXIV AND XXV.

Hans Huber, Thoughts of Home, Op. 41. **Arranged by R. Hoffman.** (Introduction founded upon a Ground Bass. Coda contains Repetition and Echo.)
Godard, Mazurka iu *B*-flat. (Cadenza, Abrupt transitions and Eingang.)
Lassen, Ballet Music from "Love above all Magic." (Each period founded upon a Pedal-note.)
Von Wilm, The Village Musicians, Op. 12, No. 3. (Drone Bass.)
Volkmann, Picture Book, Op. 11, two or four hands. (Nos. five and six contain Echo.)
X. Scharwenka, Scherzo, Op. 62, No. 10. (Repetition at end of second period.)
X. Scharwenka, Scherzo, Op. 62, No. 12. (Contains a Refrain, which occurs several

times: etc.)

CHAPTER XXVI.

SPINNING SONG.

Liszt, Spinnlied.
Löw, Gretchen at the Spinning-wheel, Op. 139.
Thomé, Chanson du Rouet.
Godard, Chanson du Rouet, Op. 85.
Joseffy, Spinnerlied.
Ketten, Marguerite au Rouet, Op. 12.
Raff, La Fileuse, Op. 157, No. 2.
Napravnik, Spinning Song, Op. 43, No. 4.
Cooper, Spinning Song, Op. 76.
Lynes, Spinning Song in *G.*

HUNTING SONG.

Von Procházka, Hunting Song.
Van Laer, Hunting Song, Op. 5.
Jefferey, Hunting Song, Op. 7.
Kirchner, Hunting Song, Op. 181.
Rheinberger, Hunting Song, Op. 5, **No. 1.**
Kornatzki, Hunter's Horn.

Gade, Boat Song.
Raff, Boat Song, Op. 8.
Nicodé, Boat Song, Op. 13, No. 3.
Hensell, Boat Song, Op. 13, No. 2.
Goldner, Barcarolle, Op. 47, No. 1.
A. G. Robyn, Barcarolle, Op. 37, No. 1.
Sternberg, Barcarolle, Op. 22, No. 9.
Moszkowski, Barcarolle, Op. 15, No. 6.
Rubinstein, Barcarolle, Op. 30, No. 1 in *F*-minor.
Hopkins, Midnight Barcarolle.
Stamaty, Barcarolle.
W. Perkins, Barcarolle in *G*.
Barnett, Barcarolle.
Pabst, Barcarolle.
Tschaikowsky, Barcarolle in *G*-minor.

CRADLE SONG.

Heller, Cradle Song in *D*-flat, Op. 81, No. 15.
MacDowell, Cradle Song, Op. 24, No. 2.
Neruda-Kirchner, Cradle Song, Op. 11.
Grieg, Cradle Song, Op. 38, No. 1.
Cesar Cui, Berceuse in *E*-flat.
W. L. Wood, Berceuse.
Bartlett, Berceuse.
Sherwood, Spirit Love, Cradle Song.
S. B. Mills, Lullaby.
Behr, Oriental Lullaby.
Flörsheim, Lullaby.
Gounod, Dodeliuette.
Mendelssohn, Cradle Song.
Brahms, Cradle Song in *G*-flat.
Orth, Cradle Song in *A*.
A. D. Turner, Cradle Song, Op. 36, No. 5.
Emery, Cradle Song.
Marston, Slumber Song in *B*-flat.
Geo. Schneider, Cradle Song.

CARILLONS.

Dreyschock, La Campanella.
Saint-Saëns, Carillons, Op. 72, No. 2.
Delacour, Carillons du Village.
Field, "**Midi.**" (Analyzed in Chapter XXVI.)
Gade, **Christmas Bells.**
Haberbier, Enchanted Bells, Op. 59.
Berton, Op. 13.

NOCTURNE.

Brassin, Nocturne, Op. 17.
Pabst, Nocturne, Op. 14.
Raff, Abends, Nocturne, Op. 55, No. 12.
Tausig, L'esperance, Nocturne, Op. 3.
Henselt, Nocturne in *E*-flat, Op. 6.
F. Dewey, "Night has a Thousand Eyes"
Pratt, Nocturne Impromptu.
Brandeis, Nocturne.

ROMANCE.

Clara Schumann, Three Romances, Op. 21.
X. Scharwenka, Two Romances, Op. 25.
Henselt, Romance, Op. 18.
Max Bruch, Romance.
Nicodé, First Meeting, Romance, Op. 22, No. 1.
Sherwood, Appassionatta, Op. 8.
Foote, Romance from First Suite
Salmon, Romanza.

SERENADE.

Moszkowski, Serenata in *D*.
Del Valle de Paz, Serenade, Op. 28, No. 1.
Popper, Serenade, Op. 57, No. 2.
W. S. Bennett, Serenade, Op. 13.
Sgambati, Serenade from Symphony, Op. 16.
Wm. Mason, Serenade from "Mephisto."
E. B. Perry, Concert Serenade, Op. 10, No. 2.
Schumacher, Spanish Serenade, Op. 33, No. 3.
Ketten, Spanish Serenade, Op 60.
Jungmann, Spanish Serenade.

BAGATELLE.

Ph. Scharwenka, Four Bagatelles, Op. 39.
Merkel, Bagatelles, Op. 81
Heimendahl, Bagatelle.
C. Cui, Italian Bagatelle.

TOCCATA.

J. S. Bach, Four Toccatas. (210, Edition Peters.)
Bargiel, Toccata, Op. 45.
Dupont, Toccata de Concert, Op. 36.
Reinecke, Toccatina in *E*-minor.
Wm. Mason, Toccata, Op. 37.

ETUDE.

Liszt, Six Etudes de Paganini.
Rubinstein, Grand Etude in *C*.
Haberbier, Etudes Poesies, Op. 53.
Bertini, Caprice Etudes, Op. 94.   (Very characteristic.)
Moszkowski, Etude in *G*.

Nicodé, Two Etudes, Op. 12.
X. Scharwenka, Three Etudes, Op. 27.
Alkan, Etudes.
Neupert, Poetic Studies.
Lambert, Etude in *G*. (In Harmonic counterpoint)
Joseffy, Etude in *A*-flat.
Kölling, Perpetual Motion Etude.
W. G. Smith, La Cascadilla, Etude de Salon, Op. 21.
Lavallée, The Butterfly Etude.
Parsons, Forest Murmurs.
Goldbeck, Petit Etude.
Foote, Pedal Study No. 2.

PIFFERARI.

Sternberg, Pifferari, Op. 35, No. 3.
Sidney Smith, Pifferari, Op. 183.

SCHERZO.

Mendelssohn, Two Scherzos.
Volkmann, Scherzo from Symphony, Op. 44.
C. Engel, Scherzo, Op. 10.
Carreño, Intermezzo Scherzo, Op. 34.
Flörsheim, Scherzo.
St. Emery, Scherzo and Sarabande, Op. 6.
Orth, Scherzo in *D*.
H. W. Parker, Scherzo in *A*-minor.
Sherwood, Scherzos, Ops. 7 and 9.
Em. Moor, Scherzoso in *B*-flat minor.
E. Perabo, Petit Scherzo.
Lynes, Scherzino, Op. 9, No. 4.
Jadassohn, Scherzo in form of a Canon.

HUMORESQUE.

Moszkowski, Humoresques, Op. 33, No. 2, and 35, No. 3.
Nicodé, Burlesque, Op. 28, No. 2.
Ph. Scharwenka, Humoresque, Op. 13, No. 1.
Tschaikowsky, Humoresque in *G*, Op. 10, No. 2.
Em. Moor, Humoresque in *D*.
Wm. Mason, Two Humoresques, Op. 23.
MacDowell, Humoresque in *G*, Op. 18, No. 2.
Maas, Six Humorous Sketches, Op. 13.
Kroeger, Humoresque.

IDYL.

Gregh, Pastorale, Louis XV., Op. 12. (Especially recommended as a primary etat of Pastoral Music.)
Gregh, Elegie, Pastorale in *D*-flat.
Durand, Gai Printemps Idylle, Op. 76.
Gade, Idyllen, Op. 34.

Joseffy, Idyl in *F*.
Thomé, Under the Leaves, Idyl.
Sherwood, Idyl from Suite, Op. 5.

CHAPTER XXVII.

ROMANTIC SINGLE FORMS.

Carl Heymann, Elfin Dance.
Gottschalk, Eolian Murmurs.
Davidoff-Rosenthal, At the Spring.
Mendelssohn, Elfin Dance, from "Midsummer Night's Dream."
Hiller, Dance of the Fairies.
Behr, Fairy Dance, Op. 351.
Gottschalk, Dance of Sylphs, Op. 86.
Prudent, Revel of the Fairies.
Renaud, Firefly, Caprice, Op. 19.
Kroeger, Elves at Play.
Seeboeck, Fairy Dance.
Saint-Saëns, Phrygian Greek Dance.
*MacDowell, Witches' Dance, Op. 17, No. 2.
* *Jensen*, Dryade, Op. 43, No. 4.
* *Jensen*, Will-'o-the-Wisp.
²*Chopin*, Presto from *B*-flat minor Sonata.
*Carreño, Dance of Gnomes.

PART VII.   CHAPTER XXVIII.

Best illustrated by thirty Inventions, and Art of Canon and Fugue by Bach.

CHAPTER XXIX.

SUITES AND PARTITAS.

Mattheson, Suite No. 5.
Kuhnau, Suite.
Couperin, Suites.
Händel, French and English Suites.
DeChambonnieres, Suite in *A*-minor.
Zipoli, Partita in *G*-minor.
Bach, Six Partitas.
Krebs, Six Partitas.
A. and D. Scarlatti, Partitas.
Paradisi, Partitas.

MODERN SUITE.

Reinecke, Suite a la Roccoco.
Grieg, Suite in five movements, Op. 40.
Jensen, Suite in *B*-minor, Op. 36.
Raff, Suites, Ops. 72 and 204.

The last five selections belong to the Ignis-Fatuus, rather than to the Feu Follet order.

Svendsen, Romantic Suite.
Hyllested, Romantic Suite. (Norwegian and Danish.)
Bargiel, Suite, Op. 31.
MacDowell, Modern Suites, Ops. 10 and 14.
Brockhoven, Creole Suite.
Hamerik, 3 Nordische Suiten.
Gilchrist, A little Suite of four movements.
B. O. Klein, Suite in G, Op. 25.
Sherwood, Suite, Op. 5.
Rivé-King, Piano Suite No. 1.
Foote, Suite in E-minor Op. 12.

CHAPTER XXX.

Bellini-Leybach, "La Sonnambula" Potpourri.
Wagner-Cramer, "Parsifal" Potpourri.
Wagner-Liszt, Walhall, Transcription from the "Rheingold."
Wagner-Tausig, "The ride of the Valkyrs" Transcription.
Pabst, Air and Variations, Op. 16.
A. Fesca, Fantaisie and Variations.
Brahms, Variations, Op. 9.
Clara Schumann, Variations, Op. 20.
Mills, Welsh Air and Variations.
Tschaikowsky, Theme and Variations, Op. 19, No. 6.

RONDO.

Hummel, Rondo, Op. 52.
Ferd. Ries, Rondo Elegante, Op. 122.
Merkel, Rondo Brillante and Rondo Amabile, Op. 154, Nos. 1 and 2.
Bottesini, Rondo.
Löschhorn, Rondo, Op. 149, No. 1.
Becker, Rondino, Op. 9, No. 1.
Buck, Rondo Caprice, arranged by Dayas.
H. Mohr, Rondo Scherzando, Op. 53.

PART VIII. CHAPTER XXXII.

Hensell, Love Song in B-flat. (Theme in Tenor.)
H. H. Huss, Ballade.
Bohm, La Fontaine, Op. 221. (Melody in Contralto, in Trio.)
Grünfeld, Mazurka, Op. 14. (Intrada in form of Anticipation, occurs several times
   before principal period. In the first E-flat period the Melody is divided between
   Soprano and Contralto as duet, and the Tenor, in antiphonal style. The Mazurka
   rhythm and the style should be observed.)
A. C. Mackenzie, Reminiscence. (This is founded upon two motives, the first
   which appears principally in the bass, and occasionally in Canon. An attempt at
   specifying the nature of the sounds might prove useful.)
Seiss, Evening Song, Op. 9.
Nicodé, Polonaise Caracteristique, Op. 5.

CHAPTERS XXXIII AND XXXIV.

SONATINA.

Steibelt, Sonatina in *C.*

Schumann, Sonatina, Op. 118.

Merkel, Sonatina, Op. 126.

Seiss, Sonatina, Op. 8, No. 1.

Reinecke, Sonatina, Op. 136.

H. Hofmann, Sonatina, Op. 41.

Von Wilm, Sonatina, Op. 20.

A. Krause, Sonatinas, Op. 10, No. 2, and Op. 12, **Nos. 1 and 2.**

Löschhorn, Sonatinas, Ops. 179 and 180.

H. Goetz, Two Sonatinas, Op. 8.

Spindler, Sonatinas, Op. 281, No. 4.

Pauer, Three Sonatinas.

Carl Venth, Sonatinas, Op. 17.

CHAPTER XXXV.

Chopin, Berceuse.*

S. Bennett, Toccata, Op. 38.

Wagner - Bendel, Three Improvisations. 1, Siegmund's Love Song from "Walküre"; 2, By Silent Hearth in Winter Tide, from "Meistersinger"; 3, Walther's Prize Song. (Excellent illustrations of this Chapter.)

PART IX. CHAPTER XXXVI.

Tschaikowsky, Andante from Op. 11. (Commencing at the seventeenth measure there are several instances of subject and counter-subject, first below, then above. This should be traced through the following eight measures from 17. The first appearance of the second Subject should also be analyzed. It is founded upon a Pedal-note and

accompanied by a Ground Bass throughout: 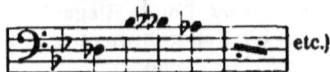 etc.)

Von Weber, La Romanesca.

Rubinstein, Romance, Op. 44, No. 1.

Blumenthal, La Pensée.

Em. Moor, Scherzoso in *B*-flat minor.

W. G. Smith, Mosaics, Op. 36.

(These selections, and the following Sonatas, etc., should be analyzed *away from the piano*, using the Symbols and Key as explained in Chapter XXXVI. The Rhapsodical forms, such as the Bendel Improvisations, and the more recent large works, should come last.)

PART X. CHAPTERS XXXIX TO XLI.

Paradisi, Neapolitan Sonata in *D*, No. 10.

D. Scarlatti, Concert Sonata in one movement:

* For a special study of Chopin the Jurgensen Edition, Moscow, revised by Klindworth, is recommended.

Turini, Sonata in *D*-flat, No. 6.

Galuppi, Sonata in *D*, four movements.

Cherubini, Sonata in *B*-flat, No. 3, Allegro Comodo.

Méhul, Sonata in *A*, Op. 1, No. 3. (Allegro, Minuet, Rondo)

Ph. Em. Bach, Sonata in *D*-minor. (No. 5 of the select Sonatas arranged v Von Bülow.)

Johann Ch. Bach, Sonata in *C*-minor. (Grave Allegro and Tempo di Gavotte)

Wagenseil, Sonata in *F*.

Hässler, Sonata in *A*-minor. (First movement in Canon Form)

Rolla, Sonata in *E*-flat.

Mozart, Sonata in *B*-flat commencing:

Mozart, Fantaisie and Sonata in *C*-minor.

Hummel, Sonata, Op. 81.

Beethoven, Op. 53, 81, or 106.

Clementi, Op. 12, No. 1, or Op. 39, No. 1.

Dussek, Op. 9, No. 2.

Weber, Sonata, Op. 39.

Mendelssohn, Sonata, Op. 105.

Chopin, Sonata, Op. 35.

Schumann, Sonata, Op. 22

Reinecke, Sonata, Op. 35 in *A*-minor.

Gade, Sonata, Op. 28.

Rubinstein, Sonatas, Ops. 20 and 41.

Brahms, Sonatas, Ops. 1 and 5.

Nicodé, Sonatas, Op. 19.

Bargiel, Sonatas, Op. 34.

Grieg, Sonata, Op. 7. (Augener, 6140.)

Ph. Scharwenka, Sonatas, Ops. 6 and 32.

Jensen, Sonatas, Op. 25.

Brandeis, Sonatas.

W. Burr, Jr., Three Sonatas.

A. Becker, Sonata in *F*-minor, Op. 40.

CHAPTER XLII.

(*See Duets and Duos.*)

PART XI. CHAPTER XLIII.

Chwatal, "Abelard and Heloise," Three Tone pictures, Op. 249.

Wettle, Grasshopper Dance.

Sherwood, The Nun and the Fountain.

Henselt, "If I were a bird." (Two or four hands.)

Massenet, Scenes from Fourth Orchestral Suite.

Dvořák, Six Silhouettes.

Kullak-Salmon, The Phantom Chase.
Fradel, The Arab's Wedding.
Hyllested, Three Character pieces.
E. B. Perry, " Loreley."
G. D. Wilson, Phantom Dance.
Strelezki, Ennui Valse.   (Very characteristic.)
Jefferey, Danse Feerique, Op. 20.

PIANO-FORTE DUETS.
CHARACTERISTIC AND DESCRIPTIVE ILLUSTRATIONS CONTINUED.

Berlioz, " Harold in Italy."
Liszt, Symphonic Poems: "Divine Comedy," "Battle of the Huns," " Mazeppa,"
" Inferno," etc. (Arranged as Duets by the Composer.)
Moszkowski, Spanish Dances, Op. 12, Duet or Duo.   (There is an American reprint
of these cheaper than the foreign editions.)
Volkmann, Seven Hungarian Sketches, Op. 24. (Echoes in No. 1, Stretto to Nos. 2
and 7. Antiphonal style in No. 3. No. 7 is a Czardas.)
Gade, Norwegian Tone pictures, Op. 4.
Grieg, Norwegian Bridal Procession, arranged by A. R. Parsons.
Buck, Revel and appearance of the Abbot, from " Golden Legend."
MacDowell, Five Moonshine Pictures, Op. 21.
H. Hofmann, Three Characteristic pieces, Op. 35.
Löw, Six Descriptive pieces, Op. 330.
Merkel, Forest Scenes, Op. 127.
Kunkel, The Alpine Storm, Op. 105. (Two or four hands.)
Gounod, Funeral March of a Marionette.
Tschaikowsky, The Seasons, Twelve Characteristic pieces, 1 Vol., Op. 37.
Massenet, The Roman Harlequin. (Pantomime.)
C. Lachmund, Japanese Overture.
Lumbye, Dream Pictures. (Augener, 8570.)

SYMPHONIC FORM, CONCERTOS, OVERTURES, CHAMBER MUSIC.
ILLUSTRATIONS FOR CHAPTER XLII.

All the Symphonies of Em. Bach, Haydn, Mozart, Beethoven, Schubert, Mendelssohn,
and Schumann, have been arranged as Piano Duets, though we regret to say that much of
this work has been poorly done. The following are, however, especially recommended, as
every student should be familiar with them.
Ph. Em. Bach, Symphony in *D*, arranged by Horn.
Haydn, "L'Adieu" in *F*-sharp minor. (Or the Military Symphony in *G*)
Mozart, The three great Symphonies in *C*, *G*-minor and *E*-flat, composed in
1788, are published together in 1 Vol. by Peters, No. 187 (a). (They are also
arranged separately as Duos.)
Beethoven, Fifth Symphony in *C*-minor, Op. 67, arranged as a duet by Reinecke.
Schubert, No. 10, in *C*. Arranged as a Duo by Klindworth. (Motive quoted in
Chapter X.)
Mendelssohn, Reformation Symphony, Op. 107.
Schumann, Symphony No. 2, Op. 61. (Arranged by the Composer.)
Raff, Symphony, "Im Walde," No. 3, Op. 153.

Brahms, Symphony No. 1, in *C*-minor, Op. 69.
(For other Symphonies see illustrations to Chapter XLIV

CONCERTOS. (*See Piano Duos.*)

OPERATIC AND CONCERT OVERTURES
(Four Hands.)

Gluck, Five Overtures.
Beethoven, Eleven Overtures.
Schubert, Seven Overtures.
Mendelssohn, Ten Overtures.
Glinka, "The Life for the Czar."
Jensen, Concert Overture in *E*-minor.
Ph. Scharwenka, Fest Overture, Op. 43.
Moszkowski, Concert Overture, Op. 19.
Goetz, "Taming of the Shrew," Augener, 8540.
Lortzing, Two Overtures.
C. C. Converse, "In the Springtime" Overture.
Chadwick, "Melpomene" Overture.

Mozart, Eight Overtures
Cherubini, Nine Overtures.
Schumann, Seven Overtures.
Von Weber, Ten Overtures.

CHAMBER MUSIC.

Nearly all the Classical Chamber Music is arranged for Piano, four hand
but these arrangements are not generally recommended except as studies i
Sight-reading, or as a preface to a regular Chamber Music Concert. Litol
Peters, Breitkopf and Härtel, Steingräber, Augener and Co., Cotta, Schot
Jurgensen (Moscow), and Ricordi (Milan), publish cheap editions of the abov

MISCELLANEOUS SELECTIONS (Four Hands).

Hummel, Sonatas Complete, arranged by Winkler. (Litolff Edition. 444 †
Mendelssohn, Sonatas, arranged by Winkler. (Litolff Edition, 983.)
Clementi, Four Sonatas, arranged by Winkler. (Litolff Edition 95.)
J. B. Cramer, Two Sonatas, arranged. (Or Edition Peters. 1321.)
Onslow, Two Sonatas, in *E*-minor and *F*-minor, Ops. 7 and 22. Edition Peter
1326.)
Gade, Three Marches, Op. 18. (Bright and original. Edition Peters, 1005.
Grieg, Suite, Op. 40. (Edition Peters, 2266.)
Nicodé, Ball Scene, Op. 26.
Ph. Scharwenka, Polish Dances, Op. 38. (The last eight measures of No 1 & &
is a Refrain. This also occurs in the middle of the movement, marked Dolce Two
four hands.)
Rheinberger, Tarantelle, Op. 13. (Augener & Co. 6965.)
Kalliwoda, Grande Valses, Ops. 27 and 169. (Edition Peters, 100.

---

* These overtures have recently been performed at Orchestral Con
Author is not aware that any piano arrangement of them exists

† Edition Litolff, Braunschweig, should not be confused with Format Litolff
(Enoch & Sons), London.

Berlioz-Redon, Serenade of Mephistopheles, from "Damnation of Faust."

Berlioz-Miramont, Valse des Sylphes.

Kuhlau, Six Sonatinas, Op. 44 and 66. (Edition Peters, 728. Litolff, 246. These wer composed as Duets aud are superior to the Solo Sonatines arranged.)

Löw, Bohemian Dances. (No 2 contains a good example of subject and counter-subject

Mendelssohn, Three Preludes and Fugues for Organ, arranged. (Edition Peteri 1788.)

Schubert, Divertissements Hongroise, Ops. 54 aud 63. (Edition Litolff, 358.)

Spohr, An Sie am Klavier Sonata, Op. 138.

Nicodé, Symphonic Variations in *C*-minor, Op. 27. (Augener, 6946.)

Kirchner, Bohemian Dances. (Augener, 6938.)

A. Rubinstein, Six Duets, Op. 50. (Augener 8607.)

N. Rubinstein, Tarantelle, Op. 14. (Augener, 8606.)

Behr, Hungarian Dances. (All Czardas. Litolff, 997.)*
   (The Adagio of No. 3 contains three-measure phrases. The Adagio of No. 4 contains several five-measure Sections. Curtailed Period in No. 7. No. 6, Uneven Phrases.)

Dvořák, Polonaise in *E*-flat. (Augener & Co., 6585.)

Hamerik, Three Suites, Ops. 22, 23, and 24.

Raff, Suite in *B*-flat, Op. 204. (Contains a Tambourin.)

Grieg, Two Suites, Ops. 40 and 46. (Edition Peters, 2266, 2432.)

Brahms, Twenty-one Hungarian Dances, two or four hands. (Especially recom- mended for peculiar rhythm and uneven mensural proportion.)

Strelezki, Wallachian Dances, second book.

X. Scharwenka, Short Suite, Op. 24. Gavotte, Minuet, Mazurka, and Waltz. (Contains two Roccoco and two Modern Dances. All good models and moderately diffi- cult.)

Sherwood, Christmas Dance, Op. 14, No. 7.

Pease, Delta Kappa Epsilon.

Buck, Pilgrimage to Salerno from "Golden Legend."

Buck, Barcarolle, from "Golden Legend."

Labitzky, Military Gallop.

Hans Huber, Songs and Dances of Switzerland.

Bülow, Carnival of Milan. Ten characteristic pieces arranged as Duets.)

Wagner-Pauer, Five Celebrated Marches. (Augener, 8646.)

C. G. Reissiger, Concert Overture in *D*.

Kelley, Scherzo. (Original Duet.)

DUOS FOR PIANO-FORTES.

PIANO CONCERTOS, ETC.

Beethoven, *C*-minor Concerto, Op. 37, arranged by Kullak. (Steingräber Rd.)†

Mozart, *D*-minor, Concerto, arranged by Kullak. (Steingräber Edition.)†

Mozart, *E*-flat Concerto, (easier) arranged by Bishoff. (Steingräber Edition.)†

Mozart, *E*-flat Concerto, arranged as a Duo by Kögel. (Edition Peters, 7212.)

Mendelssohn, Concerto in *D*-minor, Op. 40. (Steingräber.

Chopin, Concertos in *E*-minor and *F*-minor.

---

   * Edition Litolff. Braunschweig, should not be confused with "Format Litolff" (Knoch & Sons), London.

   † Two copies necessary.

Schumann, Concerto in *A*-minor, Op. 54.
Goldmark, Piano Concerto.
X. Scharwenka, Piano Concerto, Op. 32.
Raff, Concerto in *C*-minor, Op. 185.
Reinecke, Concerto, Op. 72.
Saint-Saëns, Concerto in *G*-minor, Op. 22.
Draeseke, Piano Concerto, Op. 36.
Henselt, Piano Concerto, *F*-minor, Op. 16.
Grieg, Piano Concerto, Op. 16.   (Augener, 6141.)
Bendel, Piano Concerto.
Rubinstein, Piano Concerto, *E*-minor, Op. 25   (Peters, 1171.)
Godard, Piano Concerto, *A*-minor, Op. 31.
Sgambati, Piano Concerto, Op. 15.
Maas, Piano Concerto in *C*-minor, Op. 12.
MacDowell, Second Concerto, Op. 23.
Burmeister, Concerto, No. 1, *F*-minor, No. 2, *D*-minor.
Max Vogrich, Piano Concerto in *E*-minor.
Arthur Whiting, Piano Concerto in *D*-minor.
H. W. Nicholl, Piano Concerto in *D*-minor.
C. Florio, Piano Concerto in *A*-flat.

(The Mozart Piano Concerto in *D*-minor is arranged according to the original design, i. e., the second piano part has only the tutti passages. The one in *E*-flat is arranged by Kögel as a Piano Duo, the parts being more equally distributed between the two instruments. Where the performers are of the same grade, this latter plan is recommended as being more generally satisfactory, though it loses somewhat of the antiphonal character of a Concerto, and becomes a Duo. Nearly all the Concertos are arranged according to the former design. A number of Standard Concertos are arranged with String quartette accompaniment. These are generally effective, except in such works as Liszt's *E*-flat Concerto

PIANO DUOS, MISCELLANEOUS

Saint-Saëns, Minuet and Gavotte.
Saint-Saëns, Variations on theme from Beethoven
Saint-Saëns, Dance of Death.   (Arranged by the Composer.)
Rheinberger Fantaisie, Op. 7.
Reinecke, Variations on theme from Schumann's " Manfred."
Clementi-Krause, Two Sonatas.
Mozart, Original Compositions.   (Peters, 1327.)
Mendelssohn, Capriccio, *B*-minor, Op. 22.
Bruch, Fantaisie, Op. 11.
Löw, Allegro Brillante, Op. 325.
O. Singer, Variations on original theme.
O. Singer, Rhapsodie for two Pianos and Orchestra.
Hyllested-Kölling, March Triomphale.
H. Huber, Sonata, Op. 31.

RHAPSODICAL FORM (Four Hands).

Berlioz, Episode in the life of an Artist, Op. 14.
Berlioz, Harold in Italy, Op. 16.

Berlioz, Romeo and Juliet, Op. 17.
Liszt, Twelve Symphonic Poems, arranged as Duets by the Composer.
Dvořák, Slavonic Rhapsodies, Op. 45, three books, four hands.
Dvořák, Scherzo Capriccioso, Op. 66.
Saint-Saëns, Phaeton, Symphonic Poem.
E. Lalo, Rhapsodie.
Svendsen, Carnival in Paris, Op. 9.

SYMPHONIES AND SYMPHONIC POEMS.

(MODERN ROMANTIC, AND ROMANTIC—CLASSICAL FORMS.)

Brahms, Symphonies, Ops. 73, 90 and 98.
Goldmark, " Country Wedding," Descriptive Symphony.
H. Hofmann, " Frithjof," Op. 22.
Volkmann, Symphony in *D*-minor, Op. 44.
Dvořák Symphonies, Ops. 60 and 70.
Saint-Saëns, Four Symphonic Poems.
Vicodé, " Marie Stuart," Op. 4.
Godard, Symphony, Op. 23.
Rubinstein, Sixth Symphony, Op. 111, arranged by Kleinmichel.
Lassen, Two Symphonies, Op. 78.
Paine, Symphonies, Ops. 23 and 34.
Gottschalk, " Night in the Tropics " Symphony.
MacDowell, Two Symphonic Poems, Op. 22, Hamlet and Ophelia. (Arranged by the Composer.)
Bristow, Arcadian Symphony.

ADDITIONAL WORKS BY AMERICAN COMPOSERS.

ORCHESTRAL COMPOSITIONS.

Foote, Overture, " In the Mountains."
H. W. Parker, Symphony in *C*.
S. G. Pratt, Symphonic Suite, " The Tempest."
Chadwick, Symphony, No. 2, in *B*-flat.
Chadwick, Overture, " Rip Van Winkle."
J. K. Paine, An Island Fantasy, and Overture, " As you like it."
Arthur Weld, Romance for Orchestra.
Arthur Weld, Suite, " Italia."
Hamerik, Symphonie Lyrique, Op. 33.
J. H. Beck, " Skirnismal."
Arthur Bird, Suite in *D*, Op. 6.
S. A. Baldwin, Overture, " A Journey in Norway."
Theo. Thomas, Festival March.
O. Floersheim, Symphonic Reverie.
W. O. Forsyth, Suite, No. 1.
E. C. Phelps, Elegie for Orchestra.
W. Petzel, Overture, Odysseus.
G. Hille, Concerto for Violin and Orchestra.
B. O. Klein, Love Song and Wedding Bells.

V. Herbert, Serenade for String Orchestra.
W. Burr, Jr., Andante and Scherzo for String Orchestra
Gleason, Introduction, Death Song, Yeteva's Processional, and Finale to Scene
II from " Montezuma."

CHAMBER MUSIC.

Kroeger, Quartette in *G*-minor.
Gilchrist, Quartette in *C*-minor.
A. D. Turner, Sonata for P., F. and 'Cello, Op. 34.
E. Howells, P. F. Trio
Petzet, P. F. Trio, Op. 9.
Foote, P. F. Trio in *C*-minor.
Chadwick Quintette in *E*-flat.
Geo. W. Andrews, Sonata, P., F. and Violin.
Gleason, Quartettes and Trios.
P. C. Lutkin, Romance for 'Cello.

PIANO-FORTE.

Arthur Whiting, Concert Etude.
T. Strong, Dance of Elves.   (For two piano-fortes.)
R. Thallon, " Florence," Gavotte.
Carl Venth, Prelude, Romance and Rural Dance.
H. Nast, Gavotte, Nocturne, and Polonaise.
Jno. Yoakley, Scherzando and Trio.
J. S. Van Cleve, Allegro con brio from Sonata.
J. S. Van Cleve, Nocture in *F*.
W. L. Blumenschein, Impromptu and Reminiscences.
Lavallée, Etude, Papillons.
Thos. Tapper, From my Sketch Book, (Six Nos.)
Hugo Kaun, Suite, Village Stories.

VOCAL.

F. A. Dossert, Mass in *E*-minor.
G. F. Bristow, Oratorio, Praise of God.
J. K. Paine, Oratorio, St. Peter.
J. K. Paine, Oratorio, The Nativity.
J. K. Paine, Cantata, Song of Promise.
O. Singer, Cantata, Landing of the Pilgrims.
O. Singer, Festival Ode.
J. C. D. Parker, Redemption Hymn.
J. C. D. Parker, Cantata, " The Blind King."
E. Thayer, Festival Cantata.
G. E. Whiting, Tale of the Viking.
G. E. Whiting, Henry of Navarre.
H. Mohr, Cantata for Male Chorus, Solo and Orchestra.
Gleason, Praise of Harmony.
Foote, The Legend of Hiawatha.

H. W. Parker, King Trojan.

Gilchrist, Cantata, "The Rose."

Maas, Will-o'-the-Wisp, Female Chorus.

A. W. Thayer, Hymn to Apollo.   Double Quartet.

A. A. Stanley, "The Strain Upraise."

E. Nevin, "The Night has a Thousand Eyes."

A. Foote, Love took me softly by the hand.

Jules Jordan, Bugle Song.

C. T. Howell, Love's Messenger, Female Chorus.

H. H. Huss, Motette for Chorus and Orchestra.

J. A. Beck, Moorish Serenade, (Tenor Solo and Orchestra.)

W. Burr, Jr., The Wreck of the Hesperus.

E. Nevin, A Sketch Book.   (Vocal and Instrumental.)

www.ingramcontent.com/pod-product-compliance
Lightning Source LLC
Chambersburg PA
CBHW021111270326
41929CB00009B/829